Dynamic Design

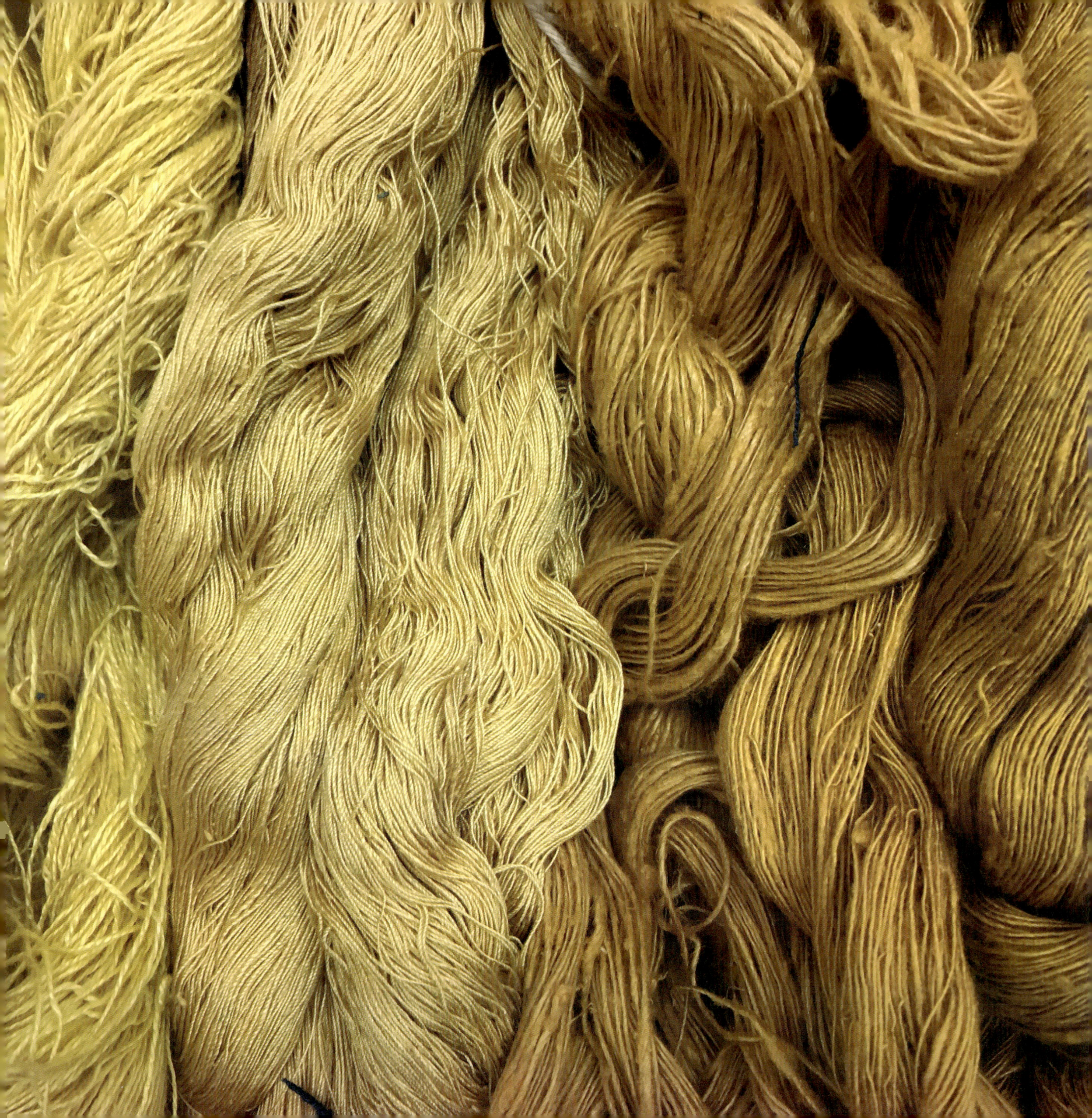

Dynamic Design

JAY HAMBIDGE, MARY CROVATT HAMBIDGE

AND THE FOUNDING OF THE HAMBIDGE CENTER

FOR CREATIVE ARTS AND SCIENCES

Virginia Gardner Troy

With contributions by Tommye McClure Scanlin and Donna Mintz

PUBLISHED IN ASSOCIATION WITH GEORGIA HUMANITIES

THE UNIVERSITY OF GEORGIA PRESS   ATHENS

Publication of this book was made possible, in part, by a generous Berry College Faculty Scholarship Grant.

Published by the University of Georgia Press
Athens, Georgia 30602
www.ugapress.org
© 2023 by Virginia Gardner Troy
Chapters 5–6 © 2023 by the University of Georgia Press
All rights reserved
Designed by Erin Kirk
Set in Miller Text
Printed and bound by Friesens
The paper in this book meets the guidelines for permanence and durability of the Committee on Production Guidelines for Book Longevity of the Council on Library Resources.

Most University of Georgia Press titles are available from popular e-book vendors.

Printed in Canada
26 25 24 23 22 C 5 4 3 2 1

Library of Congress Cataloging-in-Publication Data

Names: Troy, Virginia Gardner, 1956– author.
Title: Dynamic design : Jay Hambidge, Mary Crovatt Hambidge and the founding of the Hambidge Center for Creative Arts and Sciences / Virginia Gardner Troy ; with contributions by Tommye McClure Scanlin and Donna Mintz.
Description: Athens : The University of Georgia Press, [2023] | Includes bibliographical references and index.
Identifiers: LCCN 2022026306 | ISBN 9780820362724 (hardback) | ISBN 9780820357416 (ebook)
Subjects: LCSH: Hambidge, Jay, 1867–1924—Criticism and interpretation. | Hambidge, Mary, 1885–1973—Criticism and interpretation. | Design—Philosophy. | Hambidge Center for Creative Arts and Sciences.
Classification: LCC NC703 .T76 2023 | DDC 745.40973—dc23/eng/20220714
LC record available at https://lccn.loc.gov /2022026306

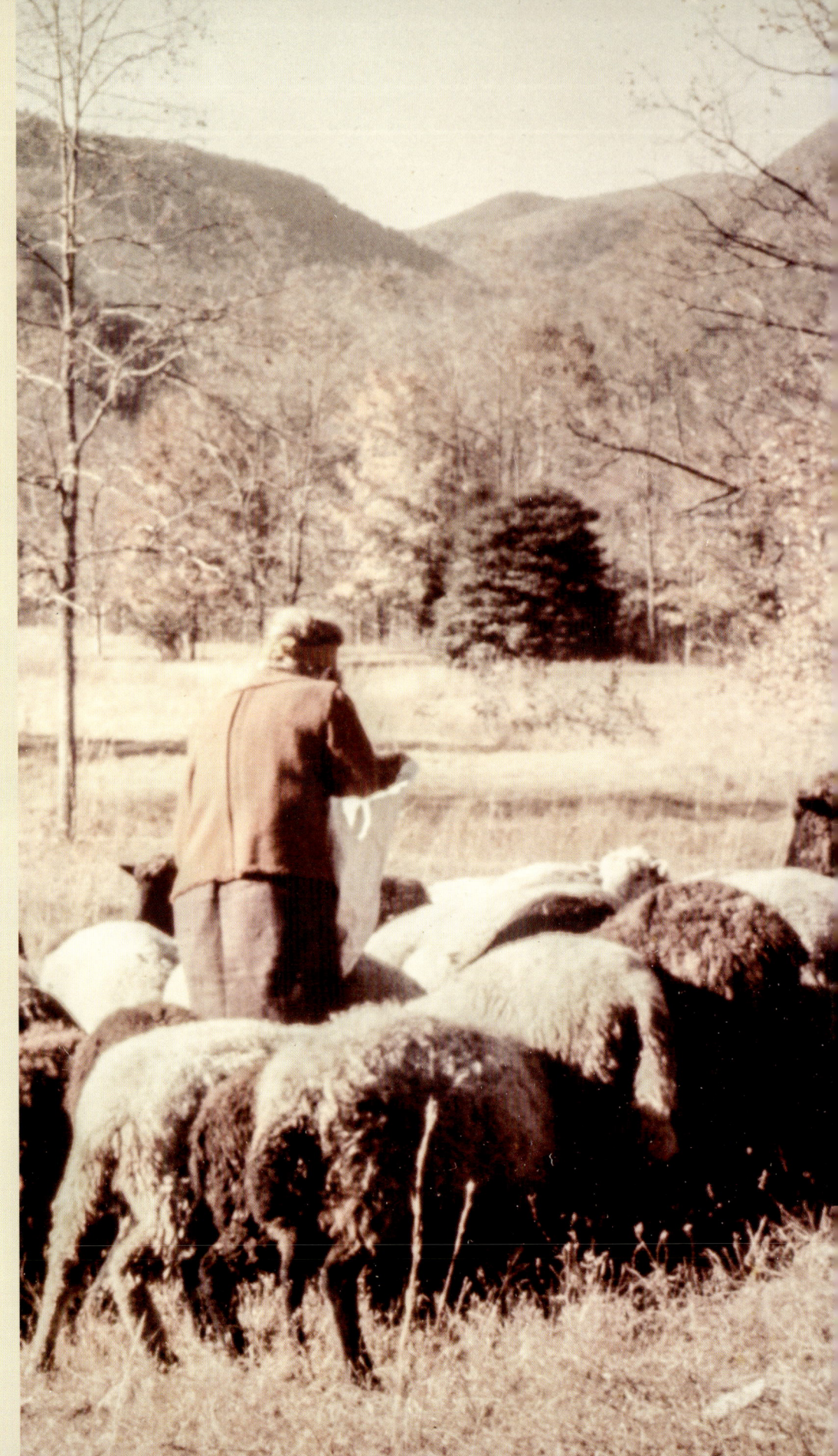

CONTENTS

Acknowledgments   vii

Introduction. Jay Hambidge and Mary Lee Crovatt Hambidge: An Overview   1

Chapter 1   Nineteenth-Century Foundations, Twentieth-Century Lives: The Early Years to 1914   11

Chapter 2   Dynamic Symmetry: Jay Hambidge and His Circle   24

Chapter 3   Mary Crovatt Hambidge and the Formation of Her Handcraft Technique and Philosophy in Greece and New York, 1920–1935: Forming Utopia   43

Chapter 4   The Weavers of Rabun and Rabun Studios in Historical Context   68

Chapter 5   Memories of Hambidge Center Experiences: Workshops and Residencies, by Tommye McClure Scanlin   98

Chapter 6   The Hambidge Center Today: An Artist's View from the Inside, by Donna Mintz   115

Conclusion   130

Timeline   133
Notes   143
Bibliography   155
Index   161

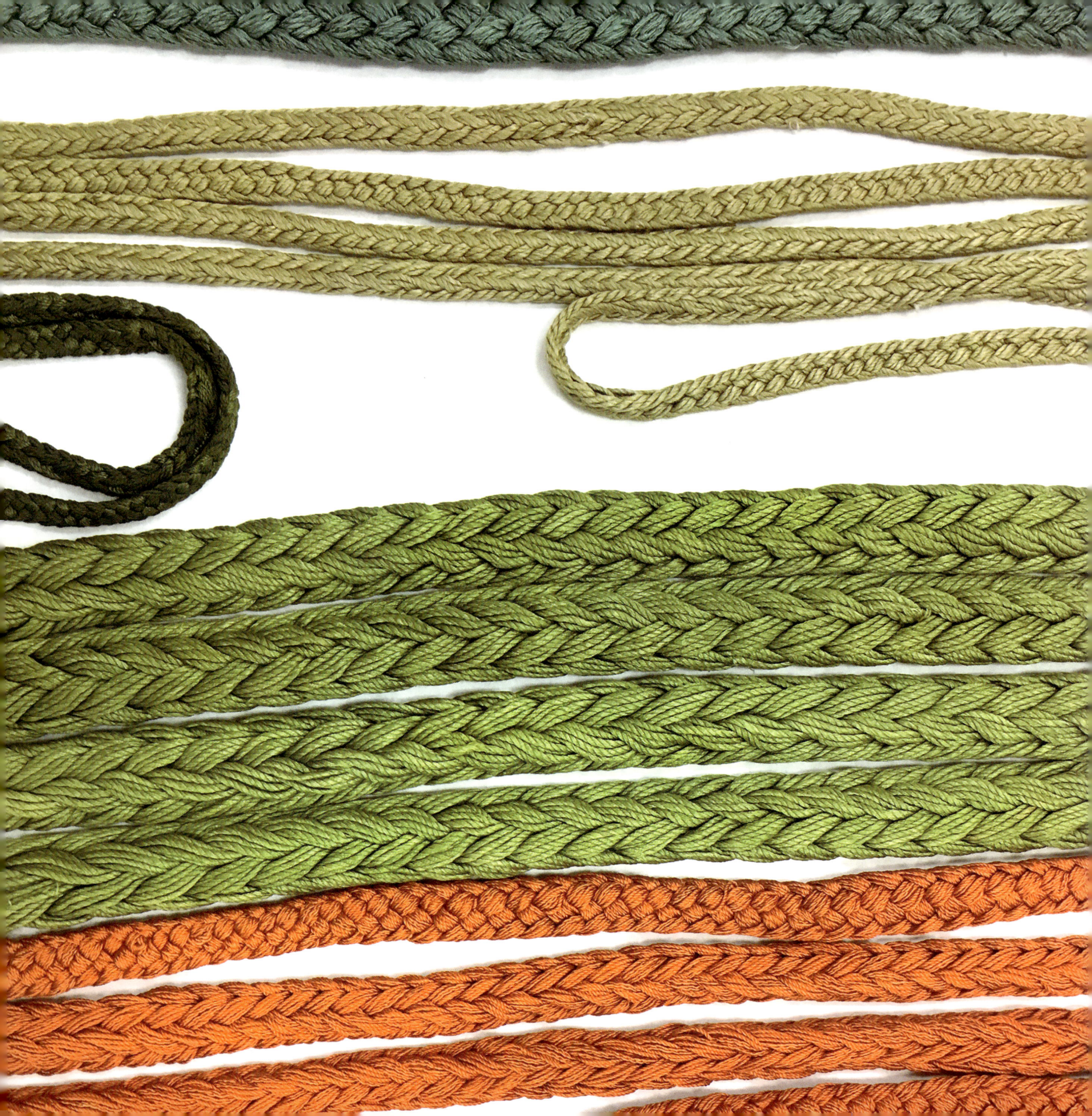

ACKNOWLEDGMENTS

Jay Hambidge and Mary Crovatt Hambidge made significant contributions to the development of art and design in the twentieth century. Their legacy continues with the Hambidge Center for Creative Arts and Sciences. In this book I seek to put their stories into a focused historical context and chronology.

I discovered the woven work of Mary Hambidge while assisting with an exhibition of her textiles at the Atlanta History Center in the late 1990s. I pursued further research, supported by a residency at the Hambidge Center, which resulted in my article "The Great Weaver of Eternity: Dynamic Symmetry and Utopian Ideology in the Woven and Written Work of Mary Crovatt Hambidge" in the summer 1999 issue of *Surface Design Journal*, which won an Award of Merit in the Surface Design Association Critical Writing Competition. Much has happened since then. Contemporary scholarship in fields dealing with textiles, crafts, women designers, artist couples, handcraft guilds, Appalachian arts, and many other topics has collectively changed our understanding of twentieth- and twenty-first-century art and design.

This project, which required intensive archival and collections research that has revealed significantly new information and insights, could not have been completed without the assistance and expertise of many individuals and institutions over the years.

The staffs at the Hambidge Center for Creative Arts and Sciences, the Atlanta History Center, and the Hargrett Rare Book and Manuscript Library at the University of Georgia have generously facilitated access to their rich collections. At the Hambidge Center I thank Jamie Badoud, along with

Dayna Thacker, Christine Jason, Katheryn Derryberry Banks, and former associates and directors Judy Barber, Karin Schaller, and Bob Thomas. The Atlanta History Center is the main repository of Hambidge archives and collections. I thank Executive Vice President Michael Rose and the collections staff and archivists at the Kenan Research Center for granting access to this collection and generously providing photography and licensing. I thank the staff at the University of Georgia's Hargrett Rare Book and Manuscript Library for providing access to the collection as well as photography and licensing. At the University of Georgia Press I thank editor Patrick Allen for supporting this project from the beginning, and I thank the anonymous reviewers who provided insightful suggestions. I also thank UGA Press editor Jon Davies and designer Erin Kirk for their skillful attention to editorial and design decisions.

I thank the staffs at the Archives of American Art; Yale University's Beinecke Rare Book and Manuscript Library; Syracuse University Special Collections; New York Public Library Special Collections; Tennessee State Library and Archives; Parsons New School Special Collections; Benaki Museum/Historical Archives; and Greenwich (Connecticut) Historical Society.

Numerous scholars have contributed along the way, including Philis Alvic, author of *Weavers of the Southern Highlands*; Charles Buice, trustee of the Steele-Reese Foundation; Marie Frank, University of Massachusetts Lowell; Jennifer Wilson, the New School; and Artemis Leontis, University of Michigan, author of *Eva Palmer Sikelianos: A Life in Ruins*. I thank Ruth Simon McRae for her drawings. Filmmaker Hal Jacobs, who produced the documentary *Mary Crovatt Hambidge: Whistler, Wanderer, Weaver, Utopian*, assisted with images and research for this book. Mark Hambidge Brewer, a great-grandson of Jay Hambidge, provided essential details for understanding Jay Hambidge. I thank Hambidge Fellows Tommye McClure Scanlin, professor emeritus at the University of North Georgia, and Donna Mintz, artist and writer, for bringing the historical perspective into the present day with their cogent essays.

Berry College facilitated this project through a sabbatical, faculty development and travel grants, interlibrary loans, and a generous publication subvention grant. Remington Jackson, my research assistant, helped with the index, illustrations, bibliography, and other important details.

Thanks to my family and friends for their help and support along the way. I hope that the book creates fresh interest in this fascinating piece of twentieth-century art and design history.

Dynamic Design

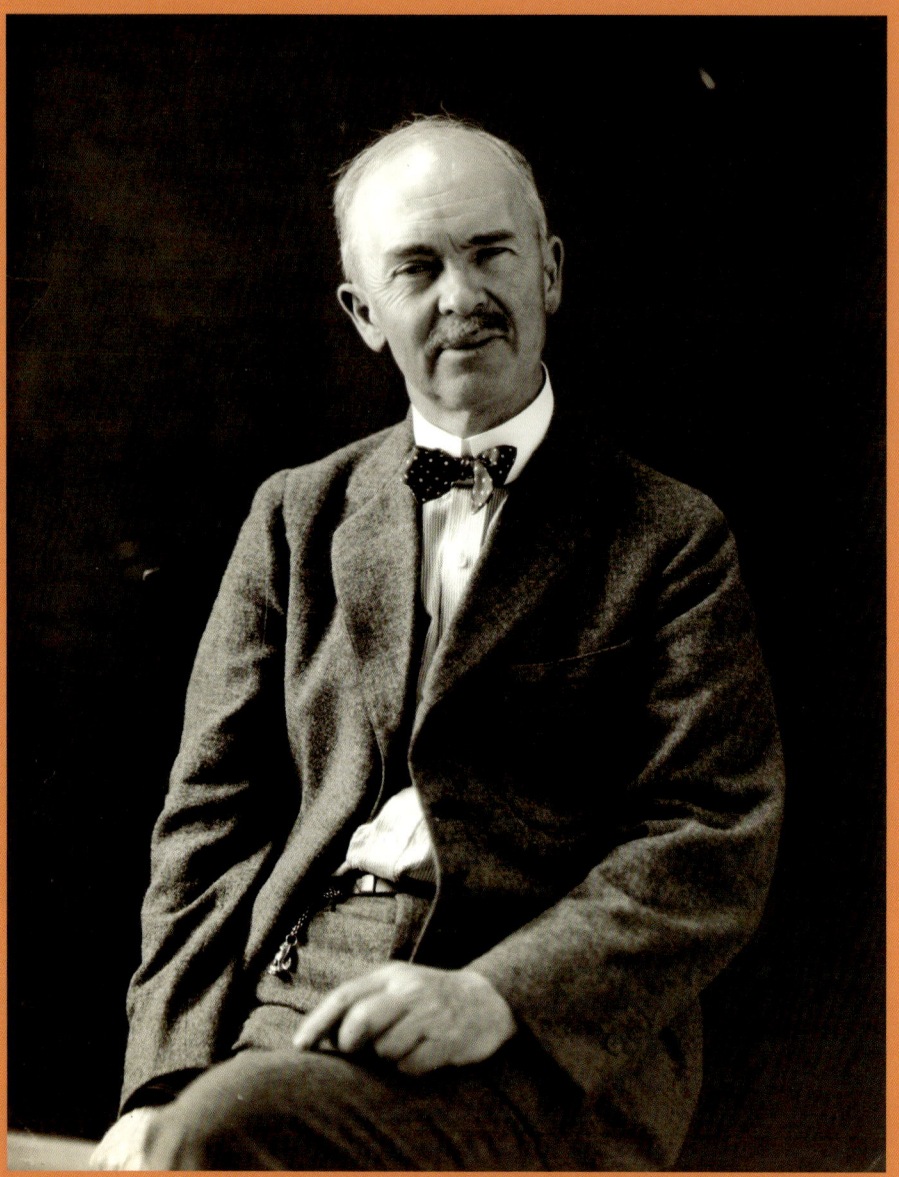

Jay Hambidge, n.d.
Courtesy of Hal Jacobs

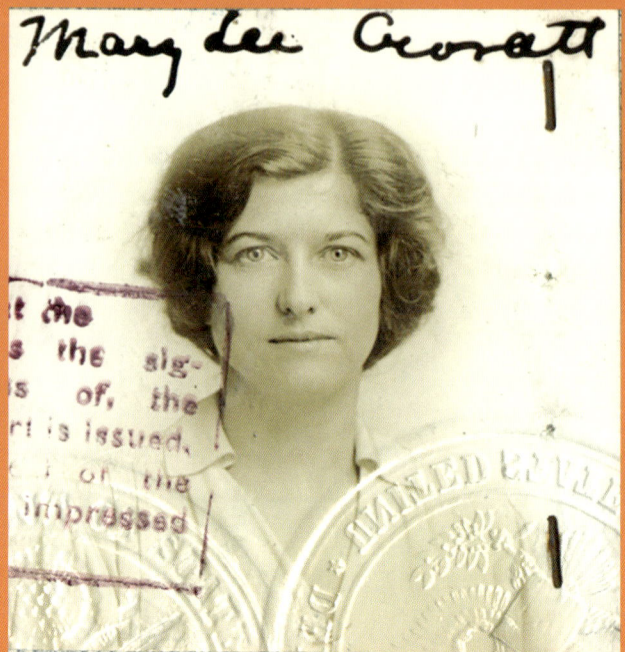

Passport photograph of
Mary Lee Crovatt, 1919.
Kenan Research Center at
the Atlanta History Center,
box 17, folder 6

Jay Hambidge and Mary Lee Crovatt Hambidge

An Overview

In this book I critically analyze the lives and work of two twentieth-century American artists and innovators, Jay Hambidge (1867–1924) and Mary Crovatt Hambidge (1885–1973). Jay Hambidge originated the concept of "Dynamic Symmetry," which is a theory of proportion that links natural human and plant growth patterns, such as phyllotaxis, to the harmonious proportions of Classic Greek design. Hambidge conceived of Dynamic Symmetry as a pedagogical tool to provide artists and teachers with a rational, mathematical system to create proportionally balanced compositions; it could be applied to a broad range of media and interpreted by a diverse range of artists.

Hambidge was not the first to apply mathematical formulas to achieve harmonious compositions in art. For example, Leonardo da Vinci and Piero della Francesca were among those who used geometric principles as compositional guides. However, Hambidge was original in his instructive articulation of the theory, published in books and journals and delivered in lectures, which resonated with a generation of American illustrators and designers seeking a rational method to organize their design compositions.[1]

Hambidge was at the height of his career in 1924, promoting Dynamic Symmetry through lectures and writing after working for decades as an illustrator for magazines such as *Century*, when he suffered a stroke and died suddenly just a week after his fifty-seventh birthday. He and Mary Lee Crovatt had spent the previous decade together as a couple, having met in April 1914 in New York City. Their activities and correspondence demonstrate their close and mutually supportive bond. Jay dedicated his 1920 book, *Dynamic Symmetry: The Greek Vase*, "To M. L. C.," and she was the

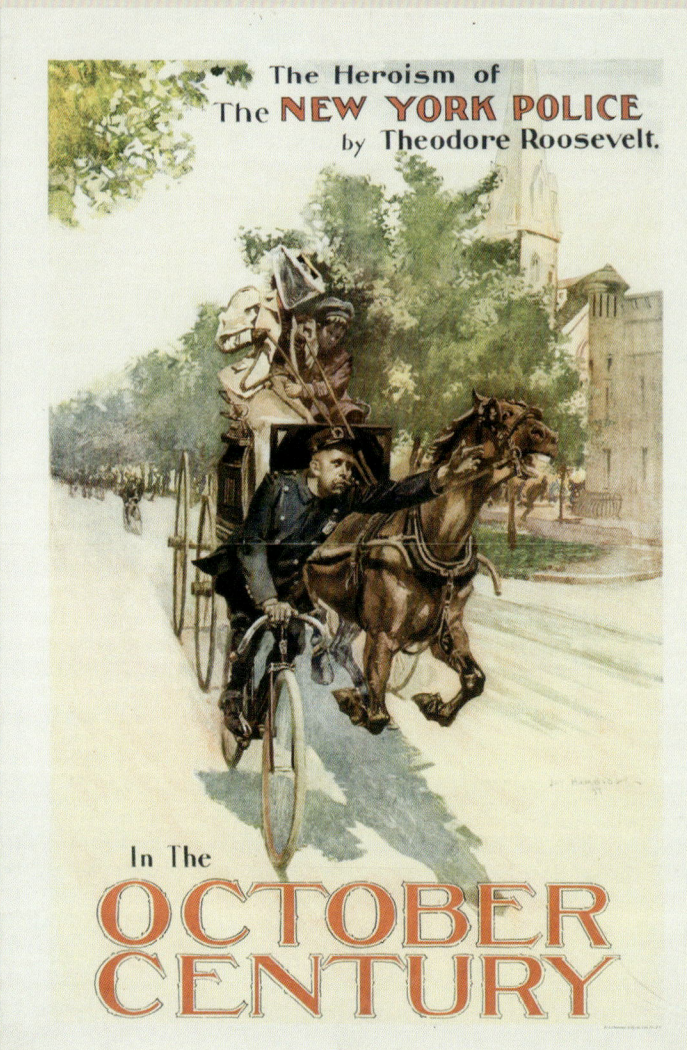

Jay Hambidge, "One of the Bicycle Squad." Image for article written by Theodore Roosevelt, *Century* 54, no. 6 (October 1897): 813

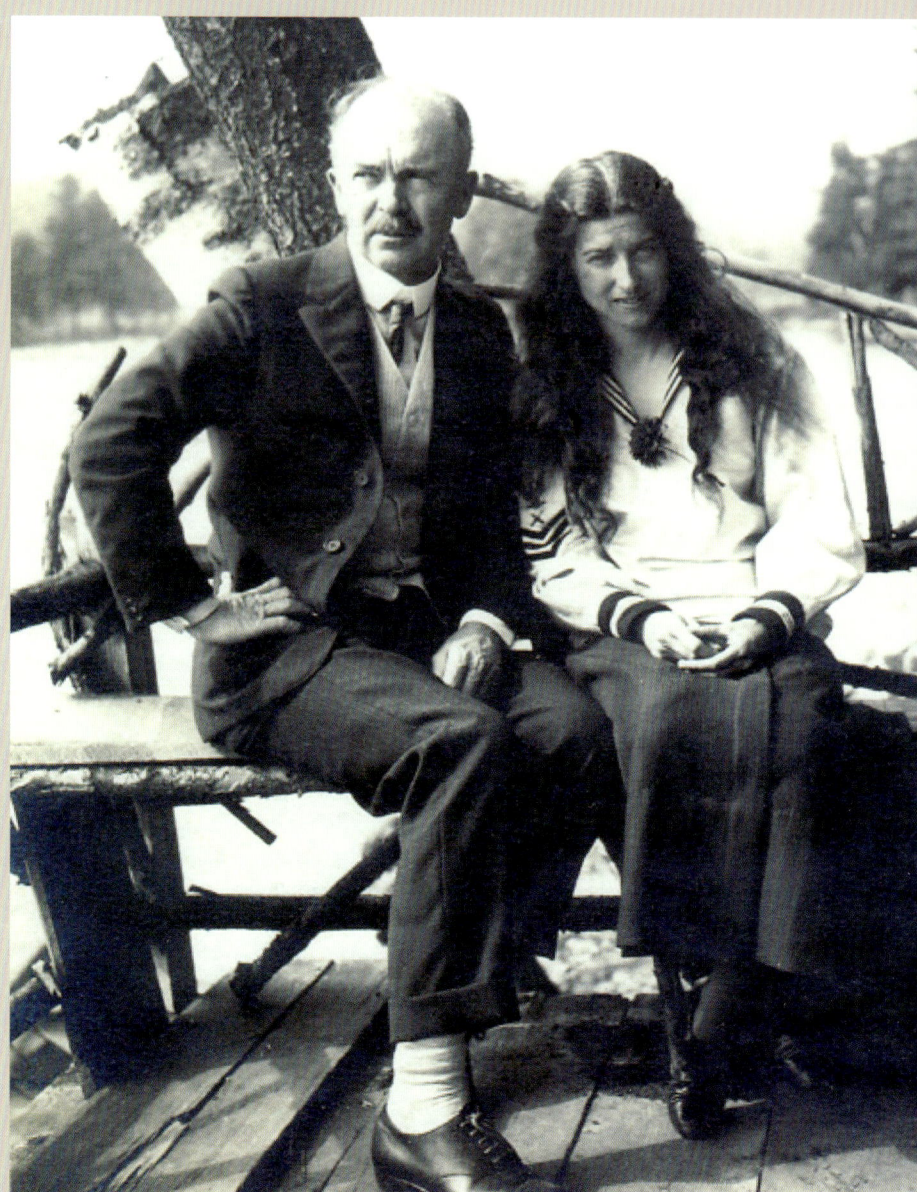

Jay Hambidge and Mary Crovatt, n.d. Kenan Research Center at the Atlanta History Center, VIS 1.940S

beneficiary of his estate. After Jay's death, Mary referred to herself as Mrs. Jay Hambidge.

A pivotal trip to Greece in 1920–1921 had changed Mary's life forever. She had accompanied Jay on a Yale University–supported research trip to Athens so that he could take measurements of the Parthenon and other architectural monuments to bolster his theory of Dynamic Symmetry and to conduct research for a new publication. While in Athens, Mary connected with Eva Palmer Sikelianos and other expatriate women living there, who were involved in reviving the ancient art of handweaving in the workshop of Kyria Elene Avramea. Mary wrote, "Up to this time I did not know that there was such a thing as a hand loom or hand weaving. But when I walked into a large factory in Athens one day and saw the peasant women there working at the big looms, I knew instantly that this was what I wanted to do. I saw as in a vision a new world for dynamic colour and design."[2] She learned to weave there, began to dress in Greek-inspired clothing that she made herself, and stayed in Athens a good six months after Jay departed for a lecture tour.

Then and there Mary began to envision how the traditional artistic production of handweaving could be adapted to contemporary use. Like Jay, she was not alone in her admiration of the ancient Greek past. Isadora Duncan, for example, had passionately studied and translated the movements and costumes of Classic Greek dance as a liberating alternative to traditional Western dance. Indeed, Greece, both before and after World War I, was a mecca for expatriate Westerners who studied Greek architecture, drama, poetry, and costume.[3] This was a pivotal time for both Jay and Mary: Mary was establishing her artistic voice, and Jay's theory of Dynamic Symmetry seemed destined for fame.

Both Jay and Mary adapted ancient Greek artistic ideals to create a synthesis of art and science, as well as a new pedagogical approach to the fine arts and crafts. They contributed to modernist discourses by encouraging unification between fine and decorative arts and by connecting modern designs with ancient paradigms. Indeed, as early as 1902 Jay envisioned Dynamic Symmetry as a foundation for work in textiles, furniture, and other applied arts, which he hoped to capitalize on.[4] Their theories aligned with contemporary notions of geometric abstraction and modular systems of construction in art, design, and architecture while maintaining a revivalist link to handcrafts and a unification of fine and applied arts.[5] Today Jay Hambidge is noted as an innovator who infused science and mathematics into the practice of art. His theories provided a structured system for artists

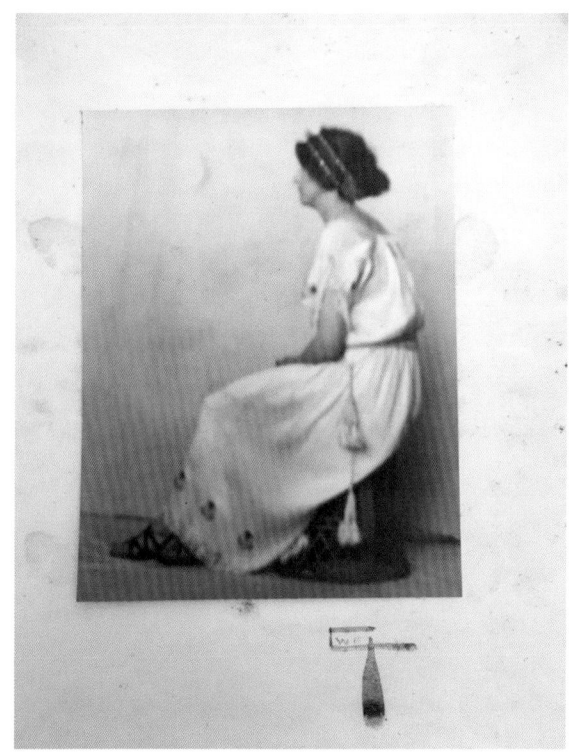

Studio photograph of Mary Crovatt Hambidge, c. 1921–1924. Kenan Research Center at the Atlanta History Center, VIS 1.940S

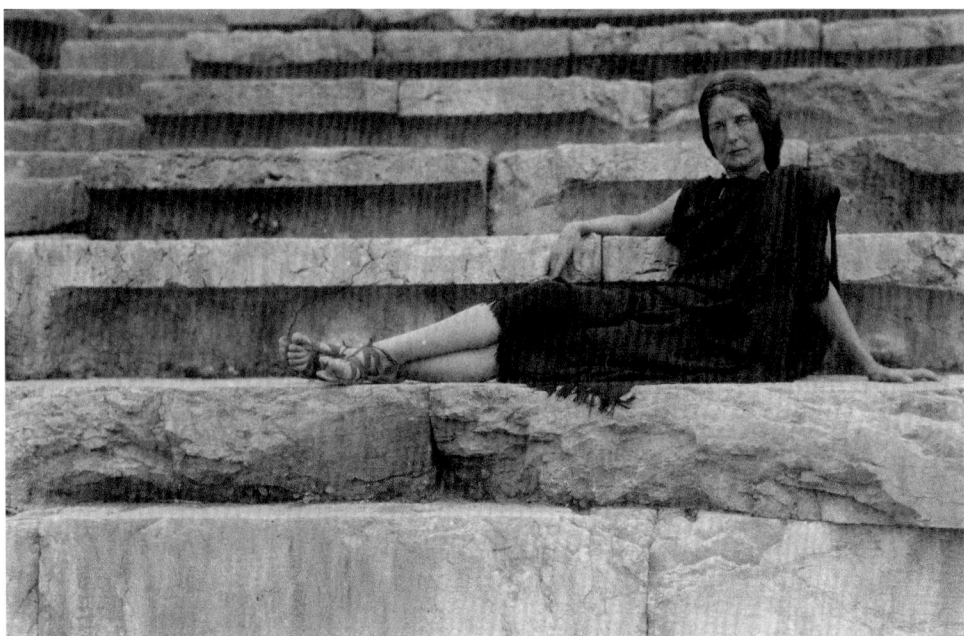

Eva Palmer Sikelianos at the ancient theater of Delphi during the second Delphic Festival, May 1930. Photograph by Elli Seraidaris (Nelly's), © Benaki Museum/Historical Archives, FA.11_N.1956

at a time when the art world was moving toward abstraction and subjective expressionism. Mary is credited with creating one of the earliest artist communities in the South and with reviving and invigorating Greek and Appalachian weaving traditions. Her woven work is technically proficient as well as beautiful in hue, pattern, and its modern interpretations of Classic Greek gowns and cloaks.

From Jay's letters to Mary during the decade that they were together (Mary's letters to him are unaccounted for), we learn that the two were planning to form an artists' community where Mary would teach and produce weaving and Jay would teach the practical application of Dynamic Symmetry. He referenced opportunities in applied arts industries and weaving collectives in the Blue Ridge Mountains region, which is not surprising given that numerous craft-based schools, colleges, and collectives were being established at the time with the goal of bringing economic reform by reviving folk craft traditions.[6] In the late 1920s Mary began to visit the northeastern mountains of Georgia, where she discovered a rich Appalachian weaving tradition. She saw parallels between the mountain weavers and the Greek weavers, and she began to envision her own weaving enterprise. By the late 1930s, with generous financial support from wealthy benefactor Eleanor Steele Reese, Mary was able to fulfill her dream by establishing the Jay Hambidge Art

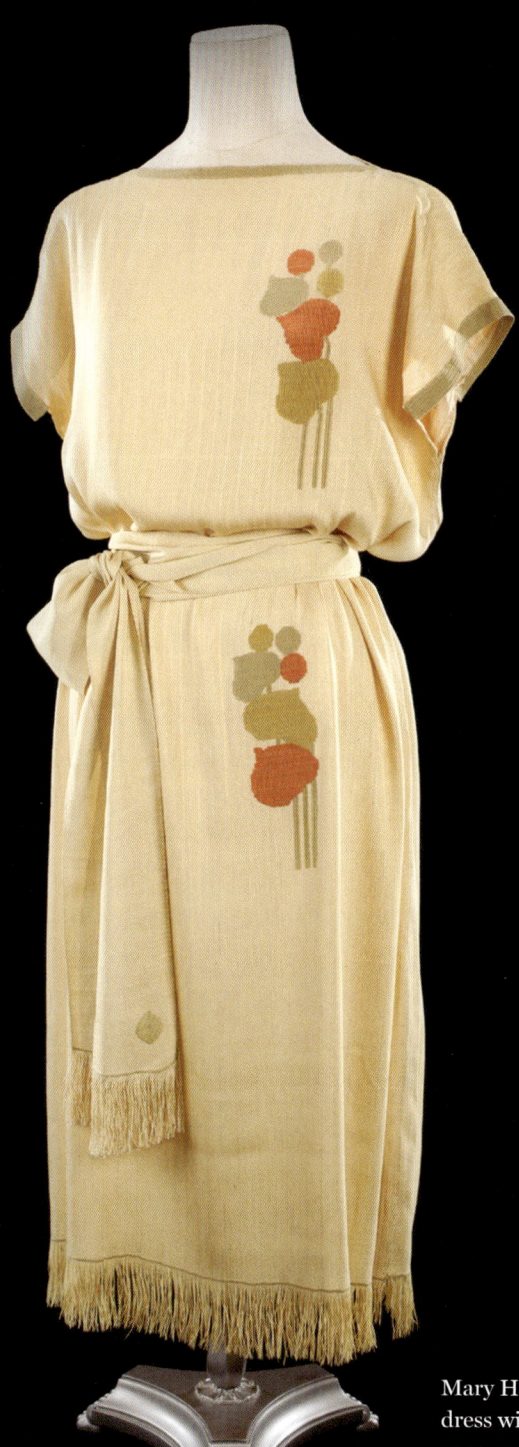

Mary Hambidge, gold silk dress with floral weft brocade, 1921–1929. Kenan Research Center at the Atlanta History Center, 1998.233

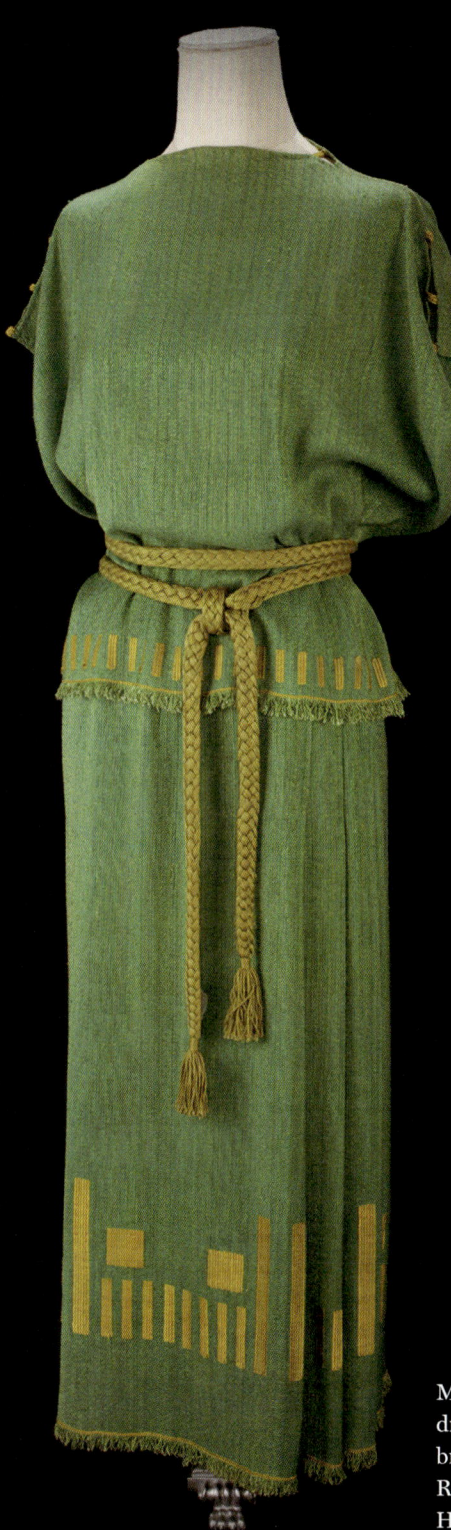

Mary Hambidge, green silk dress with geometric weft brocade, September 1925. Kenan Research Center at the Atlanta History Center, 1998.233

Foundation in Rabun Gap, Georgia, the Weavers of Rabun workshop, and the Rabun Studios boutique in New York City. Mary sought to create a retreat where art and agriculture were practiced in balance, as she believed had occurred in ancient Greece. "I think that was the secret of Greek culture, that they kept their touch with nature and the soil and all the simple things of life . . . it keeps you real," she stated.[7]

Mary wove life into Jay's theories by applying her understanding of Dynamic Symmetry to clothing and color. She began to seriously promote the merits of Dynamic Symmetry to artists and educators while compiling Jay's lecture notes into *Practical Applications of Dynamic Symmetry*. Although she was filled with determination and utopian vision in Depression-era Appalachia, forming an ambitious enterprise in the rural mountains of northern Georgia was a challenge despite economic support from Reese. Yet even with the cultural and personal complexities that living in a traditional, rural environment posed, she quickly developed positive and productive relationships with the local people due largely to her ability to provide steady employment and her successful efforts with the weaving collective to sell its products at Rabun Studios. Rabun Studios sold contemporary crafts and furniture along with woven goods, and it became a touchstone for the mid-century American studio craft revival.[8] Indeed, the studio's clientele in the 1950s included the architect Philip Johnson and the artist Georgia O'Keeffe, who appreciated the brilliant hand-dyed hues and the feel of the handwoven cloth.[9] For two decades (1937–1958) the boutique offered a little piece of Appalachia in the heart of Manhattan, a culture clash that was not lost on Mary as she became increasingly averse to big cities.

The cross-cultural and cross-historical hybrid that Mary achieved in her art, writing, and activities early in this period is extremely interesting and indicates that she, among others, was searching for an art that encompassed a new universalist ideology based on ancient principles. Her cosmopolitanism shifted by the mid-1950s, however, as she grew more disenchanted with the modern world and the encroachment of industrialization, stating, "I am afraid of this wave of industry that has invaded our part of the world and threatens to upset its equilibrium."[10] This is a particularly important transition when understood in the context of Appalachian weaving. As the big textile mills began to dominate the area, Mary retreated further into the world of nature. But her antimachine sentiments were in direct opposition to the view of another famous weaver, Anni Albers, who, working nearby at Black Mountain College from 1933 to 1949, embraced machinery

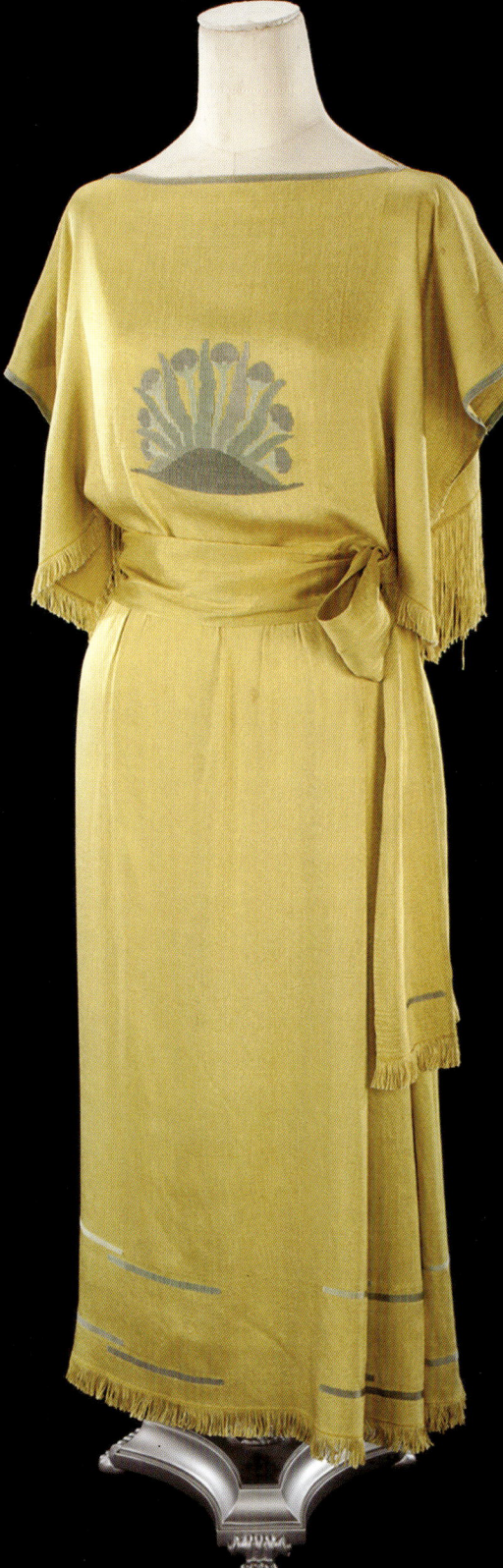

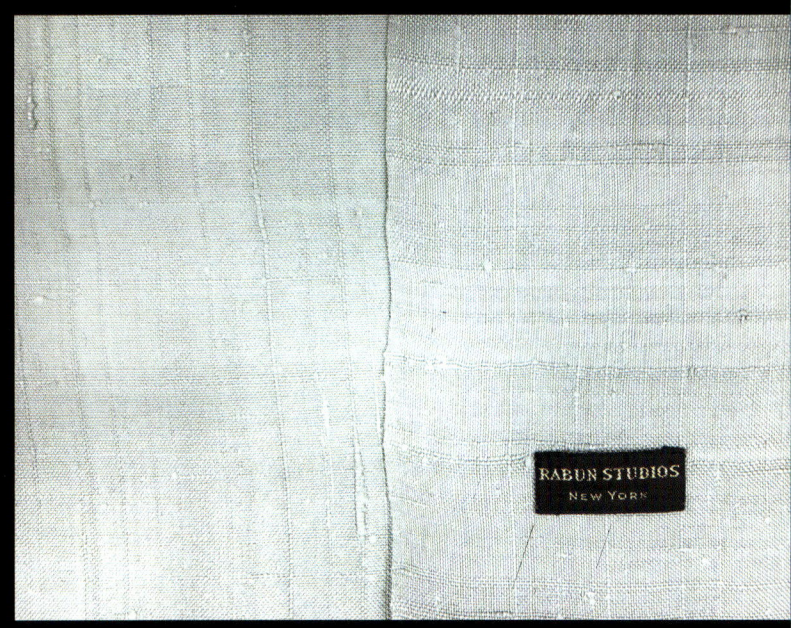

Scarf with Rabun Studios label. Kenan Research Center at the Atlanta History Center, 1998.233

Mary Hambidge, yellow silk dress with floral weft brocade, 1925. Kenan Research Center at the Atlanta History Center, 1998.233

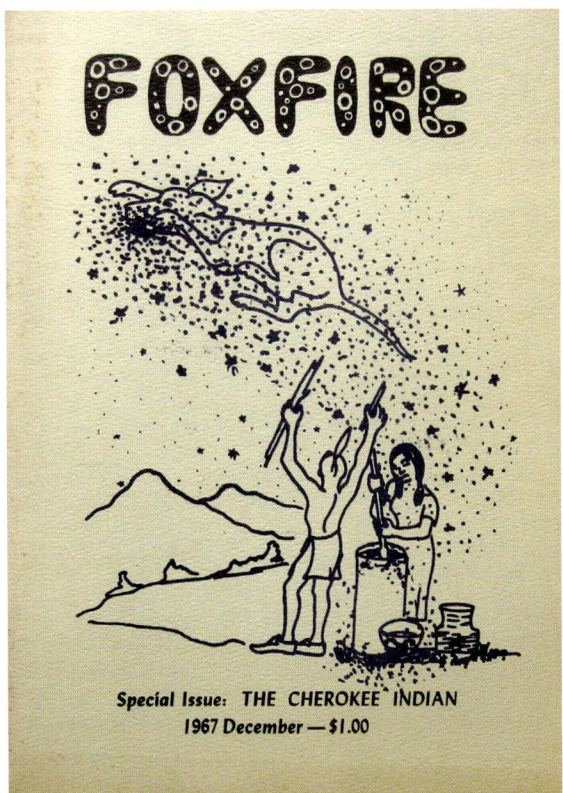

Foxfire 1, no. 3 (December 1967)

and synthetic yarns as great time-savers. Albers synthesized new materials and technology with hand production, creating prototypes for industry. She wrote in 1938, "Machines reduce the boredom of repetition. On the other hand, they permit a play of the imagination only in the preliminary planning of the product."[11]

From the 1960s until her death in 1973, Mary benefited from another wave of folk and craft revivalism, becoming a mentor to the many young people who made pilgrimages to her farm. Indeed, as Eliot Wigginton, founder of the *Foxfire* magazine series of Appalachian folk and craft culture, stated, "*Foxfire* was born on her kitchen table."[12]

Jay Hambidge and Mary Crovatt Hambidge contributed a great deal to twentieth-century visual culture. They were significant participants in the modernist phenomenon of cultural appropriation that took place in Europe and America during the first half of the twentieth century, when artwork from ancient and non-Western cultures was studied, copied, and collected.[13] Like many other Western artists, Jay and Mary sought out cross-cultural and cross-historical connections to reinforce their artistic expressions and theories while simultaneously contributing to developments in American art and design. In Jay's case, the result was tied to the rationalist and realistic style of North American art and design; in Mary's case, it was tied to the experiential and homegrown underpinnings of American craft traditions. Their ideas and their art have resonated with admirers for several generations and reflect the trends and complexities of American culture and its various waves of cosmopolitanism, utopianism, nationalism, and isolationism.

While the Hambidge Center reflected and instigated trends in American art history in the twentieth century, questions about Mary and Jay continue to be raised. Who were Jay Hambidge and Mary Crovatt Hambidge? Why do we not know more about the broader context of their work and lives?[14] There is no single reason, but a set of circumstances led to them being overshadowed by other people and events.

Jay died at the height of his career, and his papers remained untouched and unexamined for decades.[15] His writing was dense, and his theory of Dynamic Symmetry involved complex formulas based on Classic Greek art and mathematical measurements. He died before he could fully realize how his ideas were adaptable to the new machine age developing in America, which ushered in streamlined industrial design.[16] After Jay's death, Mary worked to continue his legacy while piecing together a living in the New York area by weaving fashionable garments and opera costumes before she retreated to the rural mountains of northeastern Georgia. Rabun Studios had brought cachet to Mary, but then it was closed. Mary increasingly railed against industrial progress and capitalism, and the farm, the weaving collective, and plans for a school and residency program floundered. Her subsequent lack of recognition can be partly attributed to scholarly biases, which have perceived textiles as a non-academic craft produced by women and, in Mary's case, by a woman in a remote location often disconnected from contemporary developments in art and design.[17]

Both Jay and Mary lived and worked at a time when the forces of the machine age challenged artists who clung to more traditional forms of art and craft. Neither was an academic, and neither fit solidly into a specific stylistic niche. Their art and ideas never became mainstream or associated with the avant-garde. In addition, archival documents do not provide a clear chronological picture of either of them. We do not have Mary's letters to Jay, and we know little about Jay before he met Mary. The Hambidge Center for Creative Arts and Sciences, now a robust residential artist program, evolved primarily after her death in 1973. Furthermore, while there is some scholarship on each of them separately, until now there has been no in-depth discussion of them together. Jay and Mary were important independently and collectively for different reasons. Examining those distinctions provides a wider understanding of their lives in the larger context of late nineteenth- and early twentieth-century art and design. They were from two different worlds, nearly a generation apart in age, and only together for ten years, but their lives intertwined at a pivotal moment in their development. They shared a goal to establish a place where they could integrate the arts around the concept of Dynamic Symmetry, a dream that in Jay's case was never realized. Perhaps all of these elements managed to push the Hambidge legacy to the back burner of history.

In this book, I seek to bring their history to the forefront. I provide an improved chronology based on extensive research and significant new archival discoveries. I also put Jay Hambidge, Mary Crovatt Hambidge, and the Hambidge Center for Creative Arts and Sciences into contextual perspective, exploring the impact of Dynamic Symmetry and artistic collaborations in the context of twentieth-century art and cultural history. Chapter 1 presents a broad biographical overview of Jay Hambidge and Mary Crovatt and sets the stage on the East Coast, especially New York City, as Jay and Mary begin their careers before eventually meeting in 1914. What had each accomplished at this point, and what brought them together?

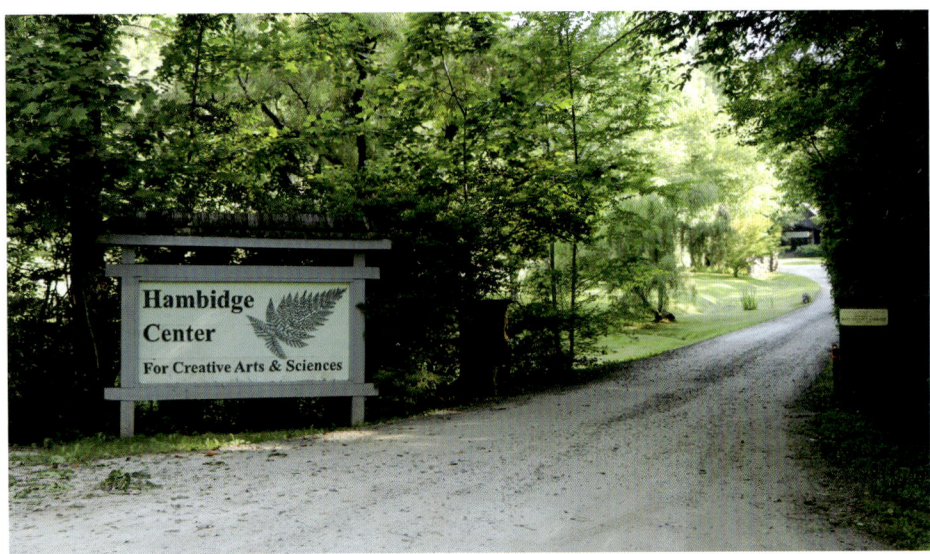

Entrance to the Hambidge Center
for Creative Arts and Sciences.
Photographer unknown, n.d.

Chapter 2 examines the principles of Dynamic Symmetry and its reverberation in the American art scene. Who was drawn to Dynamic Symmetry, and why? What did the critics have to say? Chapter 3 explores the couple's time in Greece and the aftermath in New York as Mary embraced weaving and Jay steadily lectured. Who did Mary meet in Greece, and how did she learn to weave? What did she do during the decade after Jay's death?

Chapter 4 traces the establishment and development of the Weavers of Rabun and Rabun Studios in the context of the Appalachian craft revival and the midcentury studio craft movement. I also examine Mary's approach to weaving and designing in juxtaposition to contemporary weaver-designers aligned with industry. Chapters 5 and 6 are essays written by former Hambidge Fellows and instructors, who look back on the last decades of the twentieth century and forward to the continued development of the Hambidge Center for Creative Arts and Sciences. Today, the Hambidge Center exists as a nonprofit arts center and residency program allowing artists and writers from across the world to experience the pleasures of creation in the isolation and beauty of the Blue Ridge Mountains.

The story I tell here is fascinating and complex. It begins with Jay Hambidge's theory of Dynamic Symmetry and leads to an artist residency program founded by Mary Crovatt Hambidge in the northeastern Georgia mountains. Let us see how these disparate elements came together then and have come together now.

CHAPTER 1

Nineteenth-Century Foundations, Twentieth-Century Lives

The Early Years to 1914

Jay Hambidge and Mary Crovatt met in New York City in 1914 when Mary was twenty-nine and Jay was forty-seven. Jay was already an accomplished illustrator and on the cusp of earning wide recognition for his ideas on Dynamic Symmetry. Mary, on the other hand, an up-and-coming performer, had secured only limited acting roles and whistling engagements with her pet mockingbird, Jimmy. As she later told it, she had lived for years on the verge of extinction until she met Jay Hambidge.[1]

   While none of Mary's letters to Jay are extant, there is a profusion of letters from Jay to Mary from 1914 to 1924. These letters partially trace the chronology of their work and activities, and provide some insight into their relationship. Jay's early letters to Mary described his projects and goals, and he professed his romantic love for her: "Dear Lady Dainty," "Oh Mary! . . . Your exquisite self," "I am also finding dearest, how completely I have lost myself in you," "Mary how beautiful you looked this afternoon. Your marvelously chiseled face and glorious eyes, so full of alertness, comprehension, and sympathy."[2] Jay wrote to Mary nearly every day in 1914, documenting his daily activities. For example, a note on July 13, 1914, was dashed off from the train station: "Darling Mary and Jimmy, *Scrio questi due righe in fretta* [I write these two lines quickly]. The train leaves at 7:50. I am already lonely darling. I got up this morning before six and have been thinking of you continuously. Dearest, dearest, I love you, love you."[3]

   Although no record of a marriage between Jay and Mary has been discovered, they probably were married, either by common law, which was allowed in New York until 1938, or through official means. There are references to their marriage in letters, including one from Jay himself. In an undated letter written between 1920 and 1923 from Jay Hambidge to the artist Howard Giles, which is only partially legible, Jay wrote, "Mary and I have been talking

When I returned to New York some destiny took me back to his studio and then I grew to know him better. He believed in the Handcrafts and always said "take care of the Handcrafts and the arts will take care of themselves."
—MARY CROVATT HAMBIDGE

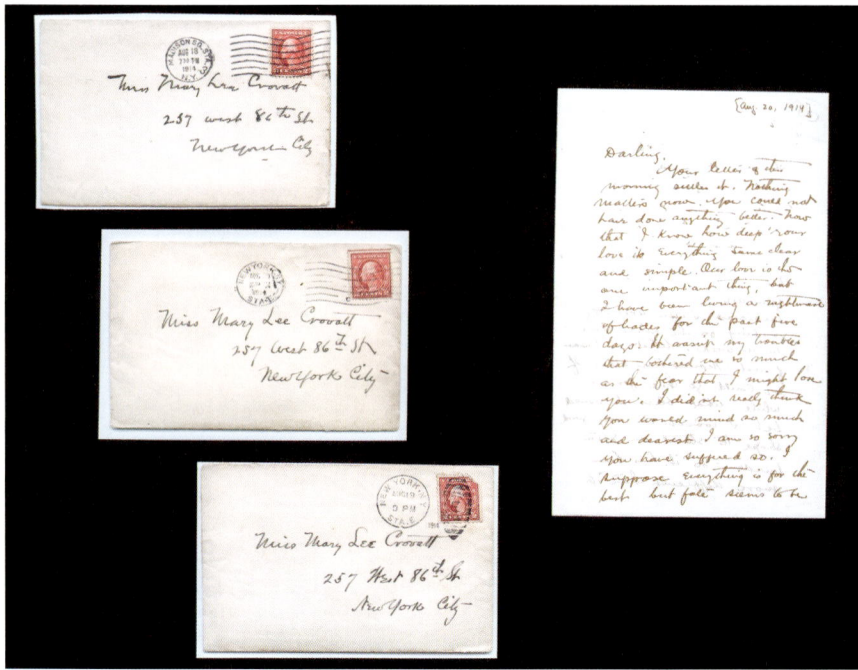

Letter from Jay Hambidge to Mary Lee Crovatt, August 20, 1914, and envelopes. Courtesy of Hargrett Rare Book and Manuscript Library, University of Georgia Libraries, Hambidge Papers, box 1, folder 2; photograph courtesy of Hal Jacobs

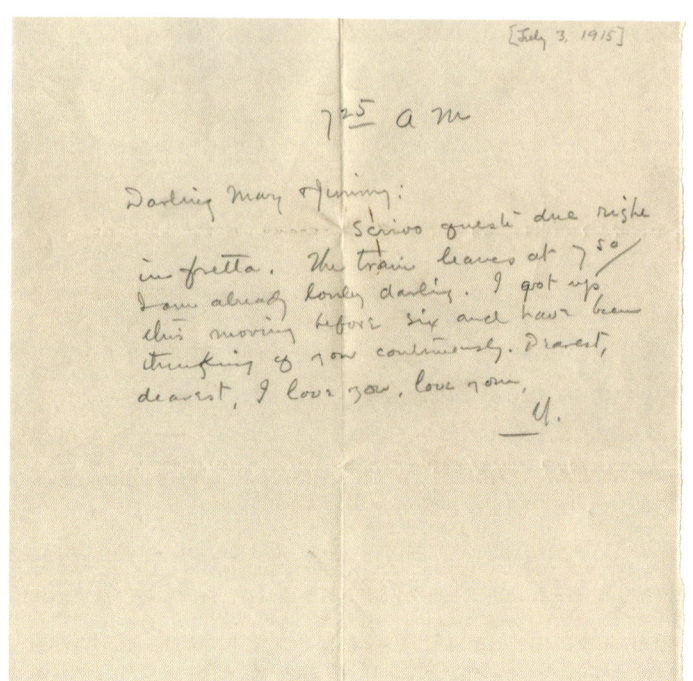

Letter from Jay Hambidge to Mary Lee Crovatt, July 3, 1915. Courtesy of Hargrett Rare Book and Manuscript Library, University of Georgia Libraries, Hambidge Papers, box 1, folder 2

things over and we have decided if the occasion is necessary our marriage may be announced." And there is a 1923 letter from the president of Yale University Press, George Parmly Day, congratulating Jay on his recent marriage: "I would like to take advantage of this opportunity to send to your wife and yourself our congratulations and warm good wishes. We had no idea that you were contemplating getting married, but the suddenness of the news has not stunned us to such an extent that we cannot at least try to tell you how happy we are to learn of your happiness, and how eager we are to have a chance to congratulate you both in person before long."[4]

Jay had been previously married. There is a copy of a divorce decree from Duval County, Florida, dated June 22, 1922 (most likely facilitated by Mary's attorney father or brother), terminating the marriage between Jay Hambidge and Cordella DeLorme Hambidge and stipulating that the complainant had resided in the state for two years, which was not the case.[5] By then, Jay had already made Mary the beneficiary and executor of his will, "in token of my love, esteem and affection for her and as a reward for her five years of laborious service in difficult research for me, which she carried on without compensation and at an actual expenditure on her part and from her own funds of five thousand dollars."[6]

Jay Hambidge

Jay Hambidge, born Edward John Hambidge in Simcoe, Ontario, Canada, was the son of a family of butcher shop owners and had six sisters and two brothers.[7] He left Canada in his late teens or early twenties and worked in Council Bluffs, Iowa, as a draftsman; in Kansas City as a printer's apprentice for the *Kansas City Times*; and then as a reporter for the *Kansas City Star*.[8] He married Cordella DeLorme (1873–1956) of Council Bluffs in January 1889, and they subsequently had two daughters and two sons: Gove (1890–1970), Ruth (1893–1986), Cordella (1903–1959), and Graeme (1906–1964). Their eldest son, Gove Hambidge, became a noted scholar of agriculture and worked with Jay on some of his publications.[9]

In the 1890s Hambidge moved his growing family to Amityville, New York, to live on what Gove called a farm, with a separate art studio for Jay.[10] Around that time a fellow Canadian, Peter McArthur, an editor of *Truth* magazine (published from 1881 to 1905), which featured a number of Jay's illustrations, moved nearby in Amityville. Together they began to develop a theory of design linking natural growth patterns of plants to the proportions of Classic Greek architecture. Jay coined the name "Dynamic Symmetry" to explain this relationship.[11]

In 1897 he was listed as a pupil of William Merritt Chase, who was then teaching art at the Shinnecock Summer School of Art and the Art Students League in New York.[12] Hambidge soon became known as a skilled illustrator whose dramatic drawings enlivened the pages of books and magazines, such as *McClure's*, *Century*, *Truth*, *Harper's*, and *Collier's*. His work was exhibited at the 1900 Paris Exposition Universelle, the 1901 Pan-American Exposition, and the 1904 Louisiana Purchase Exposition, among other venues.

Hambidge and McArthur set about convincing the editor of *Century*, Richard Gilder, to send them to London to study Greek art at the British Museum—including the prized Elgin Marbles from the frieze, metopes, and pediments of the Parthenon—and to consult with scholars and curators

Jay Hambidge, "Merry Christmas in the Tenements," *Century* 55, no. 2 (December 1897): 173. Miriam and Ira D. Wallach Division of Art, Prints and Photographs: Picture Collection, New York Public Library Digital Collections, https://digitalcollections.nypl.org /items/510d47e0-d689-a3d9-e040-e00a18064a99

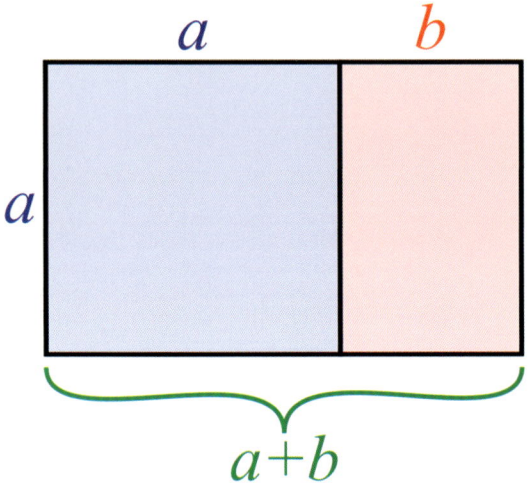

Golden ratio diagram: a/b = (a + b)/a

there. In addition, they sought to create a journal that McArthur titled the *Originator*, which would be marketed as "a magazine of attainable ideas."[13] Hambidge set sail for London with his family on March 15, 1902, and once there quickly began refining his ideas about Dynamic Symmetry.[14] He believed that Classic Greek architecture was planned and measured not by linear increments but by area and proportion based on the golden ratio.

The golden ratio is a formula achieved by dividing a line into two parts so that the longer part (a) divided by the shorter part (b) is equal to the whole length divided by the longer part: a/b = (a + b)/a. To prove his theory, Hambidge studied measurements of Classic Greek temples, such as the Parthenon, and found that the ratio of the length divided by the width was approximately 1.618, which is phi, or the basis of the golden ratio. This work received early positive recognition from artists and curators in London, particularly Francis Penrose, president of the Royal Institute of British Architects and former director of the British School in Athens. Penrose had spent time in Athens measuring temples, including the Parthenon, for his 1888 book, *An Investigation of the Principles of Athenian Architecture*. Penrose encouraged Jay to deliver a now-lost paper and slide presentation, "The Natural Basis of Form in Greek Art," to members of the Society for the Promotion of Hellenic Studies, which Jay spent months researching and polishing. By July 1902 Hambidge was urging McArthur to join him:

> I believe my work, as far as the digging and delving is concerned, is almost finished, and that it's about time for P. Mc A. to enter. I spent the entire afternoon with Penrose Tuesday, and had him check over the details of the Parthenon with me. . . . When I had finished, he frankly said I had one of the strongest and most remarkable cases he ever heard of. Penrose says I will have to take a great deal of care in preparing my paper so as to get the idea simply presented, because of the difficulty the ordinary mind has of comprehending a geometrical construction. . . . I believe that this work on Greek art will put us in a position to demand attention.[15]

Jay presented the work to an appreciative audience at the Hellenic Studies Society in November 1902. A sentence from his paper was quoted in the 1903 *Journal of Hellenic Studies*: "The Parthenon is only the most striking and complete instance of the fact that the beautiful in art involves adherence to the same law as underlies the beautiful in nature."[16] But he and McArthur had a falling-out, and neither their magazine, the *Originator*, nor their collaboration materialized.[17] Hambidge continued to pursue his exploration of Dynamic Symmetry, hoping for recognition and funding.

Hambidge shared the success of his London paper in a six-page letter to Richard Gilder of *Century* in December 1902. The letter justified his work, promoted his ideas for future applications and publications, and issued a call for sponsorship. Jay believed that he had found a rational and mathematical system of design based on ancient formulas, which could be applied to contemporary art and design. He wrote, "I now have my matters in such shape that I can go before experts in architecture, stained glass, all decorative and applied art, printing and designing of book covers, textile decoration, furniture making, vase making and decorating mosaic work. . . . It is very simple. I don't believe a science was ever evolved which was capable of such immediate application as this."[18]

Jay's comments point to his ambition to broaden the scope of his art theory by the application of his set of principles to applied arts and decoration. While Jay did not state how he would carry out this ambition, he did believe he was on to something significant, and he continued exploring various possibilities for using Dynamic Symmetry in the design of crafts, decoration, and fine art. In his letter to Gilder he also emphasized that professors and curators had confirmed his theories and opened their libraries and collections to him, thus legitimizing his ideas. He offered to give *Century* first choice to publish his work, while mentioning that he would like the Carnegie Institution to support his ongoing research and writing.

Back in New York in early 1903, first in Harlem and then in Richmond Hill, Queens, where his mother lived, Hambidge continued to fulfill illustration assignments to earn a living while making measurements and researching proportional systems.[19] *Century* provided him with steady work and opportunities to travel, although he may also have relied on photographs to complete some of his assignments. For example, it is uncertain whether he was sent to Sicily by *Century* to illustrate the ancient Greek site of Girgenti for a travel article by Scottish writer William Sharp.[20] Sharp had spent a good deal of time in Sicily and North Africa and was a skilled travel chronicler. *Century*'s illustrated two-part series, "The Garden of the Sun: Route Notes in Sicily," was not published until March and May 1906, the year after Sharp died while in Sicily. Sharp was known to have obtained photographs of the sites he visited, writing to Gilder in 1893 while pitching an idea for an article on North Africa that "from these [photographs] I think good illustrations could be made."[21]

The Classic Greek ruins at Girgenti were well-known tourist attractions and had been photographed by many during the nineteenth and early

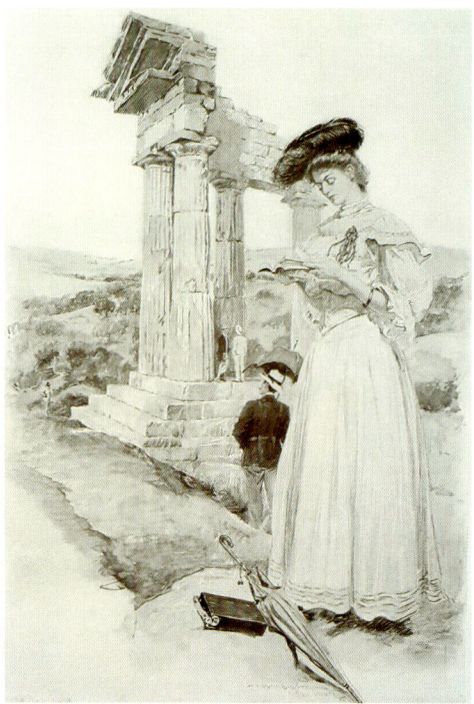 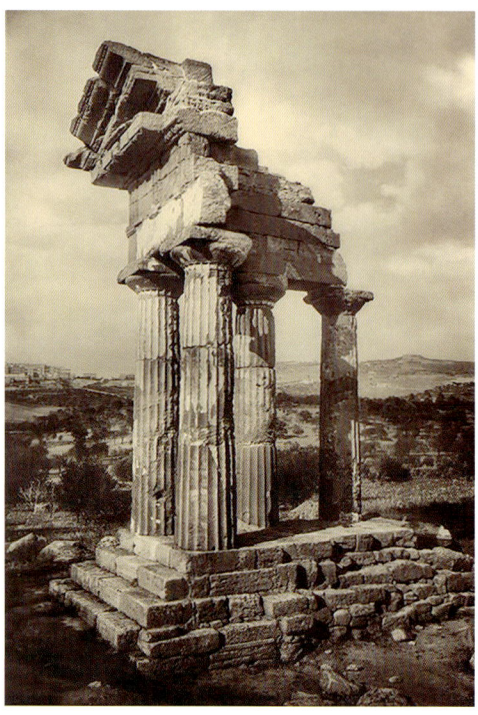

Jay Hambidge, *The Temple of Castor and Pollux at Girgenti*, *Century* 71, no. 1 (May 1906): 43

Adolph Braun and Co., *The Temple of Castor and Pollux at Girgenti*, n.d.

twentieth centuries. It is likely that some of Hambidge's thirty illustrations for parts I and II, which would have required extensive travel, research, and labor, were based on these photographs. Indeed, his drawing *The Temple of Castor and Pollux at Girgenti* in the May 1906 issue looks strikingly similar to a vintage photograph of the ruin, minus the Western-dressed figures.[22] However, a 1909 *Century* article, "After the Earthquake," chronicling the Messina, Italy, quake of 1908, included Hambidge's illustrations *The Strait of Messina Looking North* and *Eastern Coast of Sicily*, both captioned "from a sketch made on the spot by Jay Hambidge 1905." In a letter to Mary advising her about steamships to take home from Greece, Jay noted that a particular ship, the *Philadelphia*, "was the one I took to Italy."[23] In any case, whether the illustrations were drawn on site or from photographs, Hambidge's style reveals a steady and skilled draftsman who clearly planned the viewer's eye direction from foreground to middle ground to background through the use of diagonals, value gradations, and visual balance.

In 1911 Hambidge was the managing artist for the New York branch of Carlton Illustrators, an association of illustrators founded in London in 1902 by four Canadians. He used this position to pitch magazine articles and get commissions for members.[24] He studied books on botany and Greek and Egyptian architecture, and he read the work of contemporary American designers who, like him, were interested in articulating a practical vocabulary of design principles.[25] He would have been familiar with the work of Arthur Wesley Dow, a professor of fine art at the Art Students League and Columbia University's Teachers College, who published *Composition: A Series of Exercises in Art Structure for the Use of Students and Teachers* in 1899, which encouraged students to focus on arranging compositions based on the elements and principles of design, such as line, color, and value, rather than rote copying of nature, as was taught previously in most art schools.[26] Hambidge became a lifelong friend of Denman Waldo Ross, a professor of art at Harvard, who published *A Theory of Pure Design: Harmony, Balance, Rhythm* in 1907, which also advocated for employing design systems over representation, and who was an avid collector of textiles from diverse cultures and periods.[27] Dow and Ross were among the most influential early twentieth-century artist-educators who sought diagrammatic tools to streamline and rationalize image making through flat and simplified patterns based on natural forms. Their manuals provided designers, particularly textile designers and embroiderers, with new ways of looking at pattern, and they contributed to the organic patterns of the American Arts and Crafts style.[28]

Hambidge was not included in the pivotal International Exhibition of Modern Art, also known as the Armory Show, in 1913, which brought European modern art to America, but he did visit the exhibition and write about it. Hambidge believed that some of the Cubist artists sought to link science and art, but not in the methodical way that he linked them. He and his son Gove, who had just graduated from Columbia University, worked on an essay together, "The Ancestry of Cubism," which was published in *Century* in April 1914 and traced the history of artists who utilized geometry in their designs back to the medieval and Renaissance periods. The problem with Cubism, they wrote, was that the artists did not use systematic formulas or a consistent design language, but instead resorted to "personal caprice" and subjectivity by "cubifying" actual forms. The real progressive art, they suggested, was taking place in Austria at the Wiener Werkstätte (1903–1932), a collective of artists who worked in the applied arts—architecture,

V

THE ANCESTRY OF CUBISM

BY JAY HAMBIDGE AND GOVE HAMBIDGE

"CUBISM is an attempt to dissolve facts entirely in design," some one has remarked. It is a pregnant phrase that sticks in the mind and touches many veins of thought. After decades of paintings from Salon and academy, suave, su-

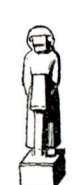

EGYPTIAN
CUBISM

perficial, blatant with the wearisome technical daring of the virtuoso, or smeared thick with a syrup of pretty sentiment, we are ready for nearly anything, provided it smacks of really creative art. The artistic mind has for so long assiduously degraded itself to the position of an observant human camera that only a strong reaction can restore something of its original self-respect. That reaction takes place among certain men who are so alive to our artistic degradation that they feel realism to be a disgusting and intolerable thing; they eschew it completely, and take refuge in pure symbolic design. At least this ultra-idealism comports more with the dignity of creative art than ultra-naturalism. It is better that an artist be poeti-

cally mad than a slave to endless copying. Art was not born to fill the position of a clerk in the outer office of nature.

But if a very meaty kernel is to be found in the basic idea of Cubism, there is much useless pulp surrounding it, and we are compelled to consider this pulp the real fruit of the movement. After a clear ex-

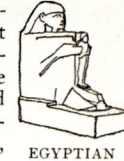

EGYPTIAN
CUBISM

amination, it becomes evident that Cubic iconoclasm is, after all, superficial, even if we consider only its leaders, and put aside all those notoriety-lovers who follow in the van, together with the egomaniacs who are bent upon toying with their pet subjective perversions, and use violent art as a means. With design for a lever, the Cubists wish to break completely the grip of realistic art. Yet what do they give us in return? Try as we may, we cannot but consider their own design ill digested and chaotic. It does not "reach" us in conditions either of normal or of abnormal appreciation. They have, indeed, substituted nothing generally constructive for that which they

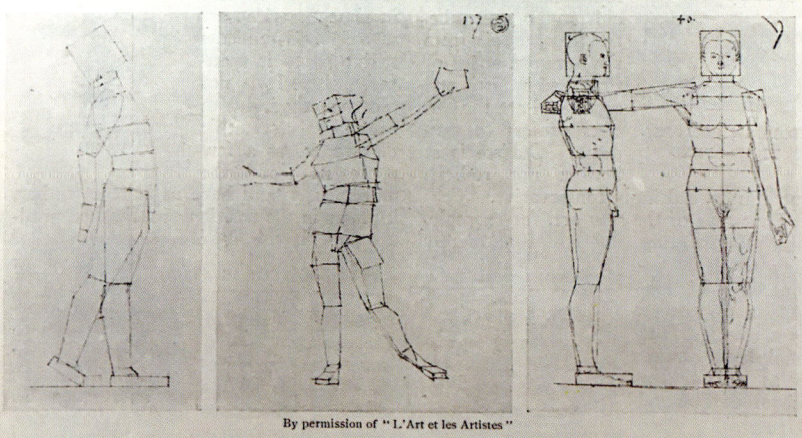

By permission of "L'Art et les Artistes"

CUBISTIC TREATMENT BY ALBRECHT DÜRER

Jay Hambidge and Gove Hambidge,
"The Ancestry of Cubism," *Century* 87
(April 1914): 869

furniture, jewelry, glass, textiles—using a design vocabulary based on geometric structures and patterns. They often designed works for specific architectural spaces, just as some medieval and Renaissance artists had done before them, similar to what Jay envisioned for his own enterprise. "Here, in this [development] out of architecture, lies the cause of that curious quality in early paintings which has made them preeminent for design."[29] The idea of providing a geometric framework for contemporary artists to utilize in order to achieve compositional dynamism was something Jay would spend the next decade developing, refining, and defending.

At this time in 1914, according to Gove, Jay's family fell apart. Cordella was very sick, and Jay began living with his sisters Sarah (Sally) and Cecelia (Celia), who were successful seamstresses in Manhattan. He also rented a studio in Manhattan, leaving Cordella and the children alone in Queens. Not long after, Cordella and the younger children moved to California to live with her mother, never to see Jay again.[30] And that year, Jay Hambidge began his relationship with Mary Lee Crovatt.

Mary Lee Crovatt

Mary was born in coastal Brunswick, Georgia, an important shipping and railroad hub and a gateway to the posh clubs and homes on Jekyll and St. Simons Islands—the Golden Isles of Georgia—an area that had been home to Native American peoples and a destination for ships carrying kidnapped African people for the slave trade. She was born into an affluent and influential family and lived in a home staffed with servants, including "Mammy Sue," a formerly enslaved woman who was the nurse for Mary and her two older brothers.[31] Mary's brother Alfred H. became an attorney and served in the U.S. Infantry in World War I, and her brother William C. joined the U.S. Marine Corps and attended Emory University.[32] Mary received a formal education at the Lee School for Girls, an academic finishing school in Cambridge, Massachusetts, from 1901 until returning to Brunswick in 1904.[33] Her course notebooks show that she studied art history, Greek language and philosophy, theater history, speech and diction, English, French language and conversation, and German.[34]

Her father, Alfred J. Crovatt, was a successful businessman, a partner in the law firm Crovatt and Mabry, a Glynn County court judge, and the mayor of Brunswick for two terms beginning in 1883. Her mother, Mary Lee Schlatter, was the daughter of the vice president of the Brunswick and

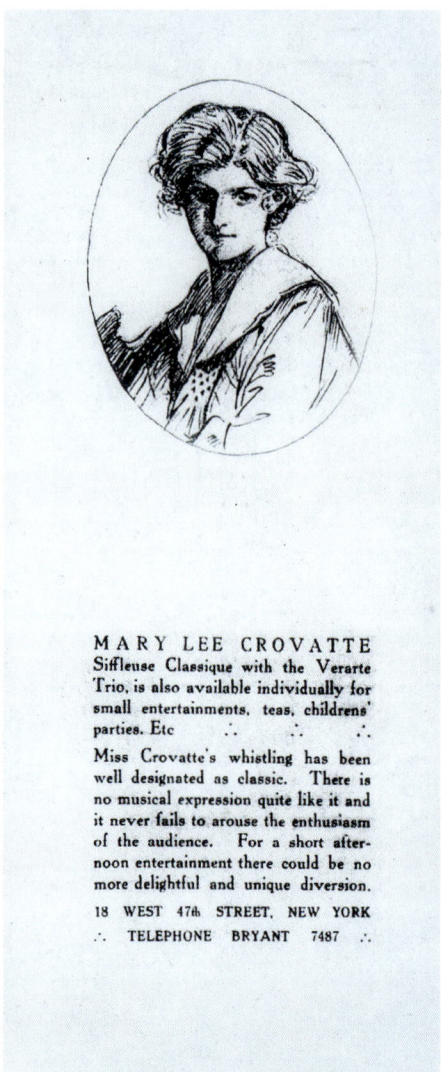

MARY LEE CROVATTE
Siffleuse Classique with the Verarte
Trio, is also available individually for
small entertainments, teas, childrens'
parties. Etc ⸫   ⸫   ⸫

Miss Crovatte's whistling has been
well designated as classic.   There is
no musical expression quite like it and
it never fails to arouse the enthusiasm
of the audience.   For a short afternoon entertainment there could be no
more delightful and unique diversion.

18 WEST 47th STREET, NEW YORK
⸫ TELEPHONE BRYANT 7487 ⸫

"Mary Lee Crovatte," whistling
advertisement. Courtesy of the
Hambidge Center for Creative
Arts and Sciences

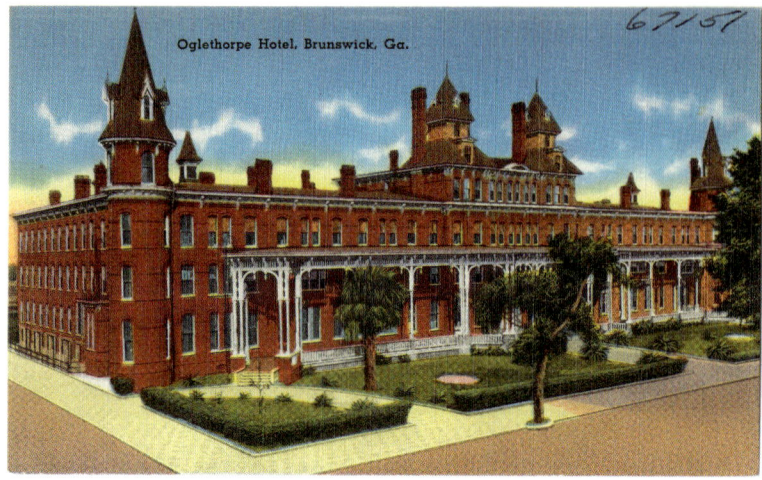

Oglethorpe Hotel, Brunswick, Ga.

Postcard of
Oglethorpe Hotel
in Brunswick,
Georgia, n.d.

Western Railroad. Both families were instrumental in the founding of the Jekyll Island Club in the mid-1880s and in developing the island's land, rail and telegraph systems, race course, water rights, and hotels.[35] According to the bylaws of the Jekyll Island Club, entrance fees to the club were $100 per share, and charter members, who most likely had contact with the Crovatts, included industrialists, bankers, and art collectors, including Cornelius Bliss, J. P. Morgan, Joseph Pulitzer, and William K. Vanderbilt, all of New York, and Marshall Field of Chicago.[36]

Mary was clearly part of the society set of Georgia. Her name appeared frequently in the society pages of Atlanta, Brunswick, and Savannah newspapers between 1905 and 1909. For example, in 1905, among those attending "the social event of the season," the New Year reception and cotillion at the palatial Oglethorpe Hotel in Brunswick, was "Miss Mary Lee Crovatt."[37] Subsequent reports noted that Mary Lee Crovatt "has returned from Jekyll Island"; attended a "water party"; "returned from a visit to friends in New York, Boston, Philadelphia and other cities"; "is visiting friends in Atlanta"; "left Thursday for New York"; "after a pleasant visit at the North, returned home Monday"; "is visiting friends in Asheville, North Carolina"; and "is with relatives in Radnor, Pennsylvania."[38]

While her parents may have wanted her to meet an eligible bachelor in her social circles, Mary followed a different path by pursuing acting, mod-eling, and professional whistling, going by the name Mary Lee Crovatte for a short time. She performed with a mockingbird, Jimmy, whose remains she donated to the American Museum of Natural History in 1926. She took a whistling course from Mrs. Alice J. Shaw in New York, who was known as "the Whistling Prima Dona," earning a degree on October 10, 1911.[39] She had professional acting photographs taken that show her in various poses with dramatic facial expressions.[40] In 1913, she performed a whistling solo of "In Venice" at the Confederate Reunion Ball at the Oglethorpe Hotel in Brunswick.[41] She played the role of Kitty Clover in the Brunswick production of the comic opera *Princess Bonnie*, with one reporter noting that "Miss Mary Lee Crovatt, piquant and engaging in every movement and gesture, was another favorite who carried the house by storm with her sweet voice and realistic acting."[42]

By 1914 she was in New York, performing with Jimmy and staying with friends or in various women's rooming houses, which were common at the

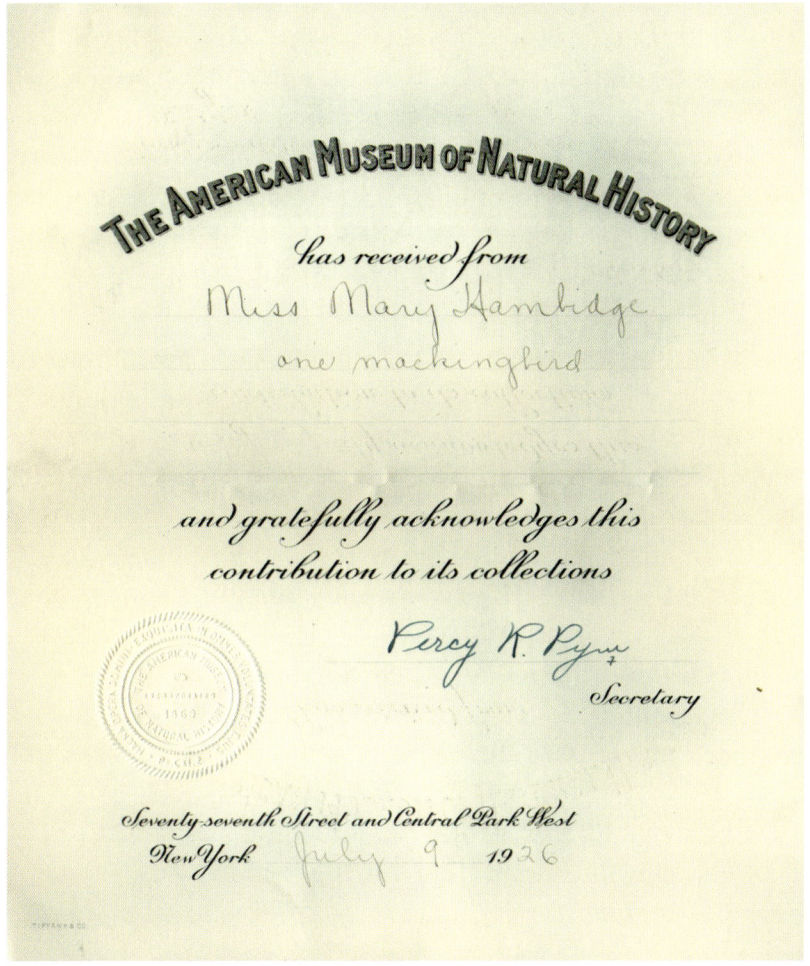

Donation certificate for Jimmy the mockingbird, 1926. Kenan Research Center at the Atlanta History Center, box 6, folder 4

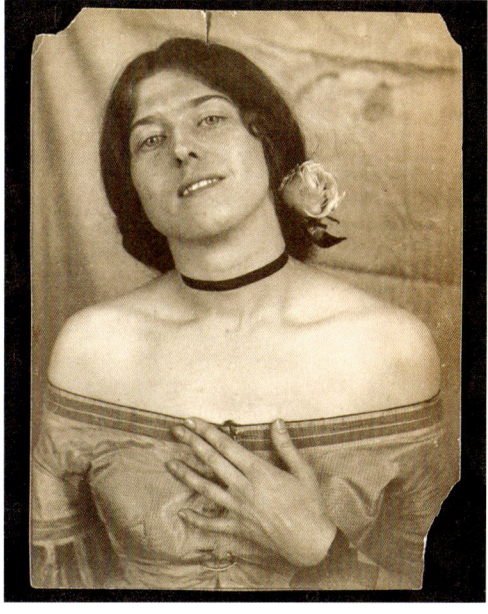

Mary Lee Crovatt, promotional photograph, n.d. Kenan Research Center at the Atlanta History Center, VIS 1.91, 1.92

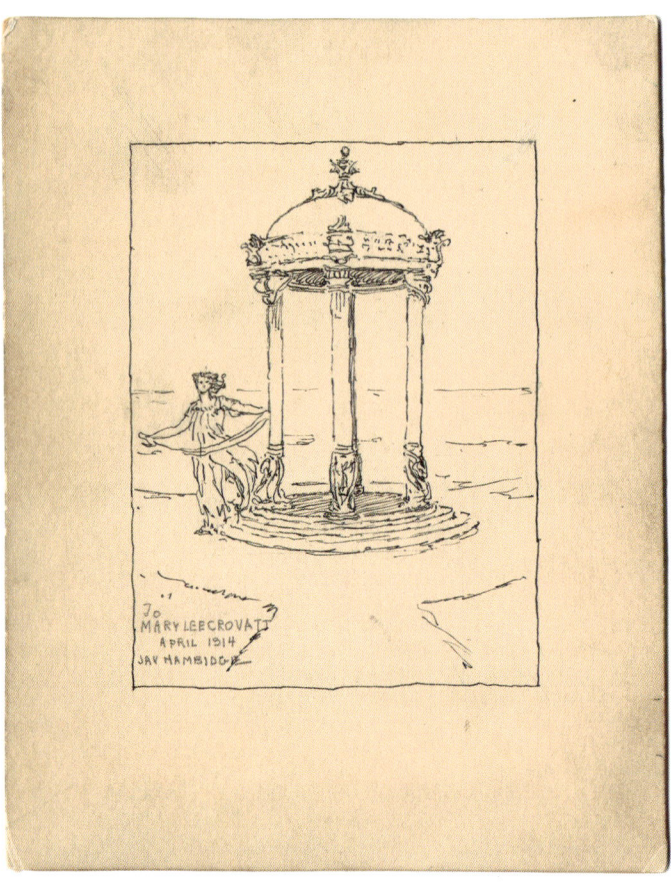

Jay Hambidge, "To Mary Lee Crovatt,
April 1914." Courtesy of Hargrett
Rare Book and Manuscript Library,
University of Georgia Libraries,
Hambidge Papers, box 1, folder 2

time.[43] The last mention of her whistling career was a 1917 performance at the home of Mrs. Charles Alexander in New York for a Junior Guild event.[44] It remains unknown what else she was doing in New York when she met Jay Hambidge. Was she posing as a model for one of his illustrations? Had he heard about her performances and sought her out? They both appear to have been at loose ends in 1914. In a letter to Denman Ross asking for funds to have Jay's lectures published posthumously, Mary wrote, "When I met him he was at his ropes end. . . . I have known his heart to pound so that the whole bed was shaken. Yet so great was his self-control that he never complained and to the very end he believed in the beauty of life and humanity. . . . With such inspiration as that what can I do but go on to the end whether I get help or not. I must justify his faith in me."[45]

The first documentation of their contact is an ink drawing by Jay of a woman with flowing hair and a long draping gown, who is stepping from a classically columned gazebo; it is signed "To Mary Lee Crovatt, April 1914, Jay Hambidge."[46] The next evidence is a little note to Mary on May 1, 1914, "I appreciated your visit this afternoon more than I can say. Sometime I should like to see you at work. Let me know the name of the theatre and some evening when you are not expecting I will be in the audience."[47] His letters were addressed to her at the newly constructed stately apartment building at 257 West 86th Street. Jay wrote from his studio in the Bancroft Building at 3 West 29th Street. This handsome building, now demolished, housed several architects' offices, the offices of *Cassier's* magazine, and the office for the Camera Club of New York, whose members included some of the most important photographers in early twentieth-century America, including life member Alfred Stieglitz.

Despite Hambidge's proximity to Stieglitz and to Stieglitz's gallery, 291 (1905–1917), which displayed contemporary European and American art, no references to Stieglitz appear in Jay's letters and writings. Jay was not among the circle of experimental, avant-garde artists and photographers championed by Stieglitz at the gallery or in the pages of *Camera Work*, which included Arthur Dove, John Marin, Marsden Hartley, and Georgia O'Keeffe, who married

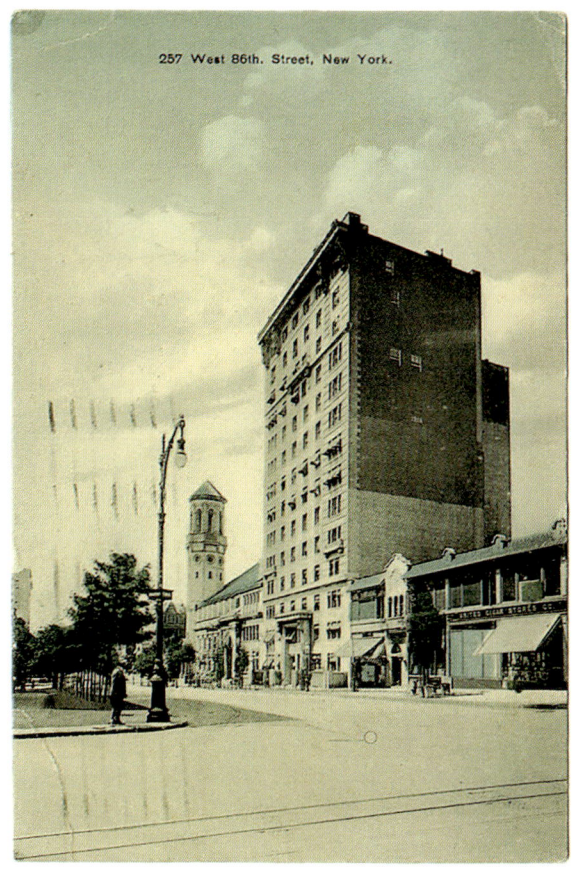

Postcard showing Mary's apartment building at 257 West 86th Street, New York, 1917

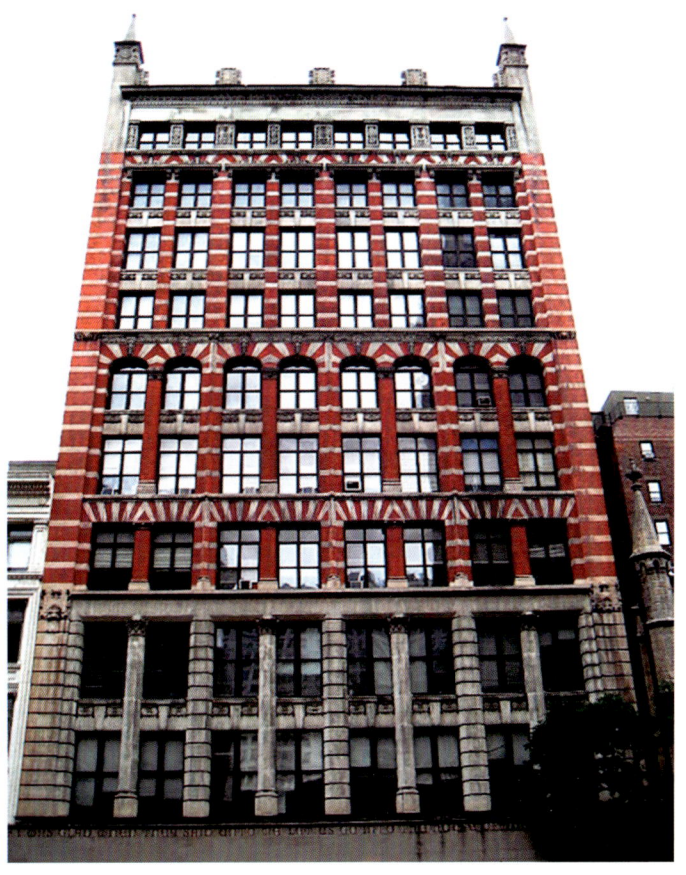

The Bancroft Building at 3 West 29th Street, New York, now demolished

Stieglitz in 1924. Jay's work was more traditional than theirs, grounded in pictorial representation rather than abstraction.

During the next decade Hambidge would find his calling as a writer and lecturer promoting Dynamic Symmetry. Mary seems to have provided a stable and supportive foundation for Jay as he pursued his career in New York, Boston, and Chicago. Jay's theories attracted numerous supporters and detractors, drawing him further into the spotlight, while Mary discovered weaving, which became her lifelong passion.

CHAPTER 2

Dynamic Symmetry

Jay Hambidge and His Circle

Much of the weakness of modern art is due to too much sex, too much sentiment, and too little design.—JAY HAMBIDGE

Jay Hambidge spent the decade between 1914 and 1924 articulating his theory of Dynamic Symmetry in books, journals, lectures, and courses. He wanted to provide an objective, mathematics-based method to guide artists in the creation of logically balanced compositions, writing, "Dynamic Symmetry is an impersonal matter, like perspective, and belongs to the technical sciences."[1] According to Hambidge, Dynamic Symmetry is not a recipe for a fixed mirror-image grid of definite lengths—which he termed static symmetry—but is a flexible, adaptable, dynamic process of dividing a rectangular picture plane into dominant and passive areas based on its diagonal, horizontal, and vertical subdivisions. He wrote, "In dynamic symmetry we have a law of pattern making capable of infinite variation and adaptable to every conceivable need of all art, as far as proportion is concerned. The problem of application is most simple as the artist may confine himself to but one rectangle all his life, because its logical subdivisions and expansions in terms of itself are infinite and encompass all the possibilities of every other rectangle of the system."[2] Hambidge's compositional theory provided artists with a method of creating designs governed by a structural logic through geometry at a time when industrial design and technical instruction began to play an increasingly important role in American culture.[3] His instructions for modern artists promoted a focus on structural composition rather than rote imitation: "Indeed, this is the lesson that modern artists must learn; that the backbone of art is formalization not realism. Art means exactly what the term implies. It is not nature but it must be based on nature, not upon the superficial skin, but upon structure."[4]

Hambidge believed that ancient Egyptian and Classic Greek sculptors and architects used a dynamic mathematical formula based on the area of root rectangles, rather than on linear length measurements, to achieve ideal proportions in vases and temples. This idea was known to other scholars before him, but he claimed to have rediscovered it and put it into modern practice. An illustration from his 1920 book, *Dynamic Symmetry: The Greek Vase*, shows a root five rectangle, which, when broken into consecutively smaller versions of itself, creates a spiral. This is also called a Fibonacci spiral, the golden rectangle, the golden ratio, or a rectangle of whirling squares (Hambidge's term), and it corresponds to growth patterns in nature, such as the spiral growth of nautilus shells. The connection between natural growth patterns, root rectangle geometry, and Classic Greek art and ceramics was something Hambidge sought to definitively prove. To this end, he began around 1917 to study and measure the proportions of Greek vases with assistance from Gisela Richter, curator in the Department of Greek and Roman Arts at the Metropolitan Museum of Art, and Lacey D. Caskey, head of the Antiquities Department at the Museum of Fine Arts, Boston. Both scholars became steadfast defenders of Jay's work and were instrumental in assisting with *Dynamic Symmetry: The Greek Vase*, in which he diagramed vessels to prove that most of the shapes corresponded to root five rectangles, as seen in his figure of a kalpis vessel.

Hambidge also benefited from his relationships with William Sergeant Kendall, dean of the School of Fine Arts, Yale University; Edward Forbes, director of Harvard's Fogg Art Museum from 1909 to 1944; and Denman Ross, professor of art at Harvard, all of whom became advocates. Ross painted an iconic portrait of Hambidge in front of a chalkboard with a Dynamic Symmetry design. Forbes and Ross were important in securing Jay a Samuel Sachs Research Fellowship in 1918–1919, which provided funds for Hambidge to study human anatomy at Harvard Medical School, to continue his study of Greek vases, and, with additional funds from Yale University Press, to travel to Athens, Greece, in 1920 to measure Classic Greek temples. The main goal of Hambidge's research was not necessarily to contribute to archaeological scholarship but to aid in contemporary artistic development by describing, illustrating, and demonstrating how Dynamic Symmetry could be applied to art and design in the modern world, including furniture, architecture, textiles, the human figure, and animals and birds. His foreword to *Dynamic Symmetry: The Greek Vase* summarized this idea:

fourth of a root-four outside and a root-five inside, one-fifth of a root-five outside. And a reciprocal to any rectangle is obtained by drawing a perpendicular from one corner.

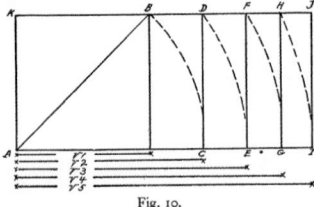

Fig. 10.

The whirling square rectangle and the root-five rectangle are placed within a square thus:

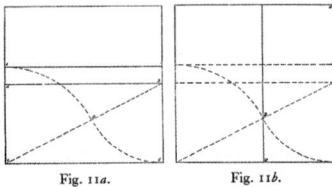

Fig. 11a.   Fig. 11b.

The square is first bisected by the line AB, to obtain a root-four rectangle or two squares. From the diagonal of this rectangle CB, unity, or BE, is subtracted to determine the point D, and CD, furnishes the side of the whirling square rectangle FE. See Fig. 11a. A line drawn through the point D, parallel to a side of the square, determines the root-five rectangle GH. Fig. 11b.

In a whirling square rectangle inscribed in a square, if lines be drawn through the eyes and produced to the opposite side of the square, a root-five rectangle is

Jay Hambidge, diagram of the root rectangle. *Dynamic Symmetry: The Greek Vase* (1920), 24

Some twenty years ago, the writer, being impressed by the incoherence of modern design and convinced that there must exist in nature some correlating principle which could give artists a control of areas, undertook a comparative study of the basis of all design, both in nature and in art. . . . The principle of dynamic symmetry is manifest in shell growth and in leaf distribution in plants. A study of the basis of design in art shows that this active symmetry was known to but two peoples, the Egyptians and the Greeks; the latter only having developed its full possibilities for purposes of art. The writer believes that he has now recovered, through study of natural form and shapes in Greek and Egyptian art, the principle for the proportioning of areas.[5]

Gisela Richter and Lacey Caskey believed that Hambidge had discovered a significant link in understanding the methods ancient potters may have used to craft their beautiful vessels. Indeed, Richter wrote that because of Hambidge's study, "we are at last in possession of the actual working scheme of Greek design."[6] Similarly, Caskey, in his preface to Hambidge's posthumously published book *The Parthenon and Other Greek Temples: Their Dynamic Symmetry*, praised Hambidge for providing enough evidence, investigated "according to a logical and scientific method," to demonstrate that the root five rectangle recurs frequently in measurements of Greek works of art.[7] Caskey applied Hambidge's methods to his own scholarship on Greek art during his long tenure at the Museum of Fine Arts, Boston.

By 1917 Hambidge had developed a considerable following of artists and illustrators, many from the Salmagundi Club, a Greenwich Village arts organization founded in 1871. He lectured at the office of *Century* magazine arts editor George Whittle, and when space became limited, at the studio of artist Edward B. Edwards, and later, when larger venues were needed, at museums and universities, such as the Art Institute of Chicago, the Metropolitan Museum of Art, Harvard University, and Yale University. Many of the artists attracted to Dynamic Symmetry worked as illustrators and decorative designers who saw in the theory a method of connecting fine and applied arts through a common system of design. Many also subscribed to Hambidge's correspondence courses, which included mail-order primers, and to his monthly publication, the *Diagonal* (1919–1920).[8] These mostly American artists, including Howard Giles, George Bellows, Robert Henri, Maxwell Armfield, Christine Herter, Maxfield Parrish, and Leon Kroll, appreciated Hambidge's mathematical method of dividing the picture plane into rational sections and angles, which provided an approach to composition governed by logic and laws rather than intuition. "Mr. Hambidge's discovery

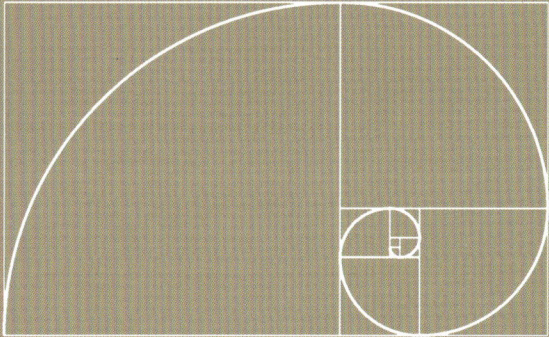

Diagram of a root five Fibonacci spiral

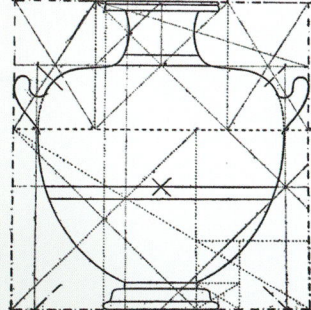

DYNAMIC SYMMETRY 87

metry, such as are furnished by temple plans, decoration, bronzes and pottery, areas and subdivisions of areas which echo and re-echo the shapes derivable from the regular solids and the summation series of phyllotaxis. That this is so the pottery designs alone abundantly show. The area of the elevation of a Greek vase of the first class, that is, the area obtained by the full height and width of such a vessel, and the secondary areas obtained by subdivision of details, such as width of foot, neck, lip and bowl and the height of such members, produce a series of shapes which could not be obtained accidentally. This is clearly disclosed by the analysis of a large krater, 10.185 in the Boston Museum

Fig. 14a.   Kalpis in the Boston Museum, showing a theme in whirling square and root-five.
(Measured, drawn and analyzed by L. D. Caskey.)

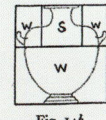 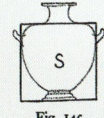

Fig. 14b.   Fig. 14c.

Jay Hambidge, diagram of a kalpis vessel. *Dynamic Symmetry: The Greek Vase* (1920), 87

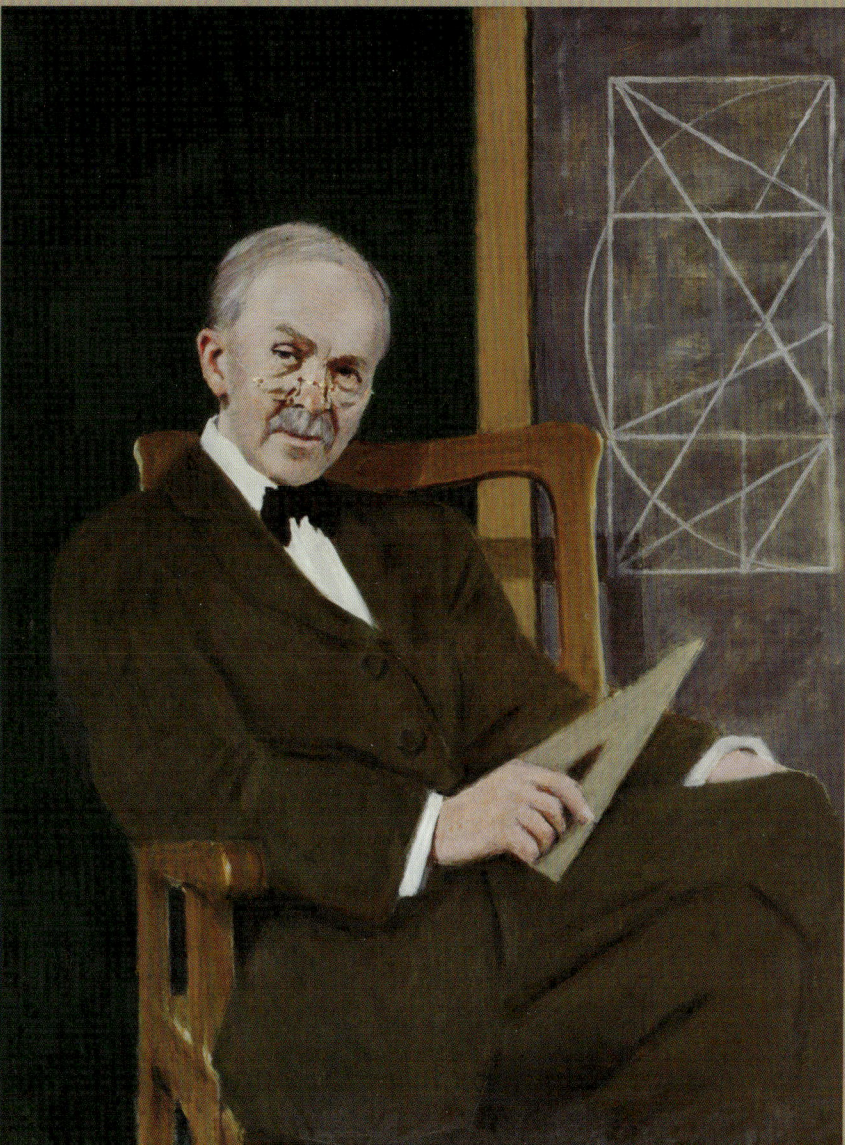

Denman Waldo Ross, *Jay Hambidge*, n.d., oil on canvas board, 102.9 × 76.2 cm. Harvard Art Museums/ Fogg Museum, Bequest of Denman W. Ross, class of 1875, 136.150.751, https://hvrd.art/o/310997

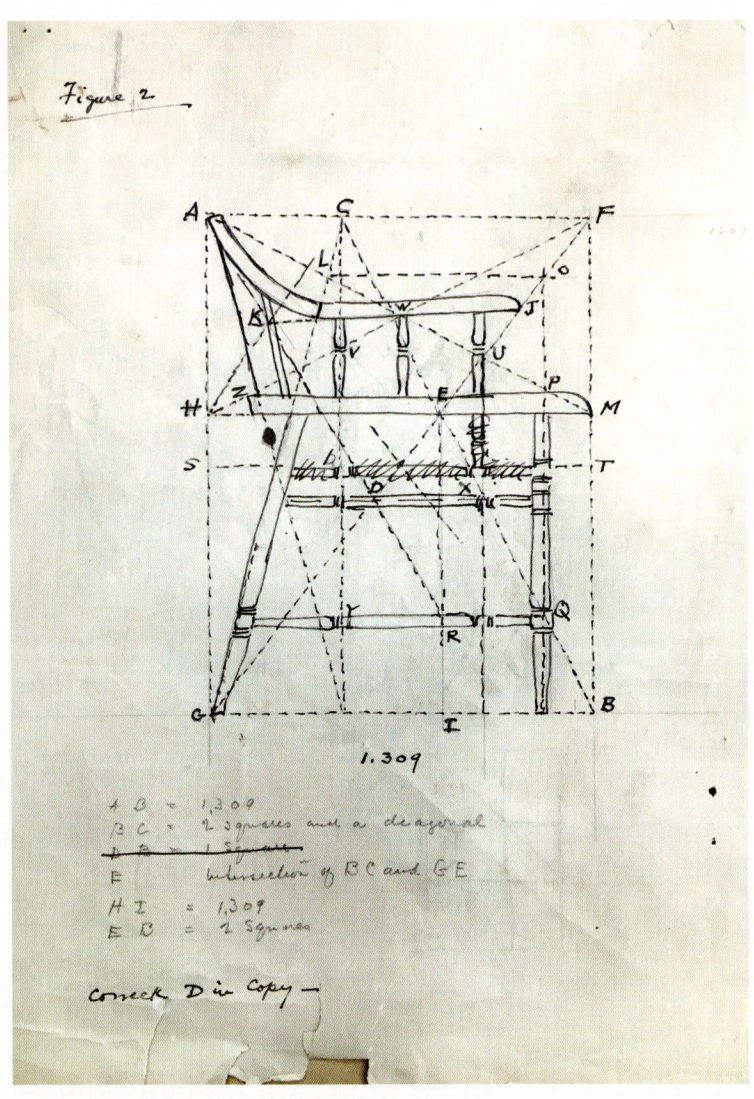

Jay Hambidge, diagram of a chair, n.d.
Kenan Research Center at the Atlanta
History Center, box 23, folder 5

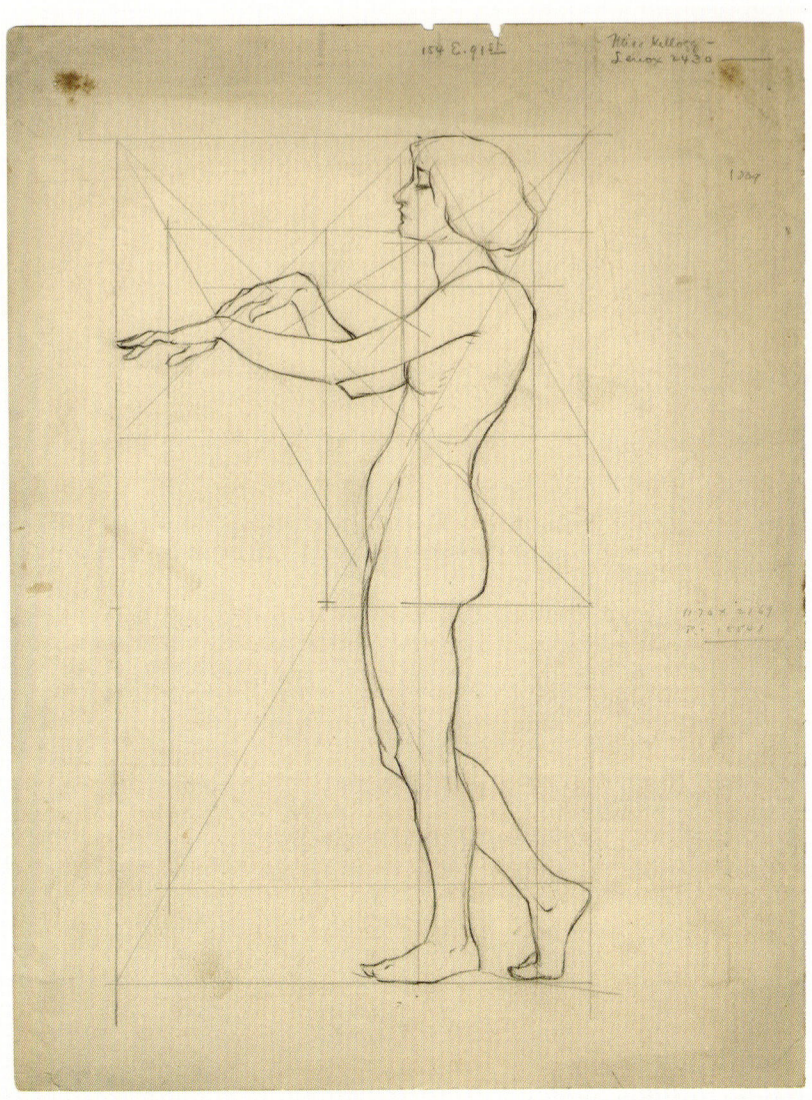

Jay Hambidge, drawing of a female figure,
n.d. Courtesy of Hargrett Rare Book and
Manuscript Library, University of Georgia
Libraries, Hambidge Papers, box 21

comes at an opportune moment," wrote Maxwell Armfield in a 1921 essay, "when the more thoughtful artists are searching for something more stable than mere personal likes and dislikes upon which to base their practice."[9] In a 1925 letter to Mary, Maxfield Parrish noted that "not a day goes by that I do not bless my fate that took me to that first lecture."[10] He later gave an idea of how engaging and inspiring the lectures were:

> A most delightful period, the evenings spent at Mr. Hambidge's last three lectures at the Fine Arts Building in New Yok: an experience whose memory seems to return again and again at the most unexpected moments: a wealth of new knowledge given by an exceptional personality, by an expert and enthusiast who inspired others with a lasting ambition. I wish those talks could have been taken down verbatim, with all the side remarks, the answers to questions, the chats after the lecture, etc. for they were as illuminating and as valuable as anything in the books.[11]

Because Jay Hambidge's instructions and writings on Dynamic Symmetry are dense and hard to follow for most people who do not have a firm background in mathematics, it is useful to hear about his theory from those who studied and applied it. Indeed, Denman Ross, in his 1924 memorial to Hambidge, wrote, "The readers of Hambidge's writings are not likely to understand his Theory or to appreciate its truth, value, and importance. The books are not easy reading. They are difficult and require special training and special knowledge. It is those who put the Theory into practice who will most easily understand what it is and what it means. Fortunately, putting the Theory into practice involves no more than a very elementary knowledge of geometry. It means the use of certain right-angled triangles on a drawing board with a T-square."[12]

Responses to Hambidge's Dynamic Symmetry were not unanimous and came from two general groups: supporters and detractors. Supporters, most of whom attended his lectures, included primarily artists and designers, museum curators, and British members of the Hellenic Studies Society, who found Dynamic Symmetry credible, understandable, and applicable to contemporary purposes. Detractors tended to be mathematicians and archaeologists, who found discrepancies in Hambidge's measurements and objected to claims that Greek artists, particularly potters, used the methods he described. Some detractors found the theory unintelligible, arrogant, and formulaic, and they ridiculed Hambidge's technical language and pronouncements. These disparate reactions, which caused quite a stir in newspapers,

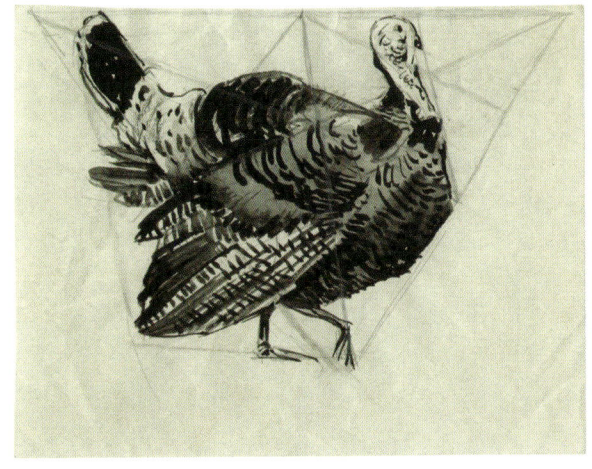

Jay Hambidge, drawing of a turkey, n.d. Courtesy of Hargrett Rare Book and Manuscript Library, University of Georgia Libraries, Hambidge Papers, box 16/17

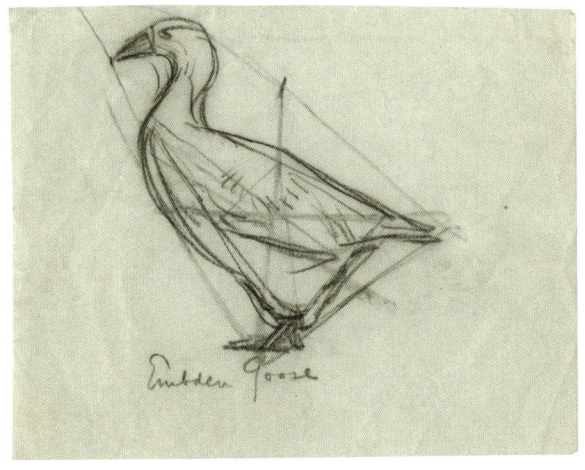

Jay Hambidge, drawing of an Embden goose, n.d. Courtesy of Hargrett Rare Book and Manuscript Library, University of Georgia Libraries, Hambidge Papers, box 16/17

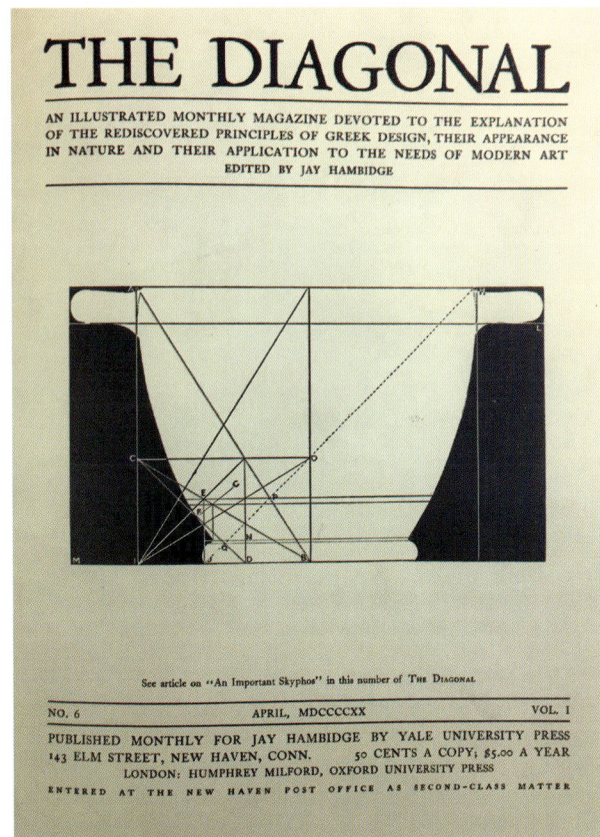

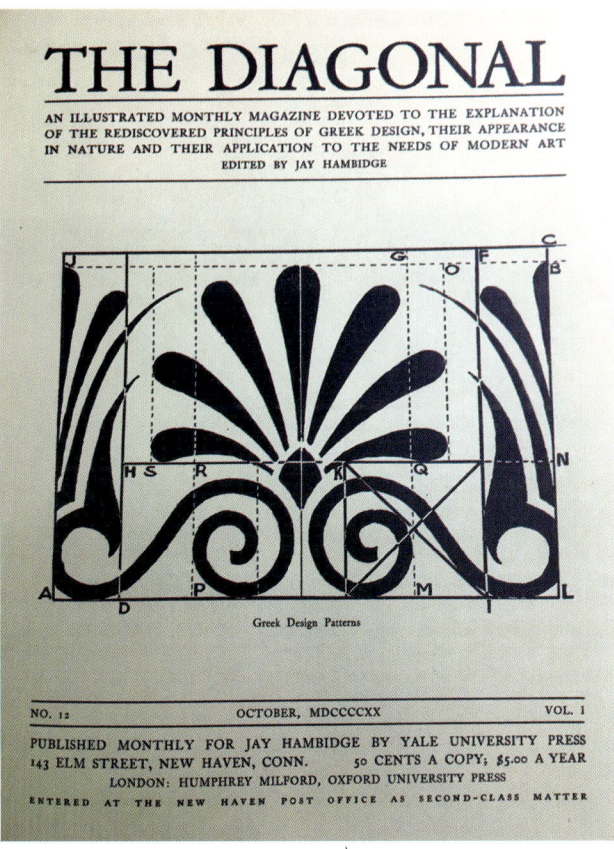

Jay Hambidge, cover of the *Diagonal* 1, no. 6
(April 1920)

Jay Hambidge, cover of the *Diagonal* 1, no. 12
(October 1920)

in journals, and on lecture circuits, would have developed into a great inter-disciplinary dialogue had Jay not suddenly died in January 1924.

Supporters

George Bellows was an artist who clearly put Dynamic Symmetry into practice. He was a student of Robert Henri at the New York School of Art.[13] Bellows and Henri were among a group of artists named the Ashcan school because their paintings depicted the dark and gritty side of American life, such as muddy streets, boxing rings, and tenement housing, as opposed to the lighter palette and style of the subject matter of American Impressionism. The Ashcan artists were seen as radical early in the century in their attempts to reframe American art, but with the advent of European modernism and abstraction after the Armory Show of 1913, they came to be perceived as conservative in their reliance on figurative realism. Believing Dynamic Symmetry to be an effective and efficient compositional formula, Bellows wrote:

> Ever since I met Mr. Hambidge and studied with him I have painted very few pictures without at the same time working on his theory. I believe it to be as profound as the law of the lever or the law of gravitation. No man who practices the arts, and this seems to be particularly true of architecture, can, with justice to himself, ignore the research that Hambidge has made. It has never been disproved, and the artist has but to learn and apply it in his work to know its helpfulness. . . . If a thing is made easier by technical understanding, then by so much is it true that having this particular phase made easier, your strength is conserved for those things which yet remain troublesome.[14]

Bellows saw Dynamic Symmetry as a tool that could be adapted according to the subject matter and the size of the canvas, writing, "It simplifies this certain difficulty of arrangement."[15] In his 1921 essay, "What Dynamic Symmetry Means to Me," Bellows wrote that Dynamic Symmetry was "probably more valuable than the study of anatomy."[16] Particularly in his famous boxing paintings, Bellows's use of the Dynamic Symmetry compositional order of diagonals crossing horizontals helped to animate the action.[17] Diagonals were important to Jay's theory because he believed that strategically placed diagonals broke up static bilateral symmetry and drew a viewer's eye to focal points in the composition.

By examining the preliminary sketch Bellows drew for his 1920 painting, *Old Lady in Black*, and reading Hambidge's discussion of it in his 1923 *Dynamic Symmetry in Composition*, one sees that Bellows placed the figure in a rectangle with a ratio of 1:1.309, meaning that when the long side is divided by the short side, the ratio is 1:1.309, a compound rectangle made of two or more basic shapes. This allowed Bellows to divide the area according to Hambidge's methods so that the corner diagonals intersect at the woman's chest and form sight lines to the focal points of her hands and face, accomplishing a dynamically balanced design scheme composed through the mathematical arrangement of intersecting planes and angles. As Hambidge explained, "Mr. Bellows has given me his dynamic layout for this picture and, like all this artist's compositions, it furnishes a simple, direct and comprehensive scheme in pattern planning. It is a composition well worth careful study, as from it the student may learn more of the principles of dynamic arrangement than he could from many lectures."[18] Jay then spent a full page explaining the various diagrammatical parts of the composition in his typically cryptic technical language:

> The rectangle of the canvas, as Mr. Bellows has indicated, is 1:1.309. The fraction .309 is half of .618, consequently the area in excess of a square is composed of two .618 rectangles, OP, PB. This area HB is similar and equal to CJ at the top of the canvas.
>
> The artist's method was the application of a square at both the top and the bottom of the canvas. These are BC and AD. These squares overlap to the extent of CD. This overlap area is composed of the square ED and the root five rectangle EH.
>
> The length of a side of the picture is 1.309. With 1. Subtracted, .309 is the result. From HA another .309 is subtracted and this leaves HC. The side of a square applied to an end of the picture is 1. Or OC. .309 from 1. Leaves .691 for HC.
>
> .691 is the reciprocal of 1.4472, i.e., a square plus a root five rectangle. The reciprocal of a square and a root five rectangle is obtained by diving 1.4472 into 1.[19]

Not surprisingly, a number of Hambidge's followers sought ways to articulate and teach Dynamic Symmetry through more comprehensible means.

Edward B. Edwards and Howard Giles were American illustrators, designers, and educators who studied with Hambidge and then taught Dynamic Symmetry at their respective institutions, the Nicholas Roerich Museum and the New York School of Fine and Applied Art. Both appreciated the underlying geometry of Dynamic Symmetry, which provided a method for them to create finely crafted illustrations. Edwards in his 1932 book, *Dynamarhythmic Design: A Book of Structural Pattern*, also sought to simplify the steps of Dynamic Symmetry in a way that could be individualized by "any number of trained craftsmen."[20] Edwards explained that he "had long been dissatisfied with the arts of design as they then existed in this and other countries and was constantly searching for a principle which would admit of the building up of a new design fabric on a logical foundation . . . and was convinced Mr. Hambidge had found such a principle."[21] Edwards's book looks and reads somewhat similarly to Hambidge's, but his instructions are more understandable, mainly because his system was directed to designers of decorative patterns, such as decorative borders on rugs and tapestries, which are often inherently geometric due to the horizontal and vertical structure of woven textiles or which use pattern repeats.

Hambidge envisioned his ideas serving a useful purpose in the applied arts; he saw the decorative possibilities of Dynamic Symmetry and sought

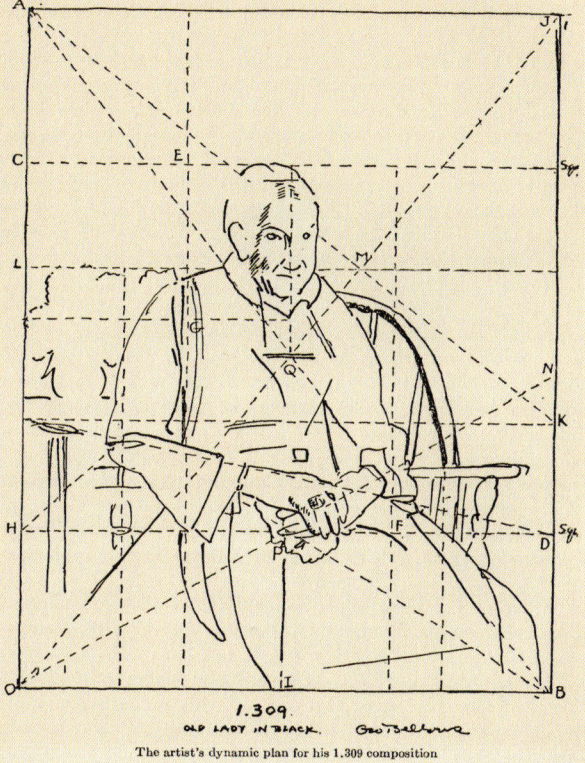

1.309

OLD LADY IN BLACK.   GeoBellows

The artist's dynamic plan for his 1.309 composition

[32]

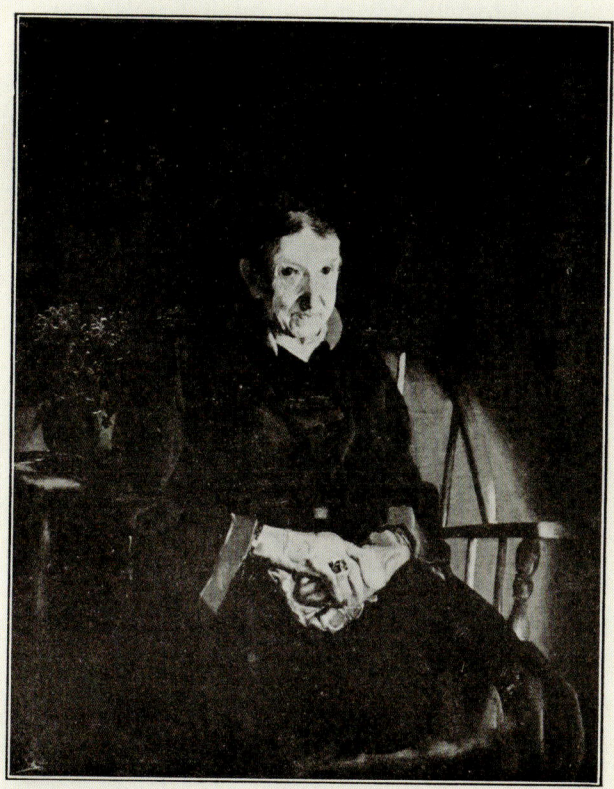

"Old Lady in Black," by George Bellows.   National Arts Club prize and gold medal

Jay Hambidge, diagram of *Old Lady in Black*
(1920) by George Bellows. *Dynamic Symmetry
in Composition* (1923), 36–37

commercial outlets for his theory and practice. In letters to Mary Crovatt written not long after they met in 1914, Jay described how he had developed a system of dyeing colors through complex dye ratios and had made color relationship charts for decorative use.[22] He had established a working relationship with New York furniture and decorative art dealer Catherine M. Traver of C. M. Traver and Co. to provide color sketches and designs for the company's modern rug, tapestry, and upholstery division in exchange for exhibiting his work at its Madison Avenue showroom and connecting him with customers. He wrote:

> One of the best known dealers in rare furniture and interior decoration is a Miss Traver, a woman I should say about 55. She has a six story house at 62nd Street and Madison Avenue and in it she has the best collection of furniture I have ever seen. She has a list of customers which includes some of the wealthiest people in America. . . . With her is another elderly woman who has specialized in modern rugs, tapestries, upholstery work, pottery, and colored inlaid woods. . . . The rugs and tapestries are woven from materials which are dyed with my colors. . . . I was really thunderstruck when I saw them. I never dreamed this color would look so well woven into materials. This morning she was at the studio and saw my color sketches. She saw at once she was reckoning with one who was a master at the game. . . . I have the same command over those [dyes] as I have over the pigment. Of course their commercial possibilities are greater than paint.[23]

Jay's method for mixing dyes according to a system of ratios has yet to be uncovered, but applying a rational method to the design of decorative arts is a significant part of Dynamic Symmetry, which appealed to designers and educators decades later.

Hambidge's system could also be applied to figurative work. Giles developed the "Jay Hambidge Discovery," a series of lessons based on Dynamic Symmetry, for his figure drawing courses at the New York School of Fine and Applied Art (now Parsons School of Design) and offered it from 1918 to 1930. Dynamic Symmetry was part of the curriculum for first-year design students through the 1949–1950 academic year.[24] Of Giles's charcoal figure drawings based on a memory of a performance of *Hamlet*, Hambidge wrote: "He looks for some dominant and characteristic angle either of the

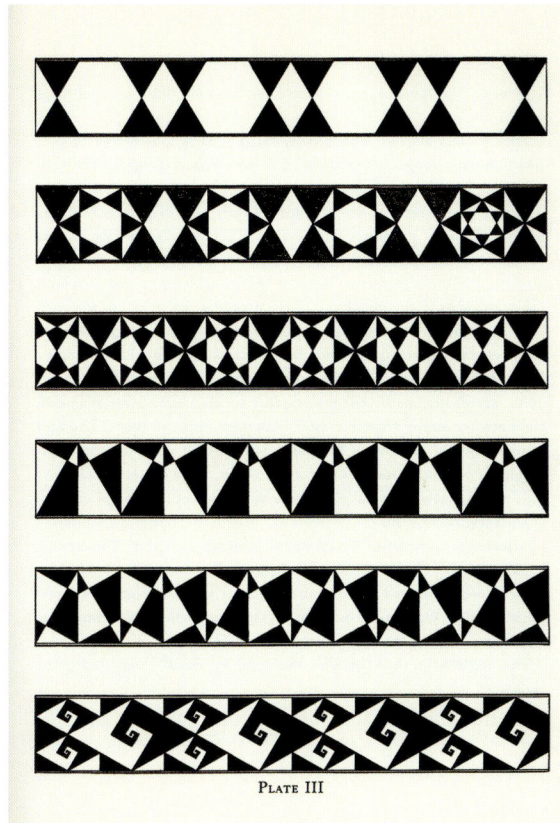

PLATE III

Edward B. Edwards, "Root Three
Patterns," *Dynamarhythmic Design*
(1932), plate 3

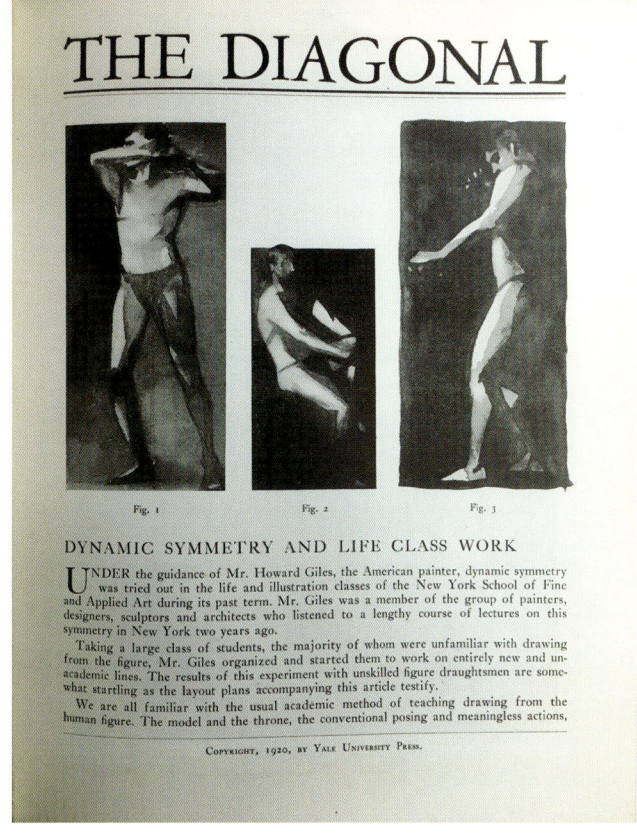

Jay Hambidge, "Dynamic Symmetry
and Life Class Work," *Diagonal* 1, no. 7
(May 1920): 138

grouping or, if it is merely a head, some basic forms suggested by the subject. He makes this the foundation of his plan and from it creates the fabric of the whole in like terms. The finished picture therefore is like a plant which has grown from a seed."[25] In the May 1920 issue of the *Diagonal*, Hambidge wrote about and included images from Giles's figure drawing course and praised Giles for banishing conventional approaches to depicting the figure through detailed verisimilitude and instead envisioning the model as a geometric construction within a rectangular compositional arrangement. "By using proper rectangles and understanding something of their modulating subdivisions much of the difficulty [in achieving correct figure proportions] is solved at once and the student is able to advance his work on any scale with assurance."[26] Giles explained his program and student results in the June 1920 issue of the *Diagonal*. According to Giles, the use of a logical, geometric approach to figural composition via Hambidge's system eliminated the need for arbitrary marks: "Dynamic Symmetry being in truth the graphic expression of logic," it ultimately provided a greater freedom of the imagination.[27]

Jay continually expanded his use of Dynamic Symmetry to a range of applications, from sculpture to modern design, a development that increased demand for his lectures. Jay was invited by George Eggers, director of the Art Institute of Chicago, to deliver the 1921 annual Scammon Lectures at the institute, which was a prestigious honor. In April of that year, having just returned to the United States from Athens via England, where he had delivered a paper at the London Hellenic Studies Society, he presented six illustrated lectures on the topic of Dynamic Symmetry in design: "The Nature of Design," "Natural Symmetry and Formalized Art," "Surveying in Its Relation to Design," "Craftsmanship, Proportion, and Symmetry," "Symmetry in Architecture, Sculpture, and Painting," and "Symmetry in Modern Design."[28] Theses lectures and others were eventually compiled by Mary Hambidge and became part of *Practical Applications of Dynamic Symmetry*, published by Yale University Press in 1932.

A reviewer in *Arts and Decoration* understood Jay quite well, particularly his explanation of dynamic versus static symmetry, and noted that his theory is "applicable to all art" but is "not a short cut": "Mr. Hambidge was convinced at this period of his research that the only way to define symmetry in art was first to define it in nature, natural architecture, and to find what principles obtained there would aid design. He found that nature contained at least two types, one as exemplified by the crystal, i.e., the equal divisions of a flower and the other by the shell or growing plant. The crystal architecture Mr. Hambidge called static, the shell and plant dynamic."[29]

There were many others who subscribed to Hambidge's theory. In May 1921 Jay was formally recognized with a reception sponsored by the League of New York Artists. Even after his death, Dynamic Symmetry lived on, especially in the realm of industrial design. The effort to equate industrial design with the timeless beauty of the past guided much of the promotional language and imagery of machine age design in America, especially in the automotive industry.[30] References to Dynamic Symmetry, which drew attention to the harmonious proportions of ancient Greek art as examples of timeless design, served as useful marketing material. For example, when the Chrysler Corporation introduced the Chrysler Six series of automobiles in 1924, Dynamic Symmetry was promoted as the guiding principle of its design; a 1925 advertisement in *House and Garden* magazine, headlined "Dynamic Symmetry in Chrysler Beauty," described the cars as "scientifically engineered to be beautiful. Three years were devoted to the study of dynamic symmetry—the science of proportion and balance."[31] A later Chrysler advertisement in *Time* magazine emphasized connections between the streamlined design of the cars and the harmonious proportions of Classic Greek architectural reliefs and column capitals in order to instill confidence in consumers: "Chrysler has sought instead to do something never done before in motor car design—to search out authentic forms of beauty which have come down the centuries unsurpassed and unchallenged and translate them in terms of motor car beauty."[32] Similarly, the Swiss-French architect Le Corbusier in his 1923 manuscript (translated into English in 1927), "Towards a New Architecture," described and illustrated ancient Greek temples as exemplars of harmonious design standards that car manufacturers should look to as the auto industry evolved.[33]

The Dynamic Symmetry formula was also used in other types of advertising and applications. For example, in 1927, Charles Mears, dean of the Cleveland School of Advertising, wrote a series of articles for *Women's Wear Daily* titled "Application of Dynamic Symmetry to Advertising Proportions": "Dynamic Symmetry doesn't necessarily transform an everyday advertising man or woman into an artist, but it does place at the advertiser's service a formula that gets dependable results."[34] Additionally, Tiffany head designer Albert Southwick, a supporter and practitioner of Dynamic Symmetry, utilized the Dynamic Symmetry rectangle for storefront and object designs.[35] Dynamic Symmetry also resonated in the fashion industry. In 1926, the Gordon Hosiery Company presented the new Gordon V Line Heel, a "stocking of sheer beauty, whose gracefully balanced heel design, based on the ancient Greek principle of dynamic symmetry, shadows so beautifully the lines with which Nature herself graces the human heel."[36]

Hambidge expended considerable energy in the study of the human figure and its proportions, devoting all but one issue of the *Diagonal* to this topic, and in the February 1920 issue he diagramed the skeleton as a vertical rectangle divided into sections corresponding to parts of the body.[37] His ideas, which equated the dynamic proportions of the human figure to the proportions of the golden ratio, impacted the way designers began to approach clothing design. Thinking beyond the traditional tailored structure

CHRYSLER . .

BEAUTY *is no chance creation*

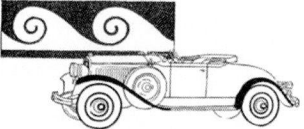

FOR the first time *in the history of motor car design an authentic system has been devised based upon the canons of ancient classic art*

The most modern thing in motor car design — Chrysler's matching of slender-profile radiator with cowl bar moulding — has its artistic origin in the repetition of motif in the historic frieze of the ancient Parthenon.

CHRYSLER designers realize fully that beauty is an elusive thing and that the pursuit of it in motor car design must not be hampered by too rigid adherence to laws and conventions . . . But Chrysler also has found that there are so many glorious precedents and inspirations in art, architecture and design, that the search for authentic and harmonious symmetry can actually be reduced to something like a scientific system in which results are certain . . . Chrysler has left nothing to chance . . . Chrysler has not relied alone upon the inspiration of individual designers . . . Chrysler has sought instead to do something never done before in motor car design — to search out *authentic* forms of beauty which have come down the centuries unsurpassed and unchallenged and *translate* them in terms of motor car beauty and motor car utility . . . The lengths to which Chrysler designers have gone in this patient pursuit of beauty will doubtless prove a revelation to those who have probably accepted Chrysler symmetry and charm as fortunate but more or less accidental conceptions . . . The Chrysler process goes far deeper than any charming but accidental conception.

Note the dynamic symmetry of Chrysler fender contours and wheels, counterparts of the "wave border" of the classic masterpieces of architecture and design.

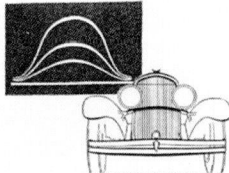

Artists know this as a "rising, diminishing series". The level road, the slightly arched bumper, the shorter arched tie-rod above, and finally the shorter and more deeply-arched radiator contour, form a series in perfect harmony.

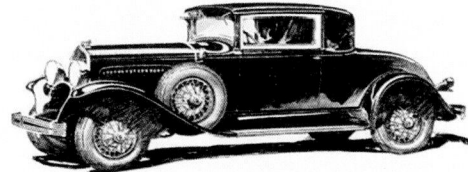

New Chrysler "75" Coupe (with rumble seat) $1,535. Wire wheels extra

All Chrysler models will be exhibited at the National Automobile Shows and in the Ballroom and entire lobby space of the Congress Hotel during the Chicago Show, January 26th to February 2nd.

Dynamic Symmetry In Chrysler Beauty

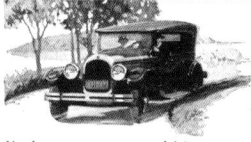

More than a year ago we remarked that the dictionary of synonyms had been worn dog-eared in the hunt for adjectives to describe motor car beauty.

There isn't a superlative left to use.

As a matter of fact, they've all been used so many times that they no longer carry conviction.

But just as surely as you know a beautiful car when you see it, you'll be enhanced by the Chrysler Six.

In every Chrysler model, you sense at once the beauty, the good taste, the smartness which we in America have been in the habit of describing as "French," or "foreign," or "continental," or "European."

More than 32,000 times last year, buyers expressed, in terms of their motor car choice, their preference for the Chrysler kind of beauty — giving to Chrysler Six a first-year sales record never before awarded to any car.

Here is a car scientifically engineered to be beautiful.

Three years were devoted to the study of dynamic symmetry—the science of proportion and balance.

The height of side body panels, for instance, was a matter of determining the exact relation between the requirements of human comfort in the car, and the most pleasing proportion from outside the car.

The "head," or "belt line," was not put on as an incident, or just because a body designer liked it. It was scientifically sized and scientifically placed to give that long, low, sweeping line which produces such a racy, foreign effect.

Most cars are pretty fair looking from some one angle; the more fortunate, from a couple of viewpoints. From the rear view, nearly all of them are weak on appearance.

One result of the scientific design of the Chrysler Six is the charm of its rear view.

Note particularly how all of the lines and curves of the front and sides gracefully blend at the rear.

There are no displeasing angles, sharp corners, awkward curves.

Then walk around in front. See how the long, sweeping lines flow out of the radiator.

It's a mere detail to the buyer, perhaps, but an interesting fact that months were spent on designing and proportioning lamps and fenders.

That inimitable grace, melting so perfectly into the bulk of the whole car, was no matter of chance.

So, too, with the wheels. Chrysler designers sought the ultimate in that much desired close-to-the-ground appearance.

But they didn't simply take any small wheel. They got exactly the right proportion. And what is the result of this new application of scientific design and proportion!

Perhaps the most important result is that air of perfect good taste—the same atmosphere that surrounds real gentlewomen and gentlemen.

The Chrysler isn't beautiful because of any fanciful tricks, or because of any ornamentation hung on it. It isn't gaudy. It isn't ostentatious.

But it is smart, refined, in good taste, harmonious, gracious, eye-compelling, simple.

In a word, it is beautiful.

And that isn't all.

Such true beauty in a car doesn't stop with looks alone—any more than it does in a man or woman.

There's an old saying, "Beauty is as beauty does."

That's the Chrysler Six.

Remember that while Chrysler engineers were scientifically building beauty of appearance, they were building with relation to human comfort.

So that Chrysler proportions are not only good to look at—they also give the most perfect riding, most accurately comfortable car you ever drove or rode in, as Chrysler owners can tell you today after a year's experience.

CHRYSLER MOTOR CORPORATION, DETROIT, MICHIGAN
Division of Maxwell Motor Corporation
MAXWELL-CHRYSLER MOTOR COMPANY OF CANADA, LIMITED, WINDSOR, ONT.

CHRYSLER SIX

Advertisement for Chrysler Six series of automobiles, *House and Garden*, May 1925, 62

Advertisement for Chrysler Six series of automobiles, *Time*, January 14, 1929, 8

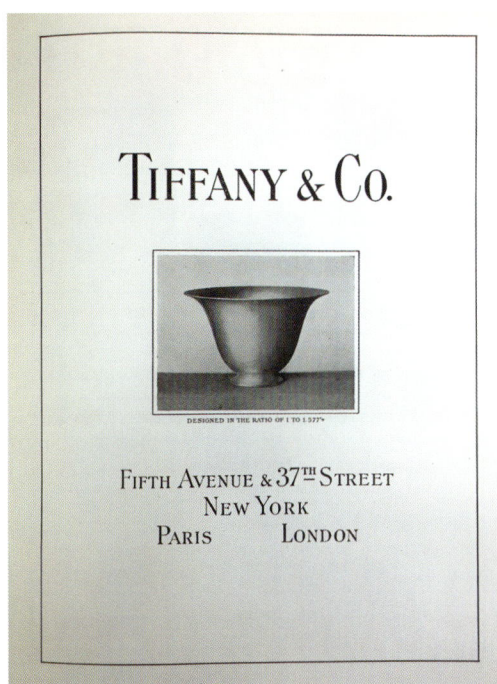

Tiffany & Co. advertisement,
Diagonal 1, no. 7 (May 1920)

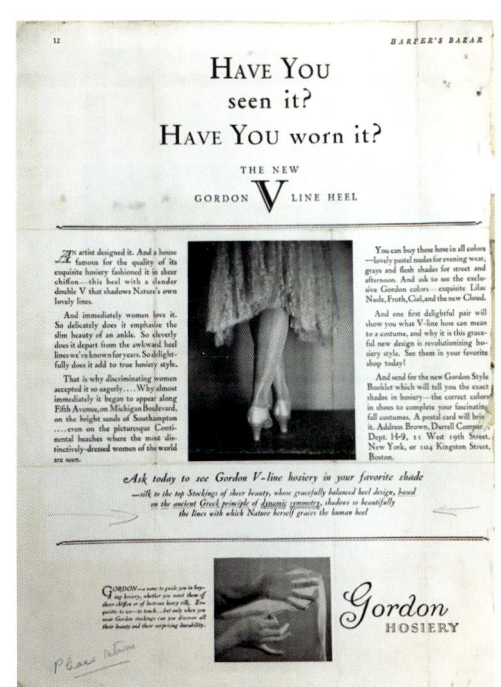

Advertisement for Gordon V Line Heel
hosiery, *Harper's Bazaar*, n.d. Kenan
Research Center at the Atlanta History
Center, os2.376

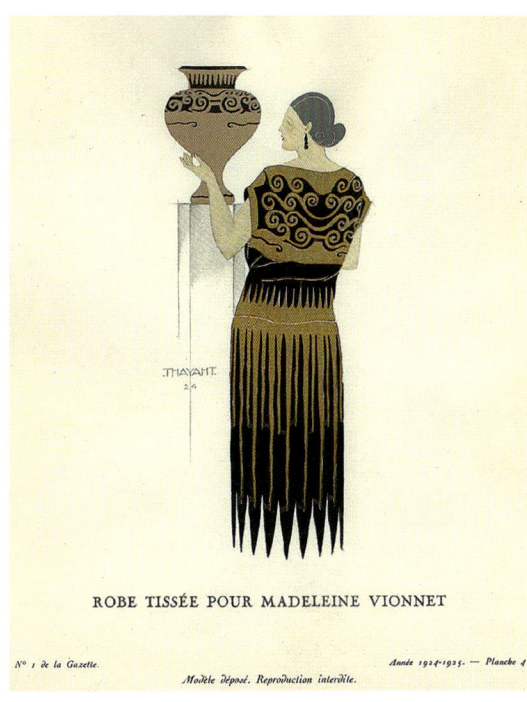

Thayaht, "Robe tissée pour Madeleine
Vionnet," *La gazette du bon ton*, no. 1
(July 1924): plate 4

of a dress, designers began to envision clothing the body in a proportionally designed rectangle, which could be belted as desired. Fashion designer
Thayaht, the palindromic pseudonym for Ernesto Michahelles, who attended Denman Ross's courses in the 1920s while studying at Harvard and
may have also attended Jay's lectures, applied these ideas about design to
his loose-fitting, rectangular, draped, and geometrically patterned clothing, which corresponded to the proportions of the body, for the atelier of
Madeleine Vionnet.[38] This type of unstructured, rectangular shift, attached
at the shoulders and sides, resembled ancient Greek gowns called chitons,
which became the basis of Mary's dress designs once she discovered the style
in Athens.

These modern adaptations of Dynamic Symmetry merged effortlessly
with developments in Art Deco and machine age streamlined design, and
they aligned with the types of application Hambidge envisioned.

Most of the opposition to Dynamic Symmetry appeared after the 1920 release of *Dynamic Symmetry: The Greek Vase*, in particular coming from those in the fields of archaeology and mathematics. Their objections are understandable since Jay himself stated that his "training has been, and disposition is, merely that of a practical artist."[39] One of the more noteworthy criticisms came from Rhys Carpenter, a professor of classical archaeology at Bryn Mawr College, in the *American Journal of Archaeology*.[40] He was suspicious of Hambidge's system, which measured area instead of linear rule, and doubted whether ancient Greeks used that method. Indeed, Carpenter wrote, "I doubt if very many people measured anything accurately to the fraction of a millimeter before modern times," and even if they did, there "is not the slightest proof that they used the method of designing by Dynamic Symmetry."[41] Carpenter was responding to a long article by Gisela Richter, "Dynamic Symmetry from the Designer's Point of View," in defense of Hambidge and Dynamic Symmetry.[42] It is "not a farfetched idea," Richter wrote, that an Athenian potter "did not make his shapes as a whim dictated, but designed them beforehand, and then executed them to given measurement[s]."[43] The back and forth regarding measurements, methods, and intentions continued for years and involved a number of mathematicians, architects, archaeologists, curators, and artists, causing Hambidge to continually defend himself instead of devoting his efforts to expanding the range and uses of Dynamic Symmetry.

A particularly vocal critic was William Dinsmoor, a professor of architecture and archaeology at Columbia University. Lacey Caskey warned Hambidge in December 1922 that Dinsmoor planned to "attack your theory," which he indeed did in a lecture in New Haven later that month.[44] Caskey later relayed to Jay a summary:

> You did well in not coming to New Haven, first because of the bad weather, second because Dinsmoor's paper was nothing but a grandstand play aimed to split the ears of the groundlings who for the most part are incapable of nothing but inexplicable dumb shows and noise. The thing was well staged. . . . The big hall was crowded and Dinsmoor's title had attracted attention. The first part of his paper had been very carefully prepared and consisted [of] a really cleverly phrased, sarcastic resume of the various theories abroad and about the proportions of the Parthenon which had been advanced in the past. I must admit that I joined in the roars of laughter. Your theory was skillfully woven into this. . . .

The effect on the audience was to put you in a class with people who ascribed the plan of the Parthenon to Hiram, king of Tyre.[45]

Beyond those who disagreed with Hambidge and sought to provide alternative solutions were those who outright mocked him. One can assume that the hostility directed at Hambidge and Dynamic Symmetry contributed to Hambidge's declining health. In a *Boston Transcript* memorial after Jay's death, the unnamed writer noted:

> To those knowing Jay Hambidge, quiet and gentle in manner, it seems difficult to realize what a storm of opposition has raged about him, while his main thought has been to give to the world certain principles which he felt would be of great benefit to the artistic world at large—principles so simple that they are to be found clearly defined in a common shell on the beach and in every leaf that grows.
> Many times has he faced an audience . . . to find it bristling with premeditated hostility, which is eventually ameliorated by his own calm presence and clear impersonal logic. The opposition has, as often in such cases, been crude and unreasoning and based on ignorance.[46]

Art critics and reporters seemed particularly hostile to Hambidge's theories. A sarcastic review of a Hambidge lecture attended by *New York World* reporter Karl K. Kitchen, "Illustrating One of the Three Easiest Ways of Acquiring Fame and Honors in New York City," included a cartoon by Herb Roth showing perplexed followers of Hambidge surrounded by question marks and exclamation points.[47] Kitchen apparently believed that Hambidge was trying to fool people with his technical language and equations, writing, "There are three ways, at least, of becoming famous in New York. Make up a long list of questions that nobody can or cares to answer. Invent 'relativity' or rediscover a theory of dynamic symmetry which can only be proved by mathematics. If you want to get your name in the papers and be the object of a lot of attention any one of the three ways can be recommended. But if you want to be honored by a lot of distinguished people the last method is the best."[48] Kitchen's sarcasm was common in the field of popular art criticism at the time, as reporters ridiculed art that was not understood. Hambidge was targeted for his seemingly unintelligible mathematical approach to design.

Jay Hambidge believed that Dynamic Symmetry could serve as a playbook for designers, and he pointed to demonstrable truths to aid in the teaching and creation of art. His theory hit a chord with some American artists and designers at a time when the U.S. art world was in flux by offering a logical

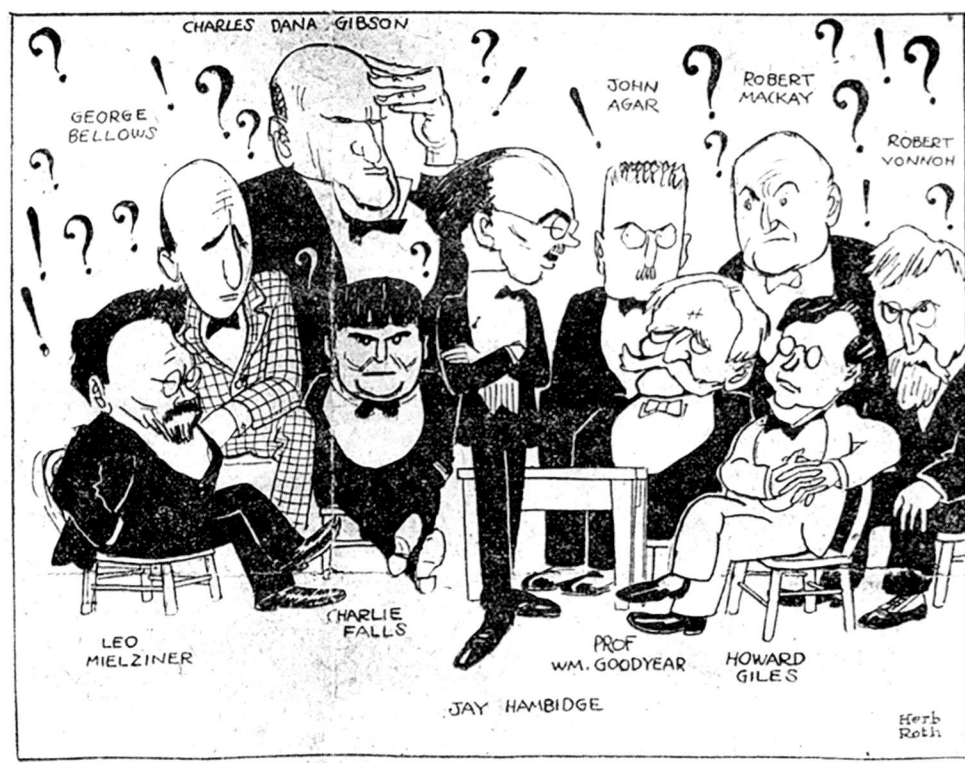

Herb Roth, cartoon for Karl K. Kitchen, "Illustrating One of the Three Easiest Ways of Acquiring Fame and Honors in New York City." The original caption read, "Perhaps the celebrated artists gathered to honor Jay Hambidge understood his theory, but most of them seemed a bit puzzled by it." Unidentified newspaper clipping, n.d., Archives of American Art, Smithsonian Institution, Hambidge Papers, microfilm box 3181, no. 963

method of ordering visual compositions and by providing a principle that gave artists control over the foundations of design. While Hambidge's theories may have appeared to be similar to contemporary investigations into rationally planned systems of design intended to unify and universalize the arts, such as the De Stijl movement, his ideas were grounded in a dedication to pictorial accuracy through design formalization rather than in utopian idealism or spiritualism. Interestingly, Mary eventually embraced the latter stance in her understanding of Dynamic Symmetry.

Mary Crovatt Hambidge and the Formation of Her Handcraft Technique and Philosophy in Greece and New York, 1920–1935

Forming Utopia

Mary Crovatt and Jay Hambidge arrived in Athens in the early autumn of 1920. He stayed in Athens until February 1921; Mary stayed through the autumn of 1921. There is little documentation concerning where they stayed, their daily activities, or with whom they associated while abroad.[1] Jay had an official document of introduction from the Yale University School of Fine Arts requesting permission to conduct his research. For some reason, Mary's passport listed her year of birth as 1893 rather than 1885.[2]

Mary often recounted the story of how she happened upon a weaving workshop in Athens while Jay was out measuring temples. Several versions of that story exist, including this draft for a 1949 Voice of America broadcast:

> It was while my husband was deeply engaged in his work on the Parthenon that I had leisure to wander about Athens, and one day came upon the Weaving Establishment on Amalia Avenue [38 Amalias Avenue] started by the women of Athens for Greek peasants. My years of study with Mr. Hambidge had prepared me for what now happened. The moment I saw the looms and the Greek women weaving at them, something deep within me, something that seemed to have been asleep in my subconscious, awakened, came to life. I knew that I had found the important thing for me. I *had* to learn to weave! I asked Kyria Elene Avramea, who was then head of the Weaving Department to let me come there and work as an apprentice. . . . I became completely absorbed by this fascinating work and by the Greek way of life. There was something so basic about it—so profound—it seemed to reach back into the ages—to relate me to all women of all time.[3]

While this narrative describes Mary's later interpretation of the moment, her enthusiasm for weaving probably involved more than just inadvertently

I can see my darling now at the loom in the old room. . . . It is all very wonderful what we have done in a short time.—JAY HAMBIDGE

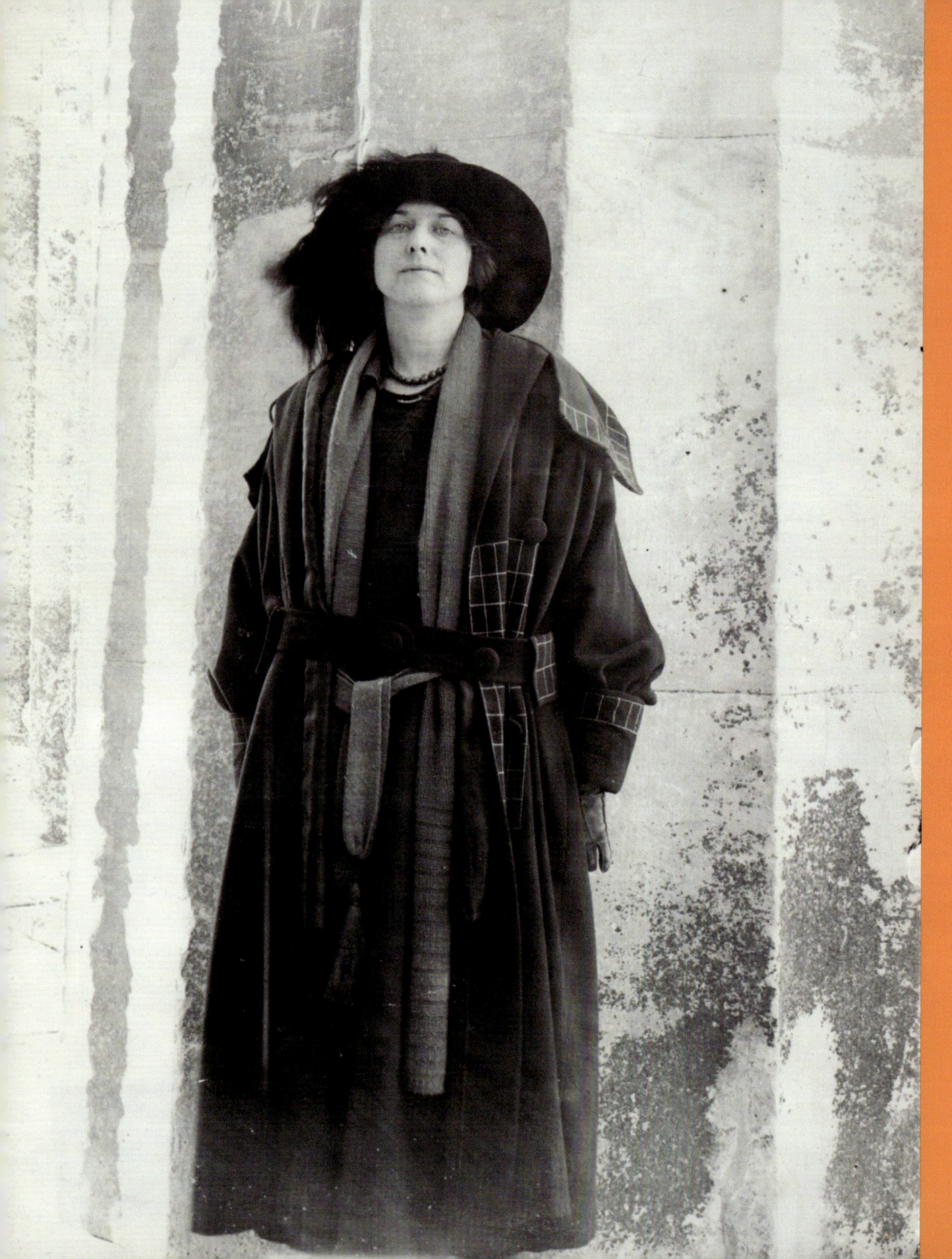

Mary Hambidge in Greece, c. 1920. Kenan Research Center at the Atlanta History Center, VIS1.93

coming upon Kyria Avramea's weaving establishment and having an immediate revelation.

Mary's introduction to weaving may well have been initiated by Eva Palmer Sikelianos, who had been living and weaving in Athens since 1906. Eva and Mary became friends and were frequent companions during the rest of Eva's life.[4] Eva lived on Serifou Street in Athens, and so did Kyria Avramea.[5] Kyria, who spoke English, was also associated with Muriel Noel, a British woman and skilled weaver married to a British ambassador, who had lived in Athens before moving to Cairo, Egypt. Eva, Muriel, Kyria, and Mary connected through weaving, as well as their class status, and remained close for years afterward. Mary learned weaving from all of these women, especially Eva, whom Muriel referred to as Mary's "teacher." Letters from

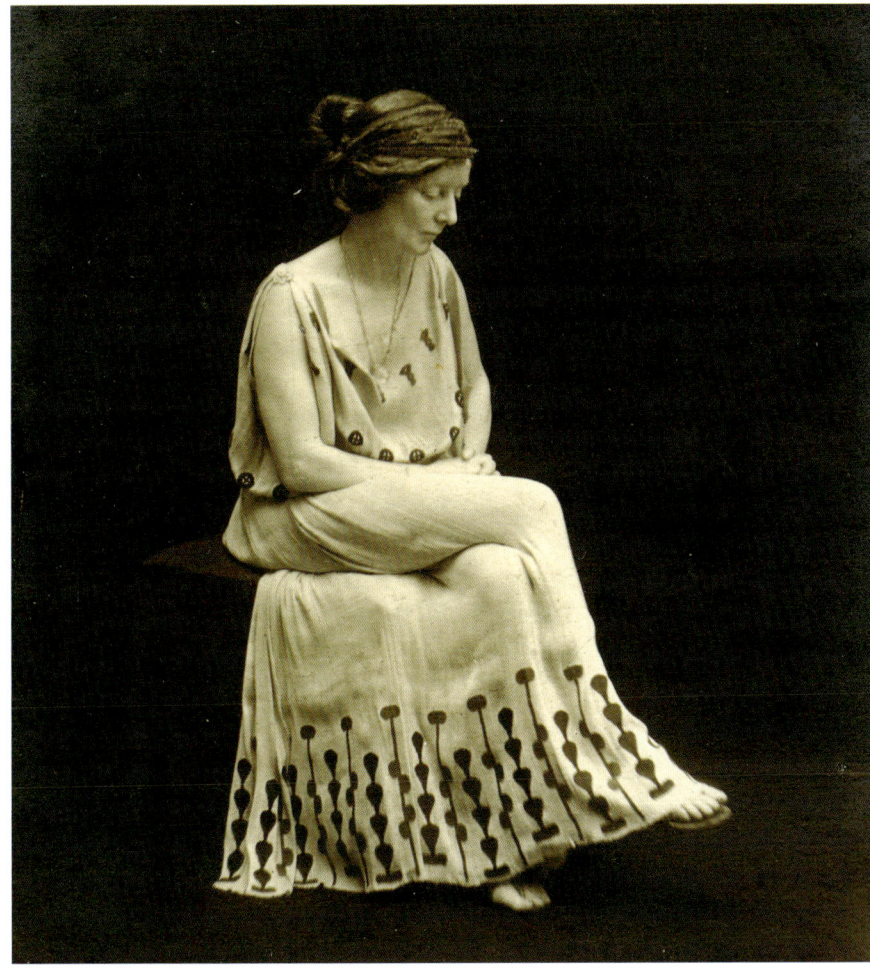

Eva Palmer Sikelianos, Delphic Festival of 1930. Photographer unknown, © Benaki Museum/ Historical Archives, F189/3/229

Muriel to Mary included weaving instructions and yarn samples.[6] After Jay departed Athens for a lecture circuit, Mary lived with Eva.[7] She came to know all of them likely not by happenstance but through networks in the strong expatriate community in Athens of educated, cultured Westerners seeking connections with Greece's ancient past and traditional crafts.

Mary may have sought out Avramea's weaving establishment—a workshop intended to revive traditional Greek spinning, dyeing, and weaving techniques and to provide skills and income to Greek families—as a way of realizing Jay's ambitions to establish a craft collective and commercial dyeing enterprise in America as he sought to do with Miss Traver in New York with his dyes for carpets and fabric. His letter to Mary stating, "I never dreamed this color would look so well woven into materials," shows that thoughts about handcrafts were part of the dialogue between them from the beginning.[8]

Their time together in Athens seems to have inspired both to discuss establishing a similar enterprise to Avramea's in America. Jay's letters to Mary while she was still in Athens reveal that he was researching weaving workshops and textile production in the American South, providing Mary with ideas about what they could do differently and better. He suggested expanding the range of Dynamic Symmetry into a commercial applied arts enterprise, which they could develop into an art school/craft workshop. In an undated letter to Mary, he wrote about his plan to expand their work in dyes, design, and weaving:

> These fabrics to be first in the form of rugs and carpets, then curtain upholstery goods, curtain wall hanging and even dress material. First we shall start with the hand made articles then use looms. I predict that within a year we shall have every woman in the Blue Ridge working madly to turn out this new creative art into the South. The New England states have had a monopoly of this sort of thing long enough. Let us beat them at their own game. From fabrics it is but a step to furniture and the completely designed home. My stained glass and pottery schemes work into this plan admirably.[9]

Jay's desire to produce objects for the "completely designed home" reveals his understanding and adaptation of the Arts and Crafts principles begun by William Morris in England. Morris advocated for the design and production of beautiful and well-crafted utilitarian objects for the home, which he referred to as "intelligent handicrafts" and which would contribute to economic and social well-being. These ideas guided many American art enterprises during the first decades of the twentieth century.[10]

In other letters, Jay discussed how their weaving and craft enterprise could jump-start the textile industry by putting "Dynamic Symmetry into the designs and giv[ing] the industry a means, perhaps a new lease on life."[11] Jay followed current developments in American textile design, writing to Mary that there was a "great deal of activity here among the artists in dyeing in the Batik way. But you don't want that dear. The dyed yarn woven into fabric is the thing. They have been training the mountaineers in the South— the Blue Ridge people . . . but not artistic."[12] Therefore, when Mary wrote, "Mr. Hambidge had prepared me for what now happened," she was likely aware that the opportunity to work at Kyria Avramea's workshop could contribute to her and Jay's success in America as founders of a school of Dynamic Symmetry and handcrafts.[13] Indeed, she later recalled, "I at once saw the possibilities of using Mr. Hambidge's ideas of colour and design in textiles."[14] Mary made sure to return to New York with ample weaving supplies, including a loom, yarns, and dress patterns from Eva, and in 1923 she corresponded with the weaving workshop at Berea College in Kentucky to purchase and ship a loom.[15]

Eva Palmer Sikelianos: A Greek-Inspired Identity

Eva Palmer came from a socially prominent family in New York City; she traveled widely, studied theater, voice, and poetry at Bryn Mawr College, and lived a cultured and privileged life. While in Paris in 1906, she met Raymond Duncan, brother of dancer Isadora Duncan, and his Greek wife, Penelope Sikelianos, sister of famed poet Angelos Sikelianos. Raymond and Penelope embraced her Greek identity, most visibly in their clothing, which was modeled after ancient Greek gowns, cloaks, and sandals and which they crafted themselves. Eva invited them to live with her at her house in Paris, where they built a loom and perfected a method of weaving cloth so that it would drape and fold in a manner resembling the gowns, called chitons, worn by figures depicted on ancient Greek vases and statues.[16]

A chiton is made by attaching two lengths of fabric at the sides, gathering and attaching them at the shoulders, and then cinching the garment at the waist with a braided belt or sash. From then on, Eva wore only such gowns, which she wove herself and to which she added a cape-like cloak attached at the neck or shoulder, called a chlamys, and occasionally a longer toga-like cloak called a himation. Just as Isadora and Raymond Duncan used Greek-style clothing to proclaim their independence from physical and cultural

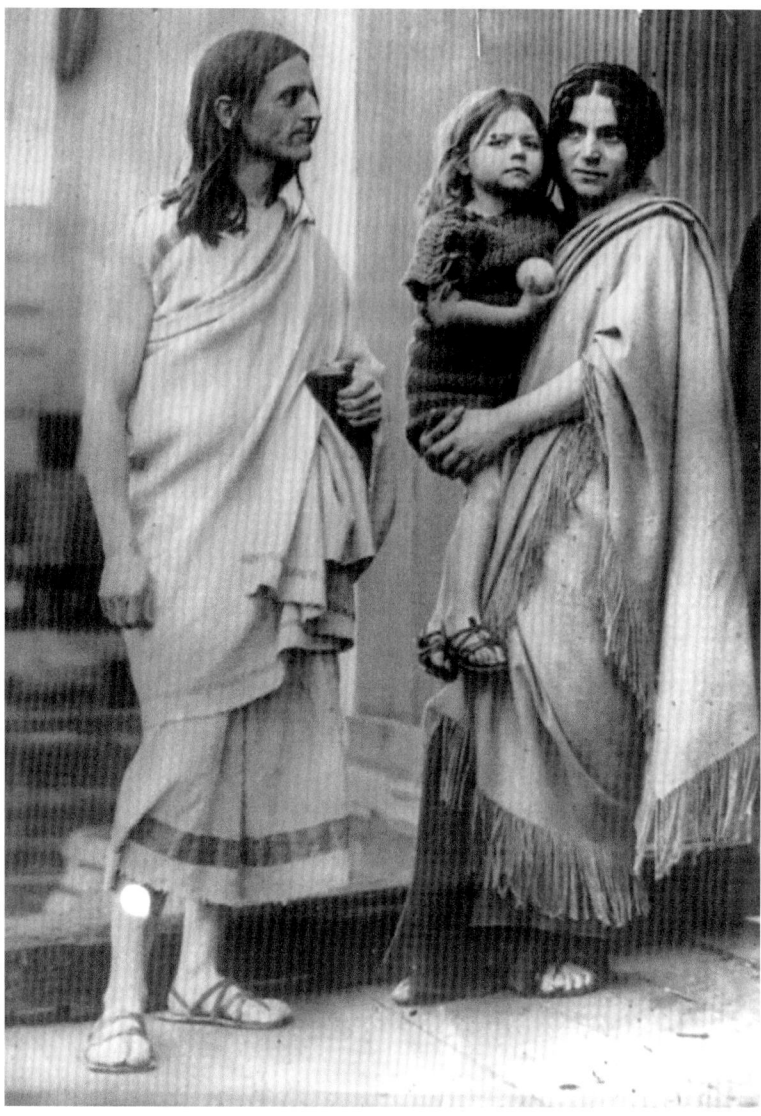

Raymond Duncan, Penelope Sikelianos, and Menalkas Duncan, 1912. Photographer unknown, George Grantham Bain Collection, Prints and Photographs Division, Library of Congress, https://www.loc.gov/item/2002715690/

restrictions, Eva's new identity through clothing gave her the freedom to break from Western fashion constraints and brought her closer to an imagined Greek past, which she would later seek to revive through theater, dance, and music in her productions of the Delphic Festivals of 1927 and 1930.

Later in 1906, Raymond and Penelope invited Eva to come to Greece with them, where they were constructing a house in the hills outside Athens. There Eva met Angelos, married him in 1907, and became his champion and financial supporter. In Athens Eva became a vocal advocate for reviving Greek national identity through handcrafts and traditional arts, while at the same time personifying Greek history through her clothing, in noticeable contrast to the Western clothing worn by modern Athenians. As Artemis Leontis noted in her book, *Eva Palmer Sikelianos: A Life in Ruins*, Eva became known as "the only ancient Greek in modern Athens."[17] She was also a consummate weaver and weaving teacher. In her memoir, *Upward Panic*, Eva wrote, "I have woven at least a hundred kinds of stuff. I have taught many people to weave," and she knew "all the different stages and processes of weaving: from shearing the sheep through washing the wool at the spring, then carding, warping, weaving, with the satisfaction of unrolling the finished stuff from the loom, and finally of sewing one's own dress, it gradually came to mean more than just an indulgence in the sort of clothes I happened to prefer. It took on, for me at least, the proportions of a solution for certain social evils."[18]

From Eva, Mary learned how to weave the distinctly flowing gowns and capes that both women wore. Specifically, based on Mary's notebooks and Eva's memoir, the gowns were woven with heavy warp (vertical) threads crossed with lighter-weight weft (horizontal) threads, which created the rhythmic folds when draped. Eva preferred a wool warp and silk weft, even though silk was not used in ancient Greece.[19] The gowns were designed as classic chitons, with edges of the cloth decorated with border designs woven in a laid-in method of supplementary weft threads. Each weaver was inspired by Classic Greek designs for her laid-in patterns:

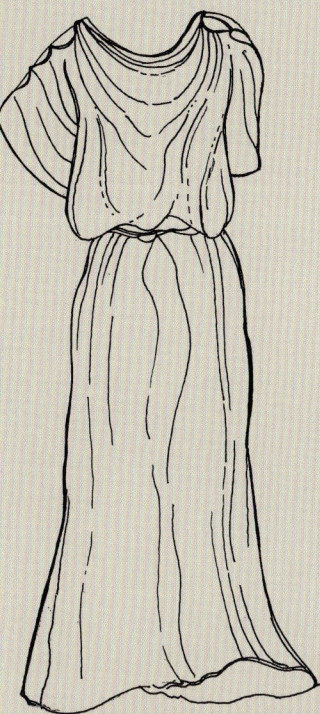

Diagram of a chiton.
Illustration © Ruth
Simon McRae

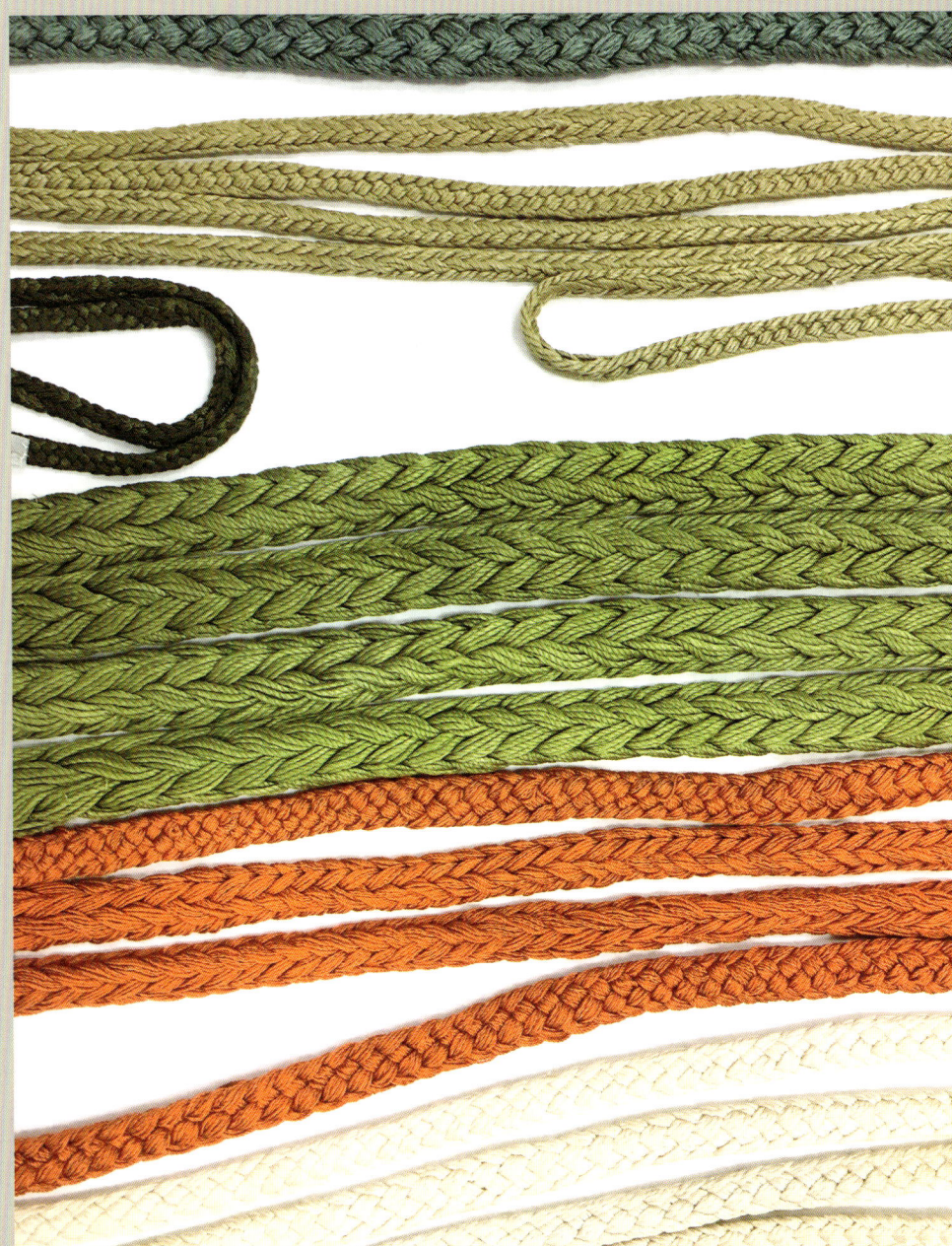

Mary Crovatt Hambidge, assorted belts.
Kenan Research Center at the Atlanta
History Center

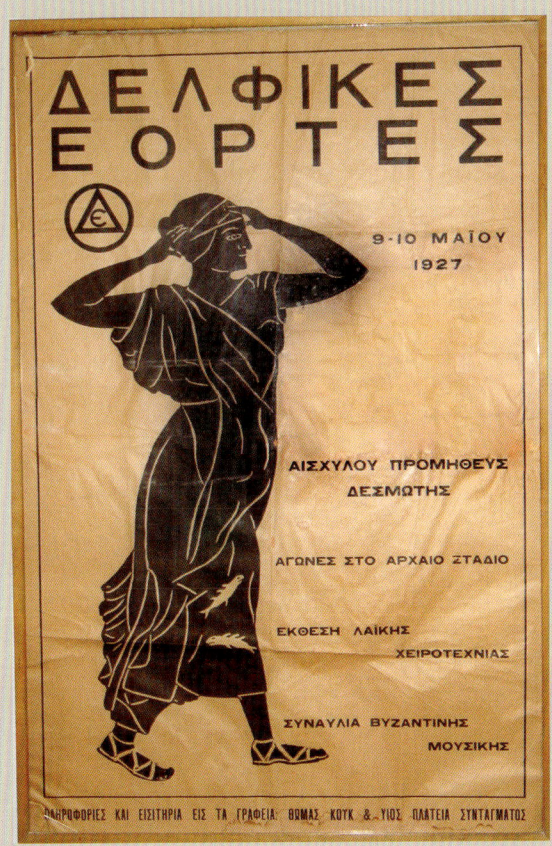

Delphic Festival poster, 1927

Eva incorporated decorative borders derived from Mycenaean ceramics and frescoes, such as sea creatures; Mary incorporated her and Jay's Dynamic Symmetry designs based on root rectangle patterns.[20] Rather than hemming the garments, Mary wove for the individual fit and let the warp fringes serve as the finishing edge. To keep the threads from unraveling above the hem fringes, she used a knotting technique that she learned from Muriel Noel called the Noel Stitch.[21]

Mary and Eva had much in common and had similar upbringings: both came from wealth and were educated at boarding schools; both sought theatrical and musical careers; and both were strikingly attractive and had abundantly long hair. Eva's was red, and while Mary's hair was recorded as

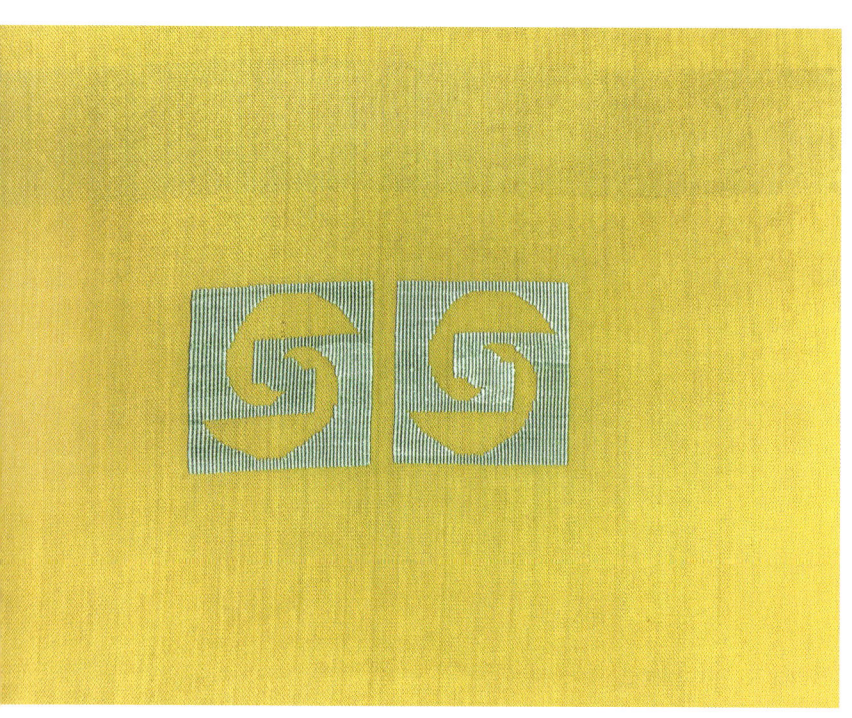

Mary Crovatt Hambidge, silk stole with geometric weft brocade, 1921–1929. Kenan Research Center at the Atlanta History Center, 1998.233

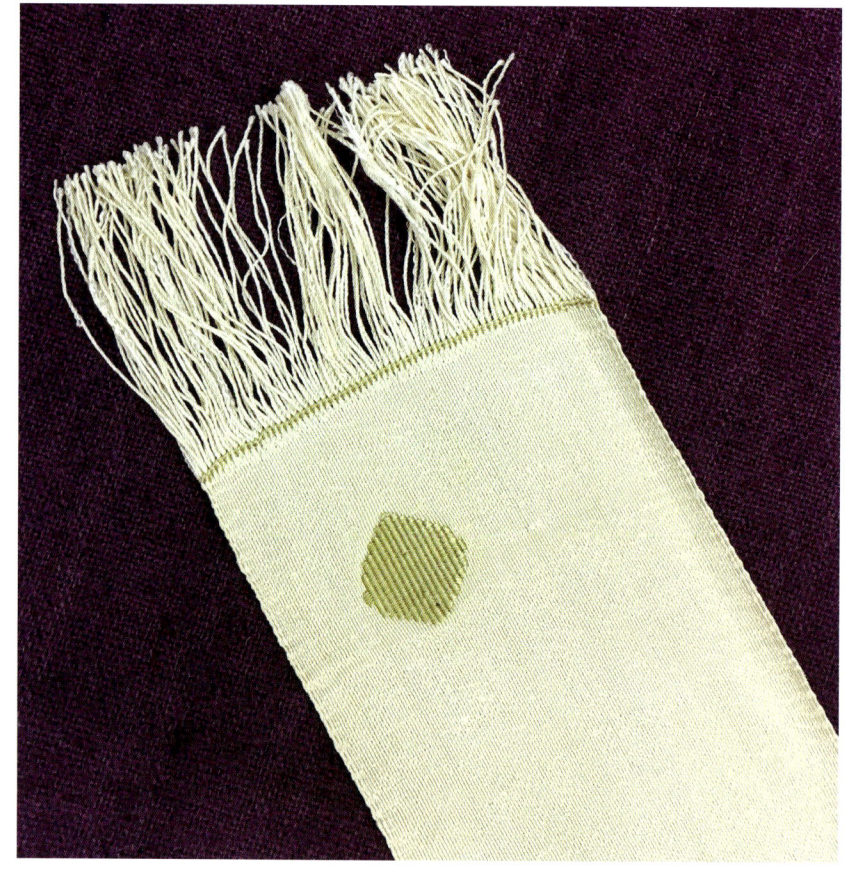

Mary Crovatt Hambidge, silk sash, 1925. Kenan Research Center at the Atlanta History Center, 1998.233

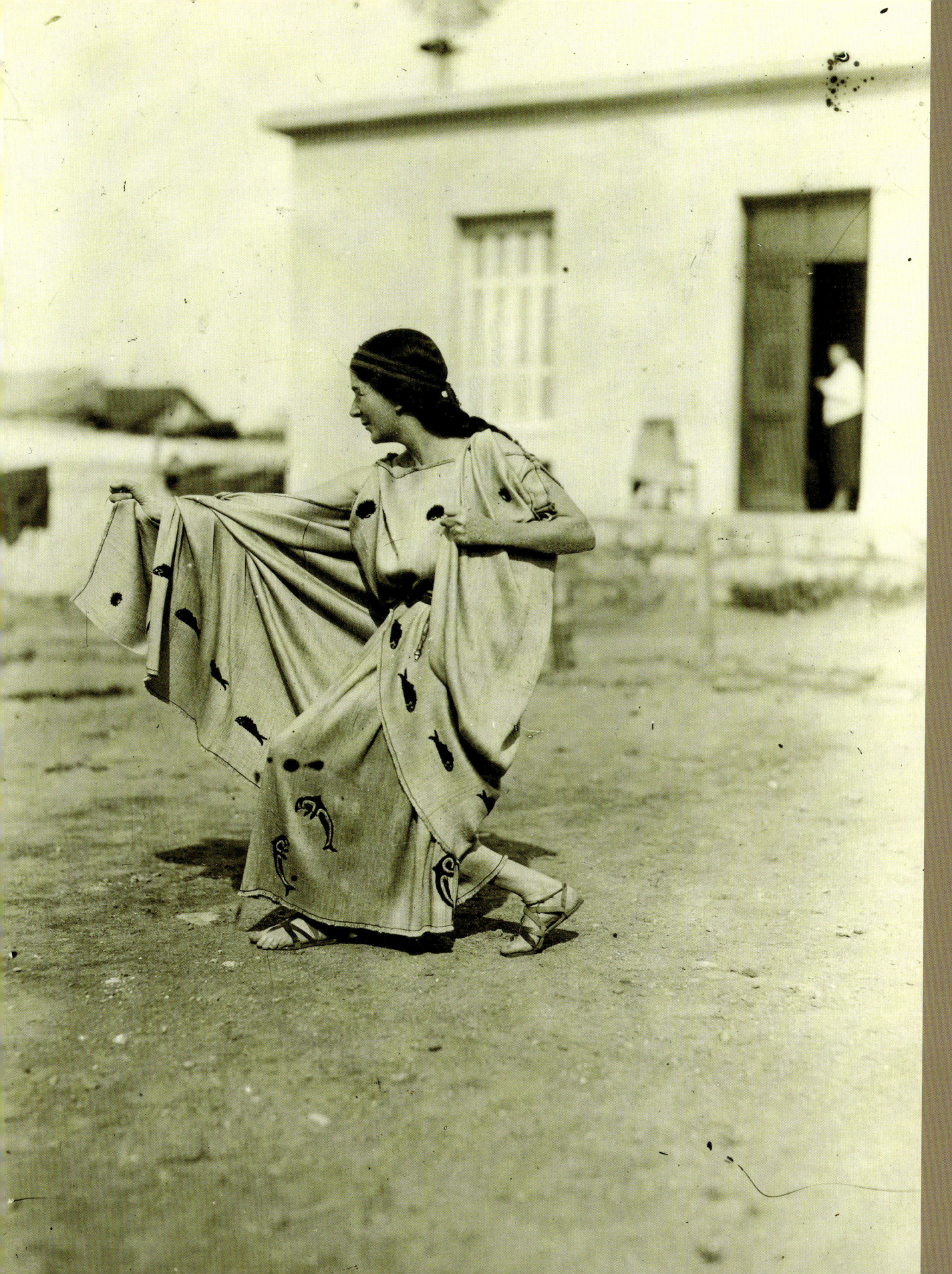

brown on her passport, she was known to have dyed it red. When they met, Eva and Mary bonded over additional shared beliefs and experiences: both underwent pivotal transformations in Greece; both became obsessed with the techniques and history of handweaving; and both embraced versions of ancient Greece that they could apply to their twentieth-century lives.

Return to the United States

When Mary returned to New York in the fall of 1921, she brought weaving supplies and a notebook documenting a year's worth of weaving instruction and production, which she would add to over the next eight years. She also returned with a determination to begin her own weaving enterprise that would unite Greek weaving techniques, Greek-style dress, and Dynamic Symmetry in color and design. Jay encouraged her weaving practice despite dismissals from her father. In a July 1921 letter to Mary while she was still in Greece, Jay had written, "The Judge [Alfred Crovatt] is a bit skeptical about weaving. He thinks you are just amusing yourself. I told him no, but he shakes his head."[22] He painted an oil of her at her loom.

Mary's ideas about fashion and clothing design had changed in Greece. Now she designed and wore clothing based on the way it draped on and in proportion to the human figure. In a draft for her unpublished manuscript "The Loom Speaks: The Law of Proportion in Weaving," she wrote, "Why did the Greeks make the dress enclosing the human figure a rectangle if they did not regard the figure as being enclosed in a rectangle? Isn't this another proof that their symmetry is based on the rectangle? . . . The drapery is a frame for the figure but a flexible frame and being so takes the *shape* of the figure but is not *cut* to shape. A drapery *cut* to shape spoils the form."[23] Mary and Jay had professional photographs taken, and from them we can see how Mary fully embraced the Greek style—from her braided chignon hair to her leather sandals to her belted chiton, now modernized with decorative borders derived from Dynamic Symmetry motifs.

Mary's weaving and fashion sense had a place in the stylish Roaring Twenties of New York. The shimmering silk, the unstructured fit that required no corset, the geometric designs, the bold colors—gold, chartreuse, rose—all contributed to the Art Deco style of the 1920s. For example, one of her outfits, featured in a New York society fashion show, was hailed as "the gown of the future":

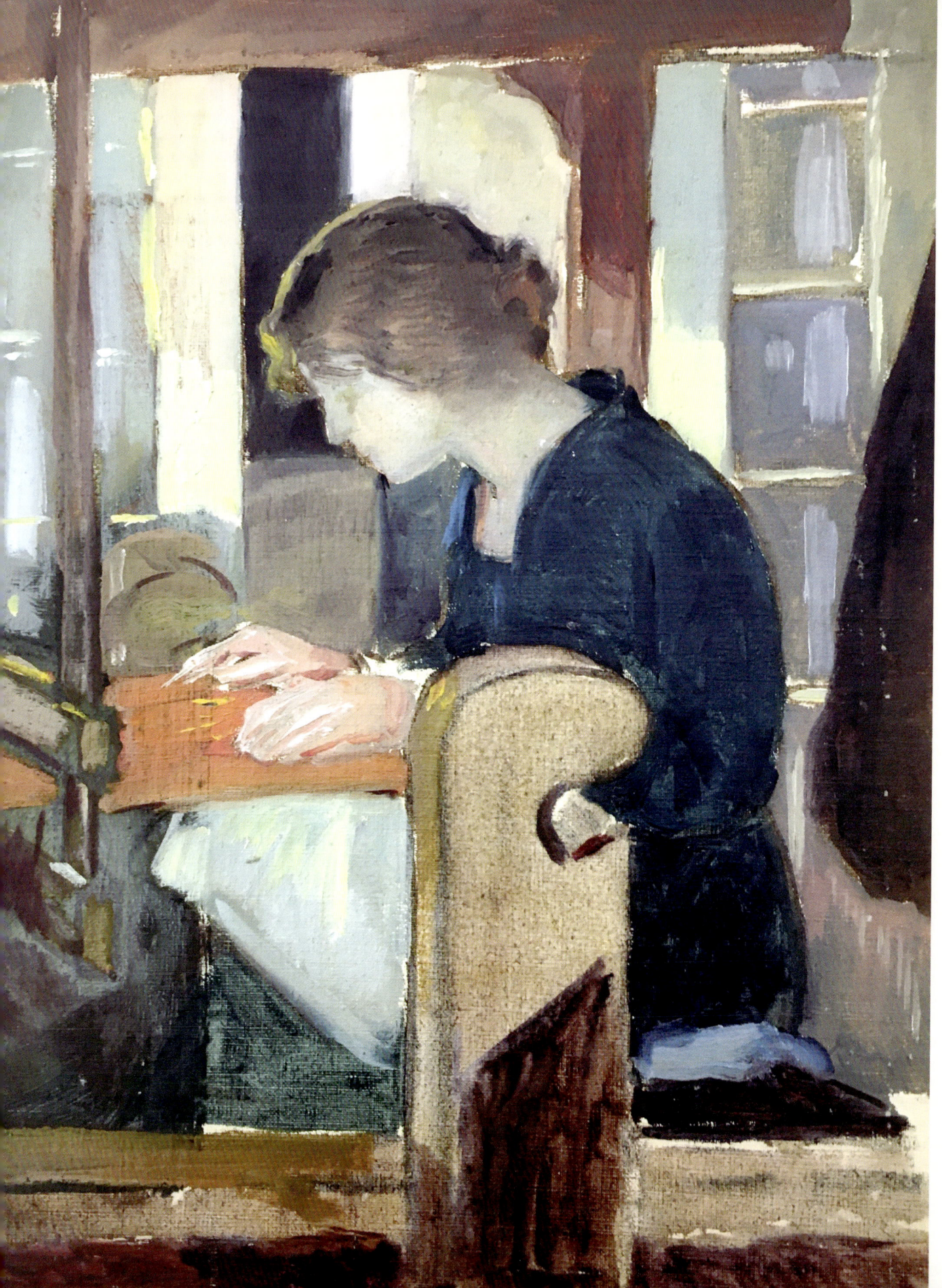

Jay Hambidge, portrait of
Mary Crovatt Hambidge at the
loom, c. 1921–1924, oil on board.
Kenan Research Center at the
Atlanta History Center, VIS 1.21

The gown of the future was fascinating. This was worn by Mrs. Otté. It was of a pale-green fabric with golden-yellow embroidery, dyed and woven according to the dynamic processes followed by Mrs. Jay Hambidge, her methods being similar to those of her husband, who made a special study of the methods of the Greeks, and who was the exponent of the dynamic symmetry in art. This gown had a rounded neck, from which it fell in straight lines, and was held in place easily with a narrow tie girdle of the self-material. It had an accompanying cape similar to the shawl-like mantles of the primitives, and, all in all, it resembled the robes worn by the tall women see[n] in canvases bearing the signature of Edward Burne-Jones, and in pictures by Lawrence Alma-Tadema.[24]

The decorative borders were not embroidered—using a needle and thread to stitch designs on top of a piece of cloth—but were woven at the same time the cloth web was being built up. In a 1925 letter to Eva, Mary described not only how she produced the designs but her hopes and dreams:

Dear Eva: Your wonderful letter made me very happy and came at a most opportune moment. I was collapsed in bed. Always after a struggle with the materialism of the world, and by that I don't mean just money but the ideas. . . . Glavkos [Eva's son with Angelos, whom Mary was helping to get settled in the United States] came over to see me and we had a wonderful dream about what we want to do. . . . I think eventually I shall have to come to Greece and live our dreams. Certain things must be done here first. I will build a little dynamic house beside you and we will weave beautiful garments, make divine pottery, plant flowers, fruits, make jams and everything which is the human expression of God. . . . I am thrilled over your dresses and they sound most beautiful only I wish I were there to do the dyeing etc. for you. One thing I have discovered I always meant to tell you about and neglected is the simple way I have found to do the designs. I make all my designs on flexible paper somewhat like this I am writing on in solid black and pin them right on to the warp with three or four pins and can follow them with no trouble. As the warp moves along I move the pins up and when the beater comes back the paper being flexible simply folds back of itself. . . . I now have a blue warp on and had planned to throw across a greener silk to get that sea like effect. I will enclose a little dolphin design that Mr. Hambidge made for me that is very lovely when finished with the formal Greek waves. We will teach the Greeks to make dynamic designs. . . . What a wonderful thing the weaving is: one can go off in the world of dreams the same time one is creating beauty. The one thing that saves me from destruction is that I do not live in this world but in the world of beauty with Mr. Hambidge that we created together, or rather that he created and opened my eyes to.[25]

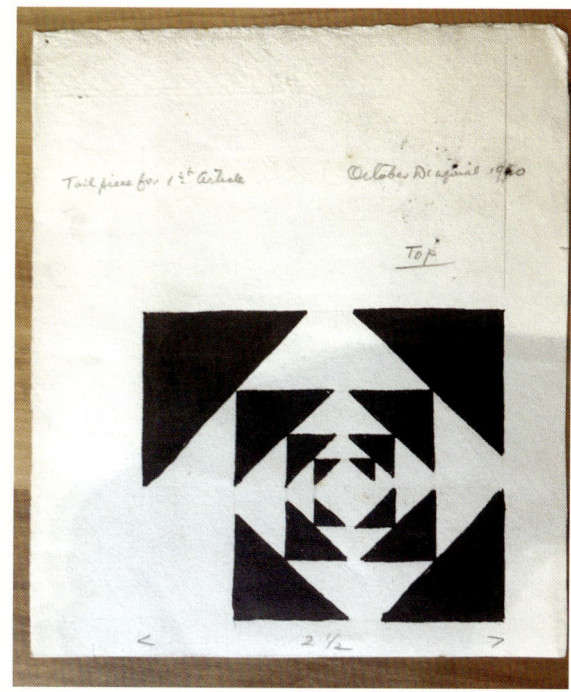

Jay Hambidge, design for the *Diagonal* (October 1920): 230, ink on paper. Courtesy of Hargrett Rare Book and Manuscript Library, University of Georgia Libraries, Hambidge Papers, box 23, folder 3

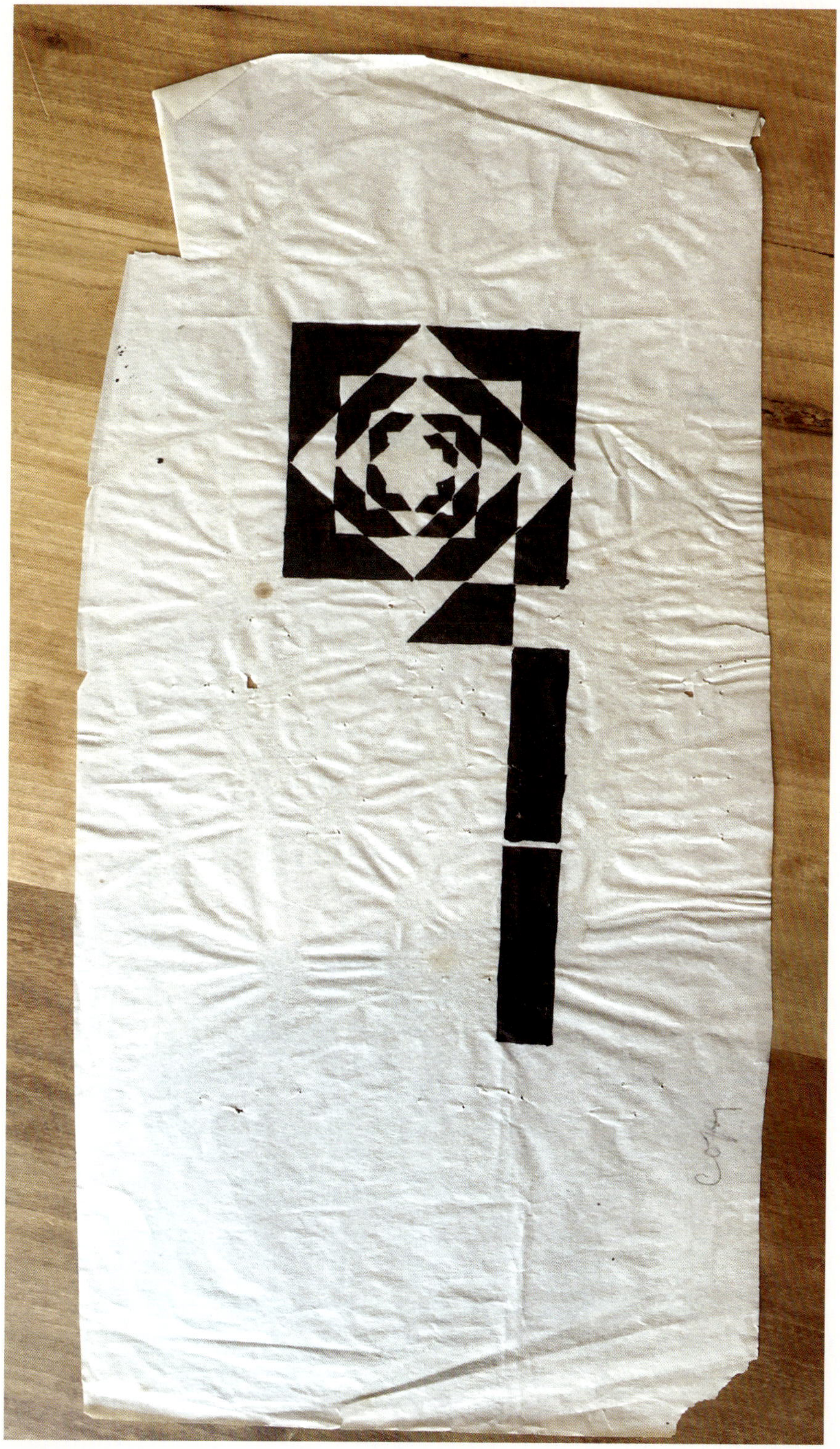

Mary Crovatt Hambidge, pattern for supplementary weft design, c. 1923, ink on tissue paper. Courtesy of Hargrett Rare Book and Manuscript Library, University of Georgia Libraries, Hambidge Papers, box 23, folder 3

This long passage is useful to get a sense of Mary's work in weaving and dyeing, her sources of inspiration, and her aversion to materialism. Weaving was a metaphor and a process that Mary associated with the beauty and purity of nature, a balance that the machine and materialism threatened to destroy. Extant tissue paper patterns for her laid-in designs show the pin marks where she pinned the design to the warp threads. Some of the patterns originated from Jay's sketches, such as his geometric spiral design in the October 1920 issue of the *Diagonal*, which Mary adapted for a weaving pattern.[26]

Mary carefully documented her weaving projects from 1921 to 1929 in her black notebook. From her diagrams and notes, one learns how she planned the clothing dimensions (some based on root rectangle proportions), materials (mostly silk or commercially spun wool, but also handspun wool by 1929), yarn colors (purple, green, orange, black, blue, gray), and border designs. Her work from 1921 when she was in Greece included "Bath Robe for E. H." (Edward "Jay" Hambidge), "Smoking Jacket," "Black Dress with Blue Embroidery—E. S." (either for Eva or under her direction), "Green Dress with Black Embroidery—E. S.," "Black Silk Coat—E. S.," "Child's Dress" with "Mrs. Noel's Stitch," and more. She recorded over forty-five individual designs, including dresses, coats, cloaks, and capes, some of which can be traced to existing outfits. For example, the heavy silk house dress she diagramed in 1922 corresponds to a dress in the collection of the Atlanta History Center; she used this motif on a number of ensembles. Her white evening dress diagram with floral motifs from January 12, 1923, corresponds to a dress that she wore for a professional photography session; the photograph, perhaps intentionally blurry, shows Mary wearing a white gown with floral motifs on the border. A collared cape begun on June 22, 1924, described as having green wave crests and fish, corresponds to her dolphin outfit.[27] From the notebook, it is clear that Mary was productive, fashion-forward, and developing exceptional weaving skills.

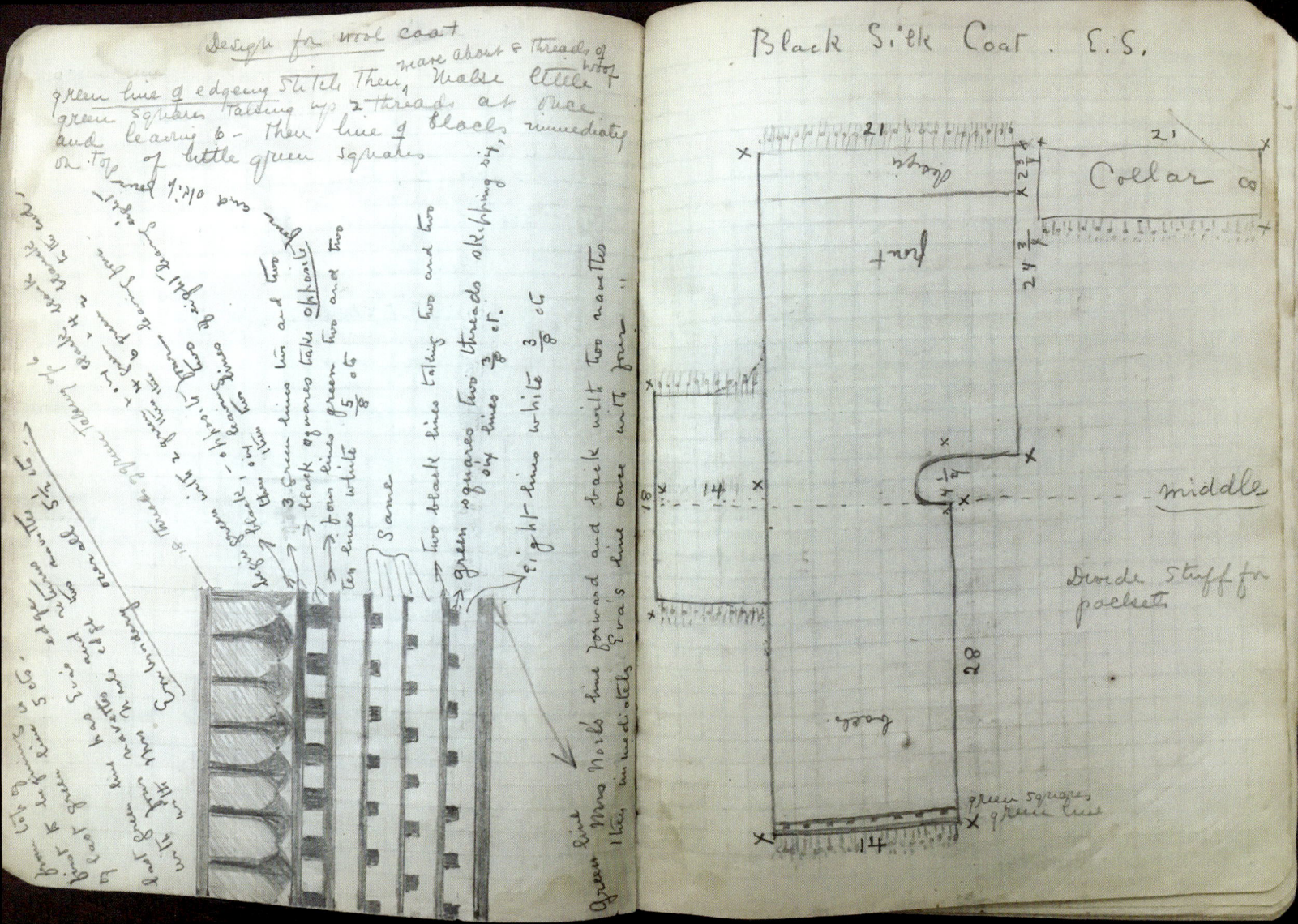

Design for wool coat

green line & edging stitch. Then make little
green squares taking up 2 threads at once
and leaving 6 - Then line of blacks immediately
on top of little green squares

Black Silk Coat. E.S.

Collar

middle

Divide stuff for
pockets

green squares
green line

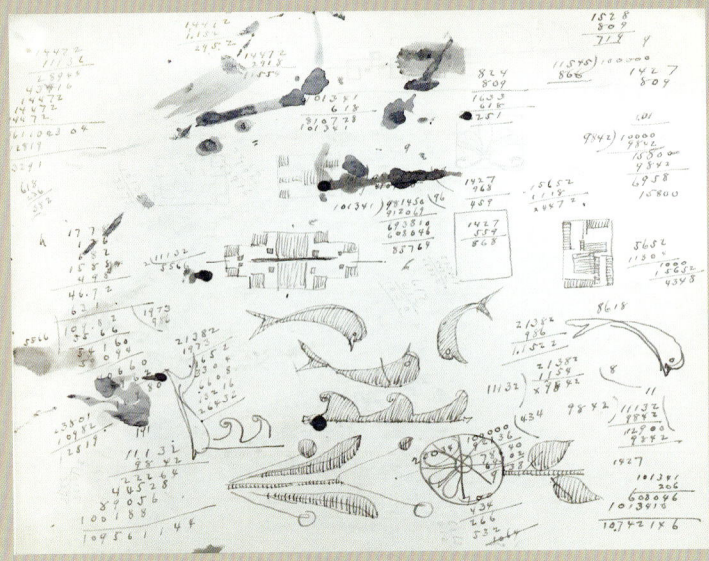

Jay Hambidge, sketch with dolphins, n.d. Kenan Research
Center at the Atlanta History Center, box 23, folder 3

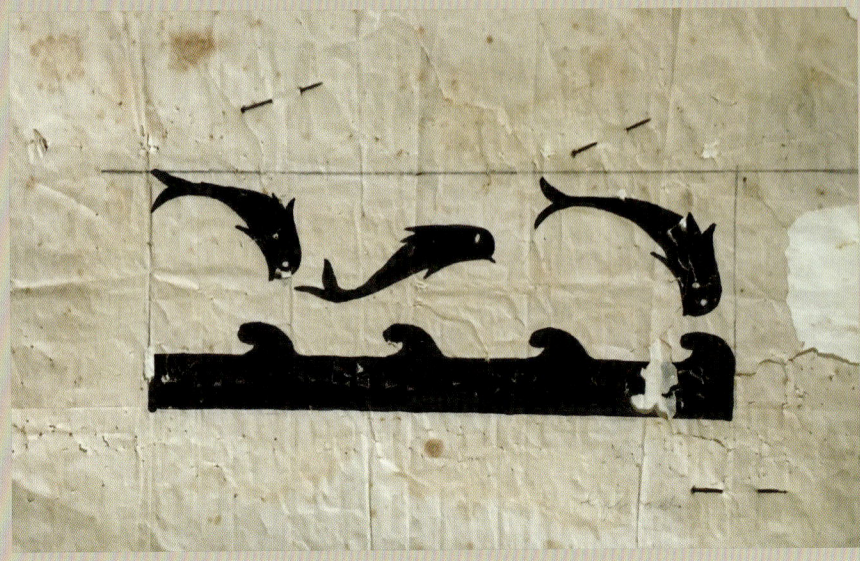

Jay Hambidge or Mary Crovatt Hambidge, dolphin pattern, ink on paper.
Courtesy of the Hambidge Center for Creative Arts and Sciences

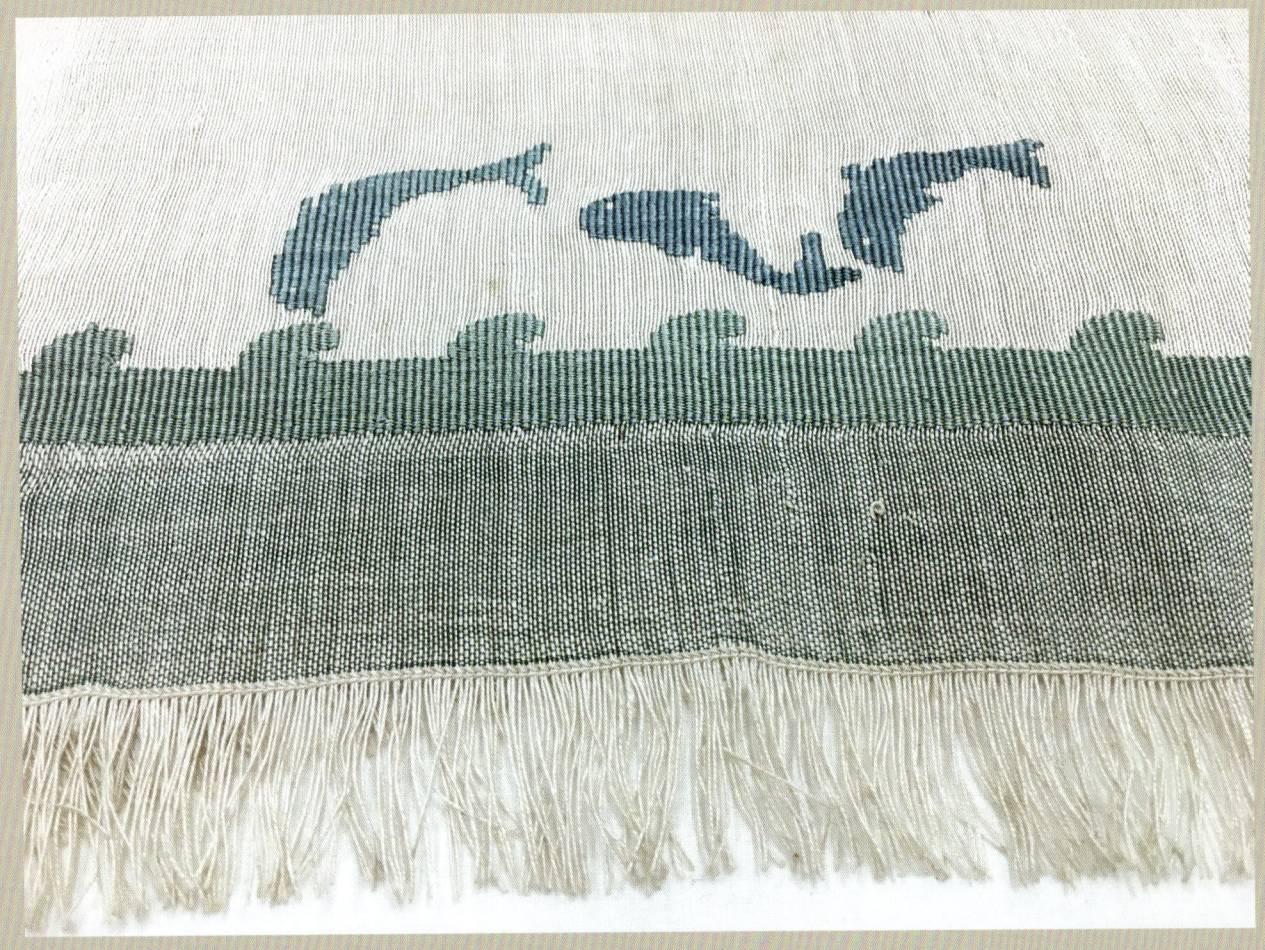

Mary Crovatt Hambidge,
detail of dolphin ensemble,
1924, linen and silk plain
weave with supplementary
weft brocade. Kenan
Research Center at the
Atlanta History Center,
1998.233

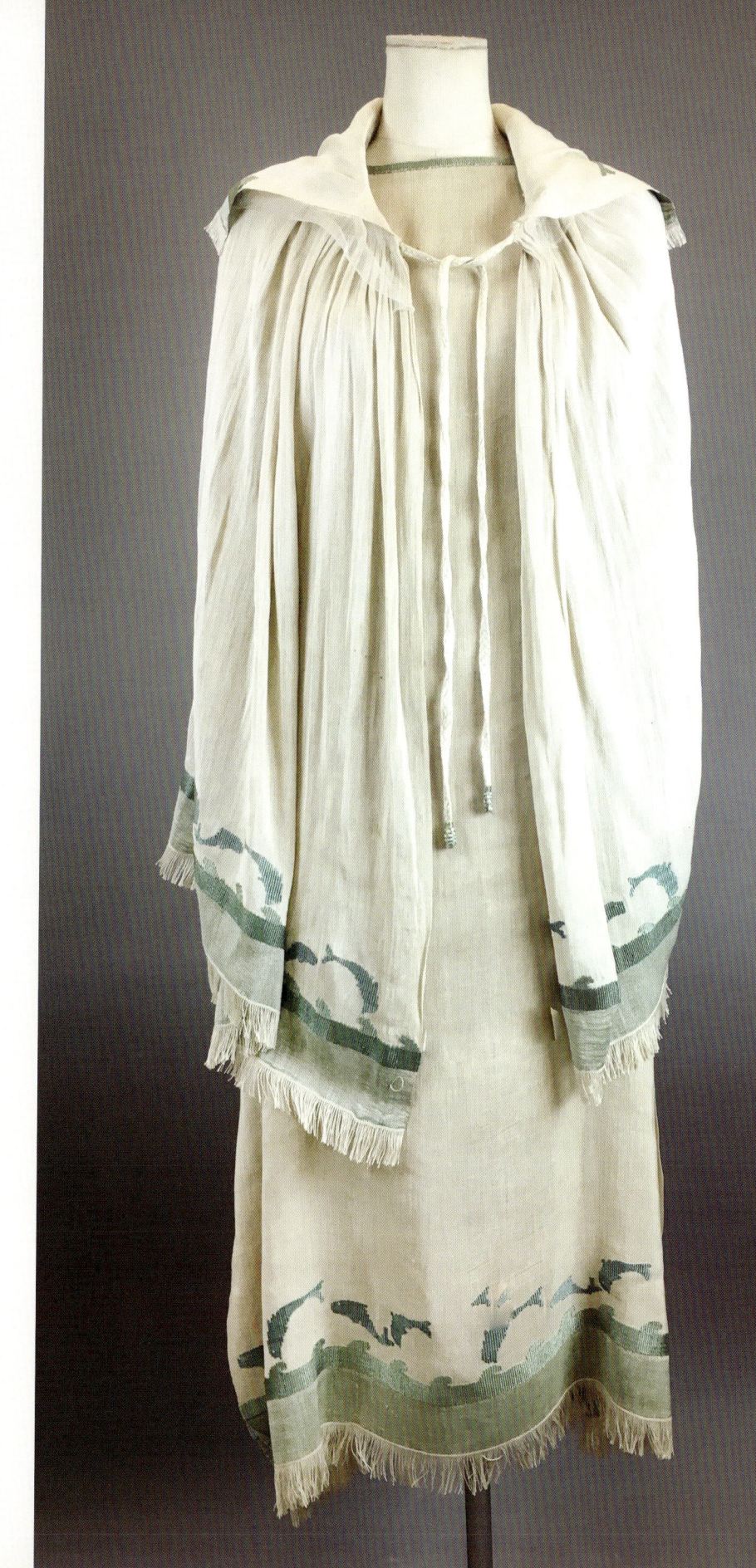

Mary Crovatt Hambidge,
dolphin ensemble, 1924, linen
and silk plain weave with
supplementary weft brocade.
Kenan Research Center at
the Atlanta History Center,
1998.233

Mary Crovatt Hambidge, notebook diagram, white evening dress with floral borders, c. 1923. Kenan Research Center at the Atlanta History Center, box 5, folder 6

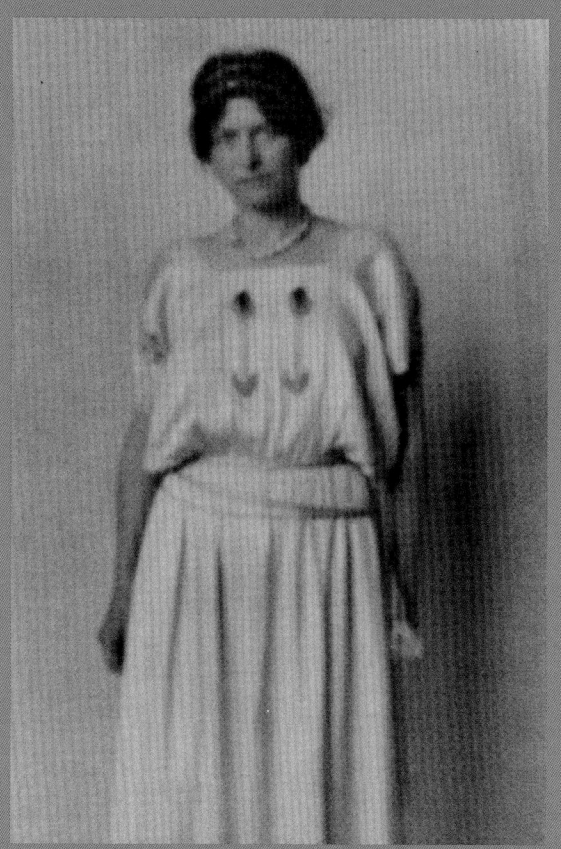

Studio photograph of Mary
Crovatt Hambidge, n.d.
Kenan Research Center at
the Atlanta History Center,
VIS 1.91, 1.92

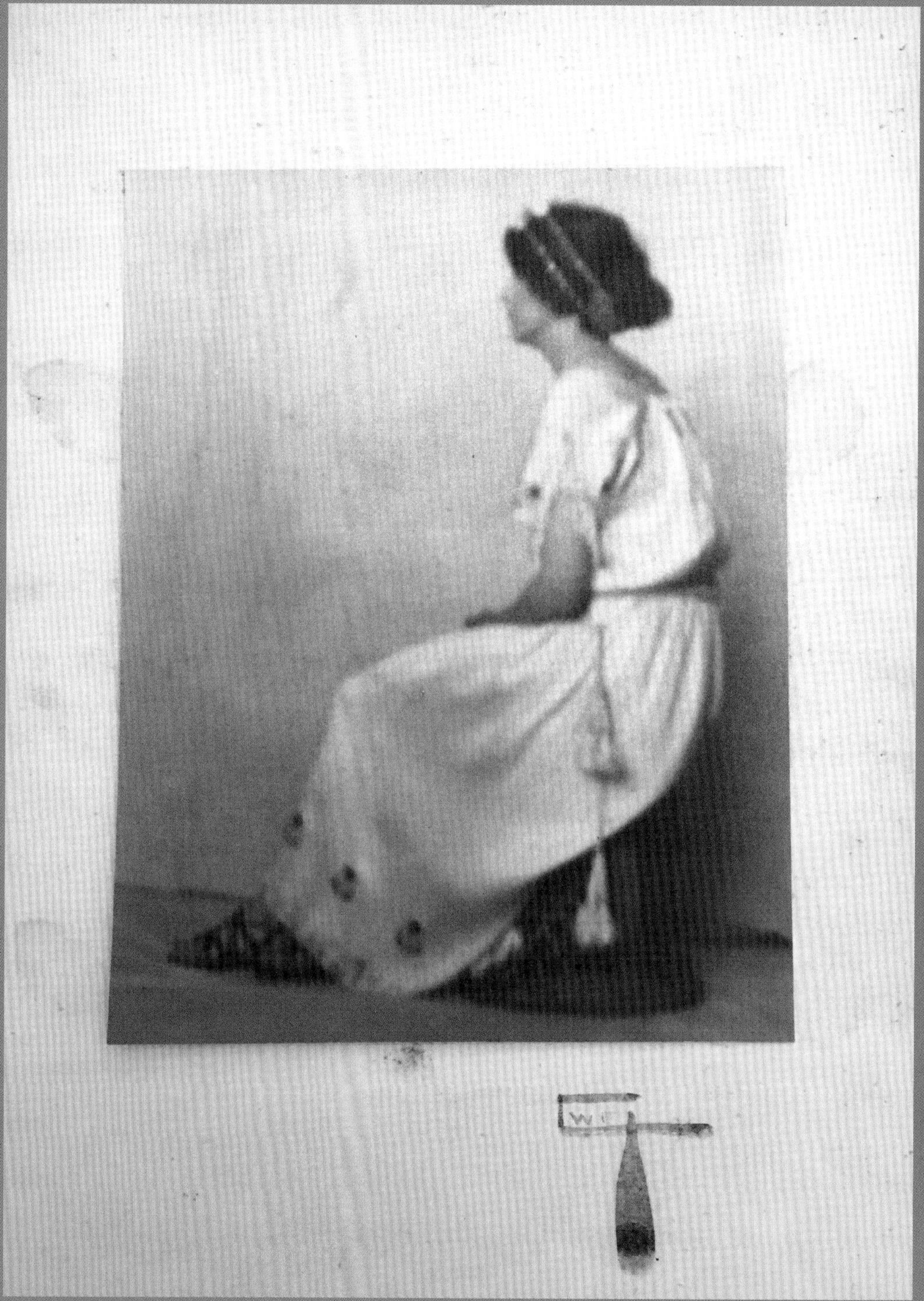

Mary Crovatt Hambidge, studio
photograph, n.d. Kenan Research
Center at the Atlanta History
Center, VIS 1.91, 1.92

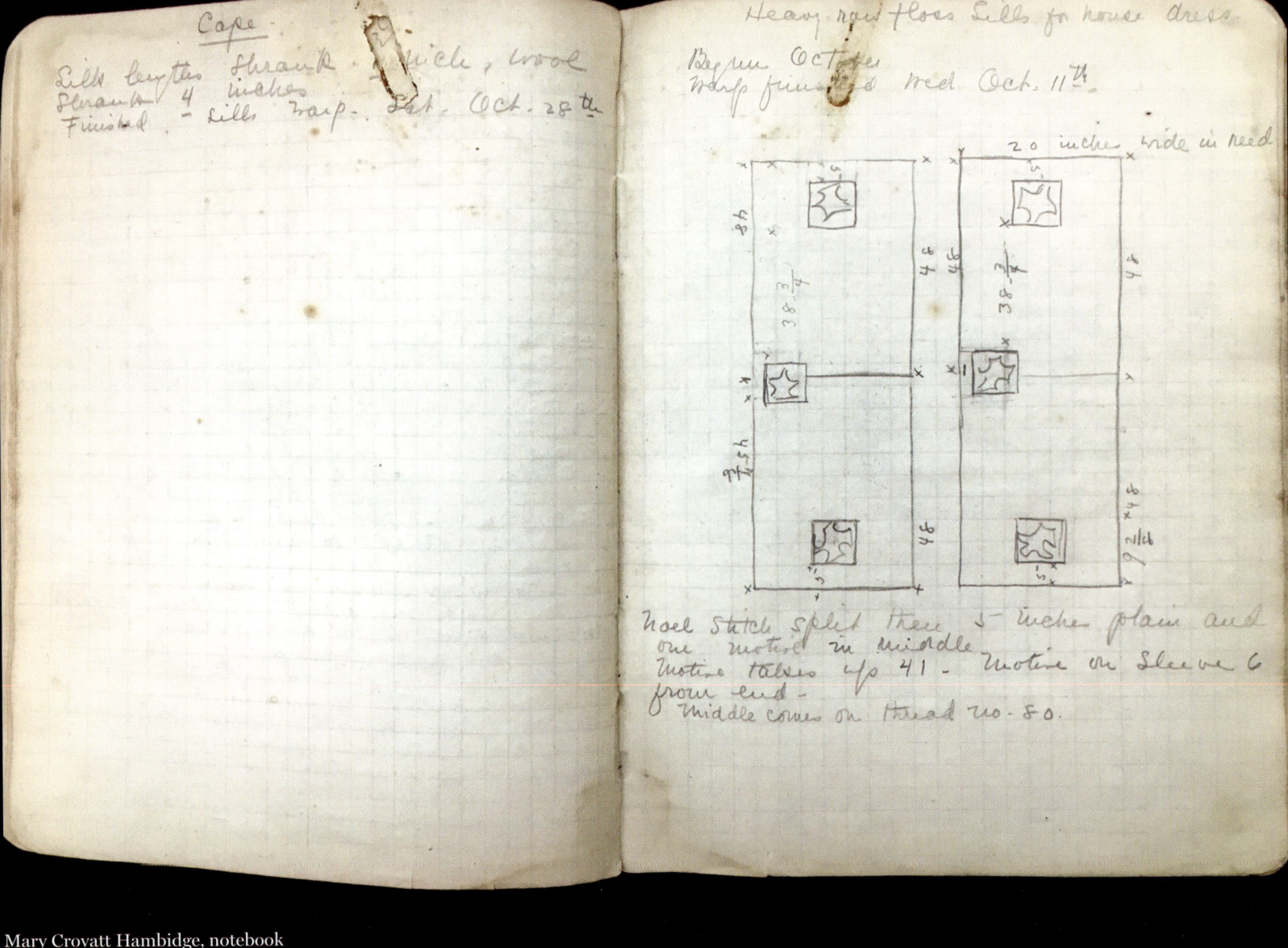

Cape.

Silk lengths shrank 1 inch, wool
shrank 4 inches
Finished - silk warp. Sat. Oct. 28th

Heavy raw floss silk for house dress.

Begun October
Warp finished Wed Oct. 11th

20 inches wide in reed

38-3/4   48   48   48   46-3/4

38-3/4   48   48   44   46   2/1ch

Noel stick split three 5 inches plain and
one motive in middle.
Motive takes up 41 - Motive on sleeve 6
from end -
Middle comes on thread no. 80.

Mary Crovatt Hambidge, notebook
diagram, silk house dress, c. 1922.
Kenan Research Center at the Atlanta
History Center, box 5, folder 6

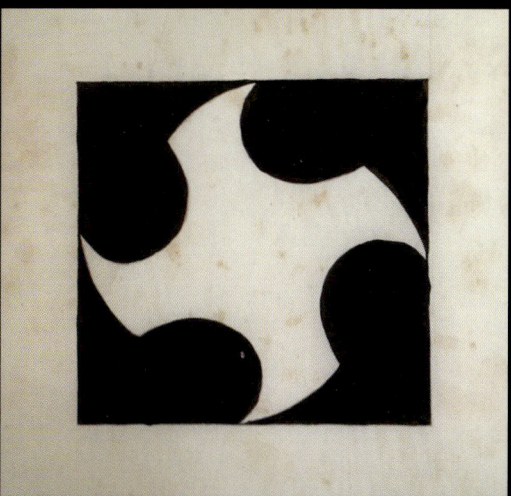

Mary Crovatt Hambidge, pattern for Dynamic Symmetry motif. Courtesy of the Hambidge Center for Creative Arts and Sciences

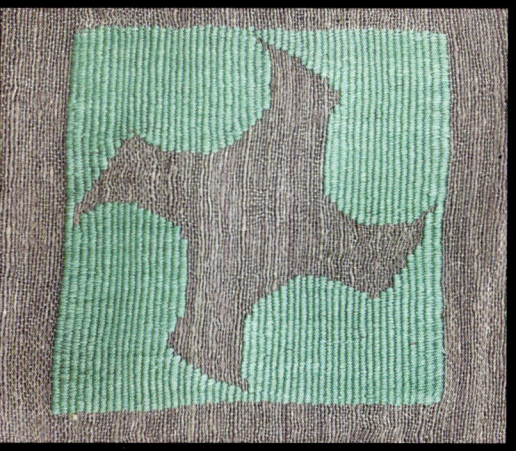

Mary Crovatt Hambidge, detail of silk skirt and blouse ensemble, 1928. Kenan Research Center at the Atlanta History Center, 1998.233

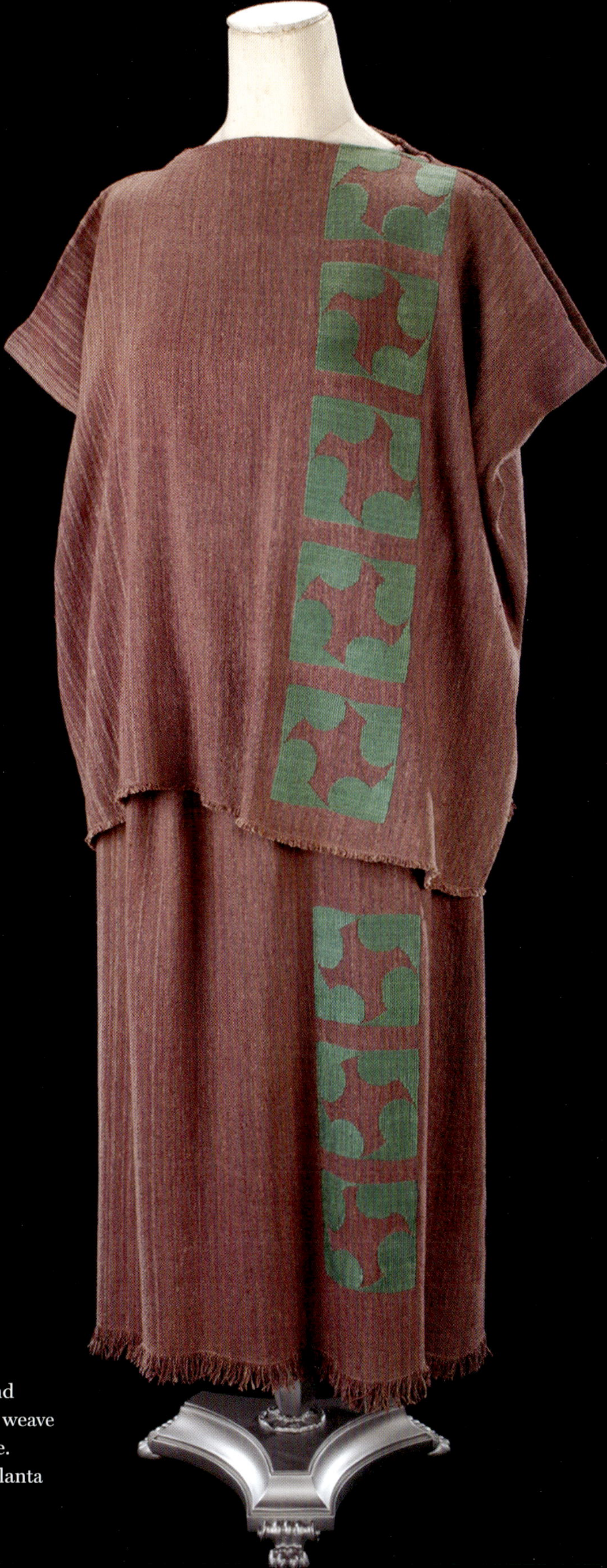

Mary Crovatt Hambidge, skirt and blouse ensemble, 1928, silk plain weave with supplementary weft brocade. Kenan Research Center at the Atlanta History Center, 1998.233

After the Death of Jay Hambidge

After Jay's death in 1924, Mary spent the next decade living in New York City; Boston; Greenwich, Connecticut; and Rabun County, Georgia. Although details regarding her exact whereabouts are patchy, records show that work opportunities and free or low rent allowed her to weave, travel, and expand her network of connections. For example, between 1928 and 1929 Eva Palmer Sikelianos, on a short visit back to the United States from Greece, occupied a Greenwich Village apartment (which they called the "Ashram") with Alma Reed, a journalist and a champion of the Mexican muralist José Clemente Orozco. The Ashram and the subsequent Delphic Circle society and gallery became gathering places, which included Mary Hambidge, who is said to have inspired Orozco to study Dynamic Symmetry.[28]

Letters reveal that in the late 1920s and early 1930s Mary began to solicit sponsors to support her developing ideas to establish a weaving and craft school. Not all of her requests were met with charitable responses. For example, she wrote to Denman Ross sometime before 1929 describing her need to have the time and resources to work: "It is only when we have leisure that we can make an art of living. If I don't have a little freedom I cannot make an art of my own life."[29] Apparently, he had sent her some money earlier, but his response in 1932, perhaps after other requests for funds, was unsupportive:

> I wish you might have followed my advice [to live with her brother and develop her ideas in the South]. I am sure that it was good advice but you did not follow it. Now you are in need of money and suggest that I, in my eightieth year, should raise the money you need to enable you to pay your rent and get away from New York and get a quiet and pleasant home in the country where you can do what you want to do for the advancement of the arts and crafts. What you ask me to do is impossible.[30]

Mary's luck changed in 1930 when she met and befriended Eleanor Steele Reese and her husband, Hall Clovis, who became the benefactors that made her dreams possible. They were wealthy socialite opera singers who were principals in a 1931 performance of Bach's *The Contest between Phoebus and Pan* at the Little Theater Opera Company of New York. Mary designed and wove over forty costumes "in the Greek style" for that production.[31] None of the costumes are extant, but her detailed instructions regarding tunic shapes, decorative border patterns, and colors reveal that she used mathematical formulas based on root rectangles for five different robe designs, including a short chlamys cloak and a longer chiton gown. She chose brown and green for the Pan chorus and blue and gold for the Apollo ballet.[32]

Mary's work in costumes brought her to the attention of famed dancer and choreographer Ted Shawn, who with his wife, Ruth St. Denis, had formed the dance company Denishawn (1915–1931), renowned for appropriating costumes and dances from a variety of cultures and epochs, ranging from Asian and ancient Egyptian to Native American.[33] Shawn was in the process of separating from St. Denis, soon to form his own company, Ted Shawn and His Men Dancers, in Massachusetts, and was receiving financial support from artist, curator, and philanthropist Katherine Dreier under the auspices of the Société Anonyme. Dreier funded the sets and expenses for the Berlin debut of Shawn's *Prometheus Bound* (1929) and the 1931 Jacob's Pillow debut of *O Brother Sun and Sister Moon*, among others. Mary was commissioned to weave costumes for the robes of St. Francis for the latter ballet, but the commission was either not completed or left uncredited. Mary appears to have overstepped her role by trying to direct the choreography herself. In a terse exchange between Dreier, Shawn, and Mary in November 1931, Mary defended her overinvolvement with the choreography, writing to Dreier, "If, in collaboration, Mr. Shawn expresses himself and I express myself and the two expressions do not coordinate the result is exactly what modern art is, a chaotic mass of disconnected detail."[34] Dreier retorted to Mary, "You must be kept very busy if you not only design costumes but instruct your clients in the dance and the character they are acting. This is of course in absolute contradiction to the policy of the Société Anonyme."[35] This exchange points to the disconnection between Mary and progressive and experimental developments in modern art. Was the disconnection due to Mary's personality, or did she really equate modern art with chaos, despite believing that her work was modern? Mary's approach to art aligned more closely with Arts and Crafts ideals than with the avant-garde and conceptual developments taking place at the time.

During the 1930s, when Mary was not in New York City or Georgia, she lived rent-free in the stately Rowland House, now demolished, in Greenwich, Connecticut, designed by Stanford White of the firm McKim, Mead & White, a situation likely facilitated by Reese and Clovis, who owned a 244-acre estate in Greenwich.[36] There she wove commissions for clients, including Reese, with assistance from Eva Palmer Sikelianos, who lived with Mary intermittently from 1933 to 1939 after suffering financial losses in Greece after funding the Delphic Festivals.[37] There are no records indicating that Mary assisted with the costumes for Eva's 1927 and 1930 staging of the Delphic Festivals in Delphi, Greece, which included epic productions of Aeschylus's *Prometheus Bound*; Eva is credited with designing and weaving all of the costumes. Nor are there records showing that Mary worked on the costumes

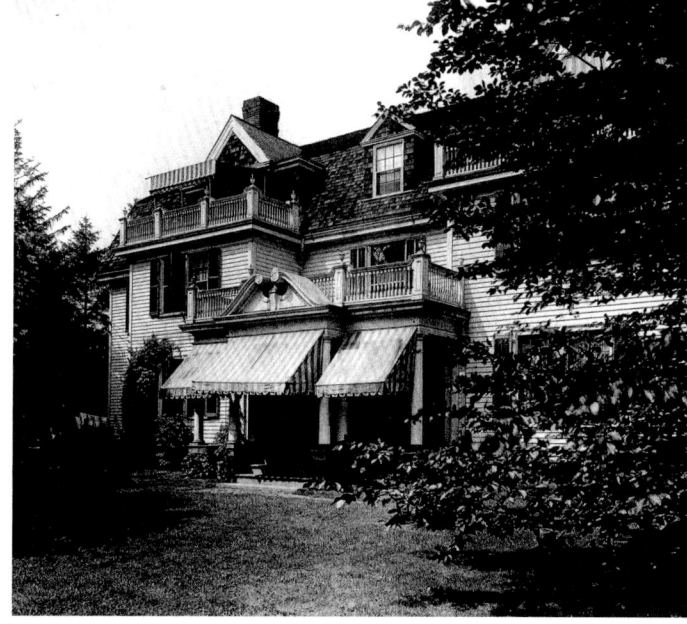

George Rowland House, 116 Field Point Road, Greenwich, Connecticut, now demolished. Courtesy of the Greenwich Historical Society

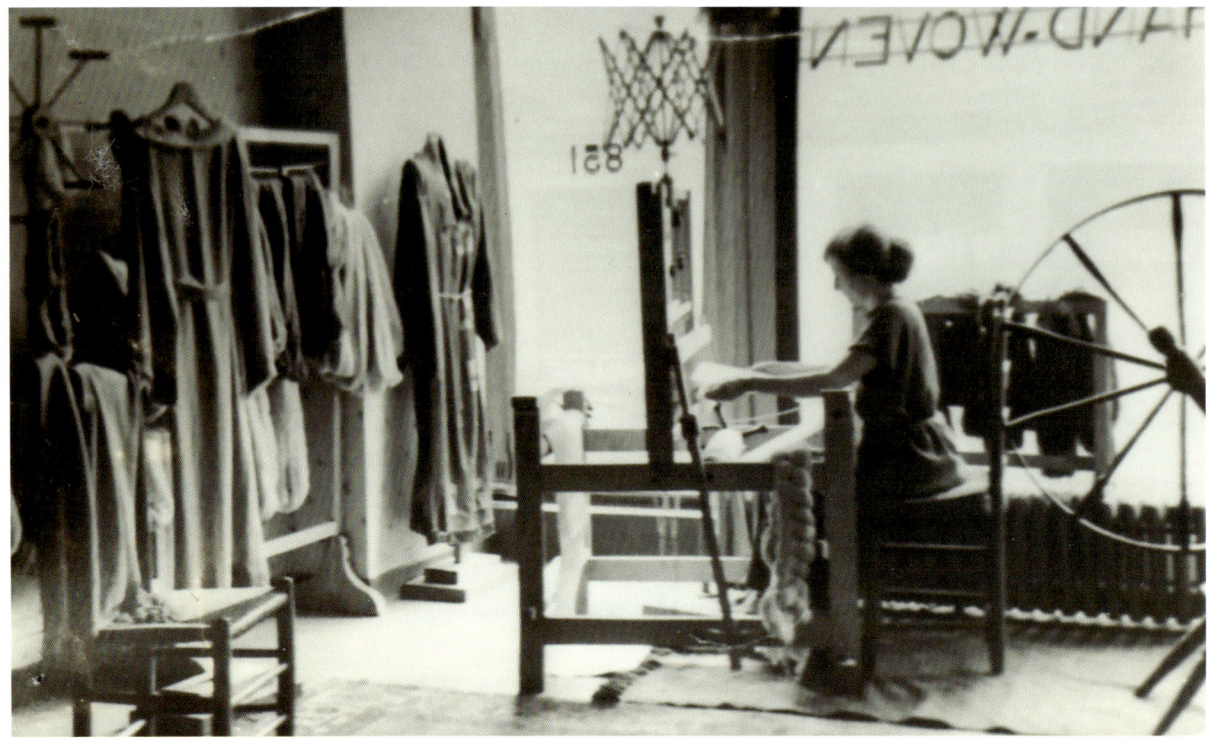

Mary Crovatt Hambidge at the loom, 851 Madison Avenue, New York City, 1936–1937. Photographer unknown, courtesy of the Hambidge Center for Creative Arts and Sciences

for Shawn's 1929 production of *Prometheus Bound*, which was before he met and began to work with Eva in 1939.[38] However, Mary did assist Eva in weaving more than one hundred costumes for Eva's production of *The Bacchae*, performed at Smith College in 1934 and Bryn Mawr College in 1935.[39]

Mary began to spend more and more time in Georgia, believing that she could create a weaving collective there similar to what she had known in Athens. She had begun to visit northeastern Georgia in 1927 where she rented a cabin called Twin Tops in Mountain City from a friend.[40] There she encountered Appalachian spinners and weavers and experienced another revelation:

> Fate brought me back to Georgia, where I was born, but to another part of the State that I knew little of. Here, buried away in the Mountains of the Northern part of the State, I found a real peasantry, very much like the people I had known and loved in Greece, living much the same kind of life. Here was the true pioneer stock of America. They had kept their craft knowledge and their native integrity but their looms had been relegated to the attics, their spinning wheels put away to be used only now and then to spin a little thread for their

men's socks. . . . When I came upon all this a great desire took possession of me to save this ancient skill and to help these people to preserve and develop the essentials of this *whole* life that they really believed in.[41]

At Twin Tops, Mary recruited a few women to spin local sheep wool for her, as well as some young women to weave, and she began to form her vision of a weaving collective using local materials and labor. "I could actually have threads spun more beautiful than those I got in Greece."[42] In 1935 and 1936 she exhibited this woven work in New York City at 851 Madison Avenue and at the Greenwich library, gaining the attention of an urban clientele, most likely facilitated by her friend and benefactor, Eleanor Steele Reese.[43]

The parallels Mary saw between the Greek weavers and the mountain weavers, both of whom she referred to as "peasants," reveal her self-identity as an elite savior who could revitalize and capitalize on the talents of the women around her. She later stated, "There was my work cut out for me—to help these people through the ideal I believed in."[44] Clearly Mary was following the path set forth by William Morris while creating a new role for herself as a reformer through weaving. She also saw weaving as a distinctly female occupation, one that could elevate a woman's quality of life: "I want the women of our country to experience the peace and contentment that this work has brought to me. I know that it will solve many problems for them as it has for me."[45] With these ideas in mind, Mary set about to make her dream a reality.

CHAPTER 4

The Weavers of Rabun and Rabun Studios in Historical Context

Rabun Studios and the Weavers of Rabun connected two disparate worlds. Rabun Studios operated in the middle of New York City, a center of art and design, while the Weavers of Rabun operated in the mountains of northeastern Georgia, a center of rural handcraft production. Mary Hambidge was the driving force behind both enterprises and the thread that united them. There are several factors to consider when explaining how Mary was able to create the Weavers of Rabun, assembling a group of old-style spinners and weavers to join her in what appears today to have been a colossal utopian undertaking in applying traditional techniques to contemporary creations. How did this worldly, eccentric outsider, who knew nothing of Appalachian craft or agricultural history, manage to wend her way into the multigenerational fabric of the area and get people to work for her and with her? How was she able for two decades to manage and supply Rabun Studios, a stylish Madison Avenue boutique, with woven goods that appealed to a wide range of consumers? How was she able to expand the exposure of both enterprises to include museum exhibitions and a presidential commission? The three primary explanations for her success were her passion for weaving, maintaining a wide network of supporters and collaborators, and having the funds to make it happen. Mary noted later that the locals at first "were very skeptical and took me only as a faddist, the chief lure being that they got a little much needed cash from the work."[1] The significance of Eleanor Steele Reese's ongoing financial support cannot be overstated; she made Mary's dreams possible.

Eleanor Steele Reese was the millionaire socialite daughter of Charles Steele, a partner with J. P. Morgan, and Ann "Nannie" Gordon French. She studied opera in Paris and New York, and in 1930 she married Hall Clovis, a principal at the Little Theater Opera Company in New York, which was around the time that Mary met them. Eleanor and Hall Clovis divorced in 1940, and in 1941 Eleanor married Idaho cattle rancher Emmet P. Reese. Although Eleanor never visited the Hambidge Center she continued her financial support and pragmatic advice throughout Mary's life, and they exchanged lengthy letters. Reese began providing funds to Mary shortly after their meeting in 1930. She was behind Mary's housing in Greenwich during the 1930s, as she and Hall had purchased an estate there in 1934. She most likely provided the start-up funds and weaving salaries for Mary's early enterprise at Twin Tops, and she later arranged for Mary to rent and eventually purchase an 800-acre property on Betty's Creek Road in Rabun Gap, which included cabins, an outbuilding, and a rock house, from the Latimer family in 1939 for $6,005.[2] Additionally, Eleanor and Hall together and then separately funded Rabun Studios from 1937 to 1958 by providing monthly infusions of cash for supplies, salaries, and other expenses.

Eleanor's many letters to Mary in the late 1930s and early 1940s show that she provided varying amounts of money to fund the farm, the weaving enterprise, and the shop. In July 1936, for example, in one of the first extant letters from Eleanor to Mary, she enclosed a check for $1,000 for expenses, a huge amount in Depression-era America. Other letters show different amounts: "Enclosing $200 to make the $500 as you asked," and "Enclosed is a check for $300 until our return from Europe." She also asked Mary to "tell us what you will need in the way of funds for July and August to buy wool and other materials."[3] Eleanor also provided professional guidance. When a customer was unhappy with the cloth and tailoring of a garment, Eleanor scolded Mary for her hardheadedness: "You cannot make a success of anything by forcing your ideals on anyone else. You must be able to give clients what they want *when* they order from samples *made* by you."[4] Eleanor also advised Mary on how to negotiate the purchase of the Betty's Creek property and provided her with the funds so that the deed would be in Mary's name.[5]

After Eleanor and Hall divorced and Eleanor married Emmet Reese, Eleanor wanted the foundation to officially incorporate, and for tax purposes, she wanted her pledge to be considered a contribution to a cause, not a gift.[6] Most likely in 1944, when the rationale and articles of incorporation were drawn for the Jay Hambidge Art Foundation, she began the $1,000 per month pledge, which continued until Mary's death in 1973; board minutes

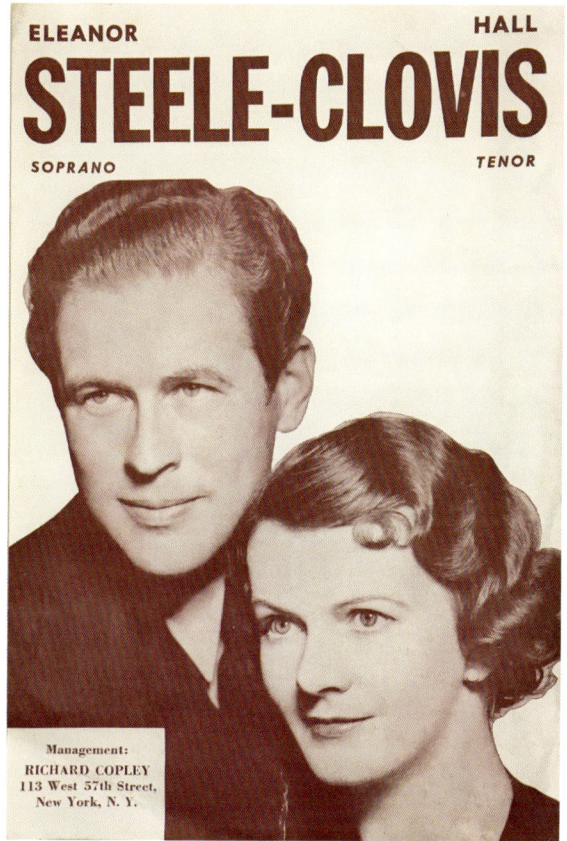

Promotional advertisement for Eleanor Steele and Hall Clovis, before 1940. Kenan Research Center at the Atlanta History Center, box 37, folders 1–4

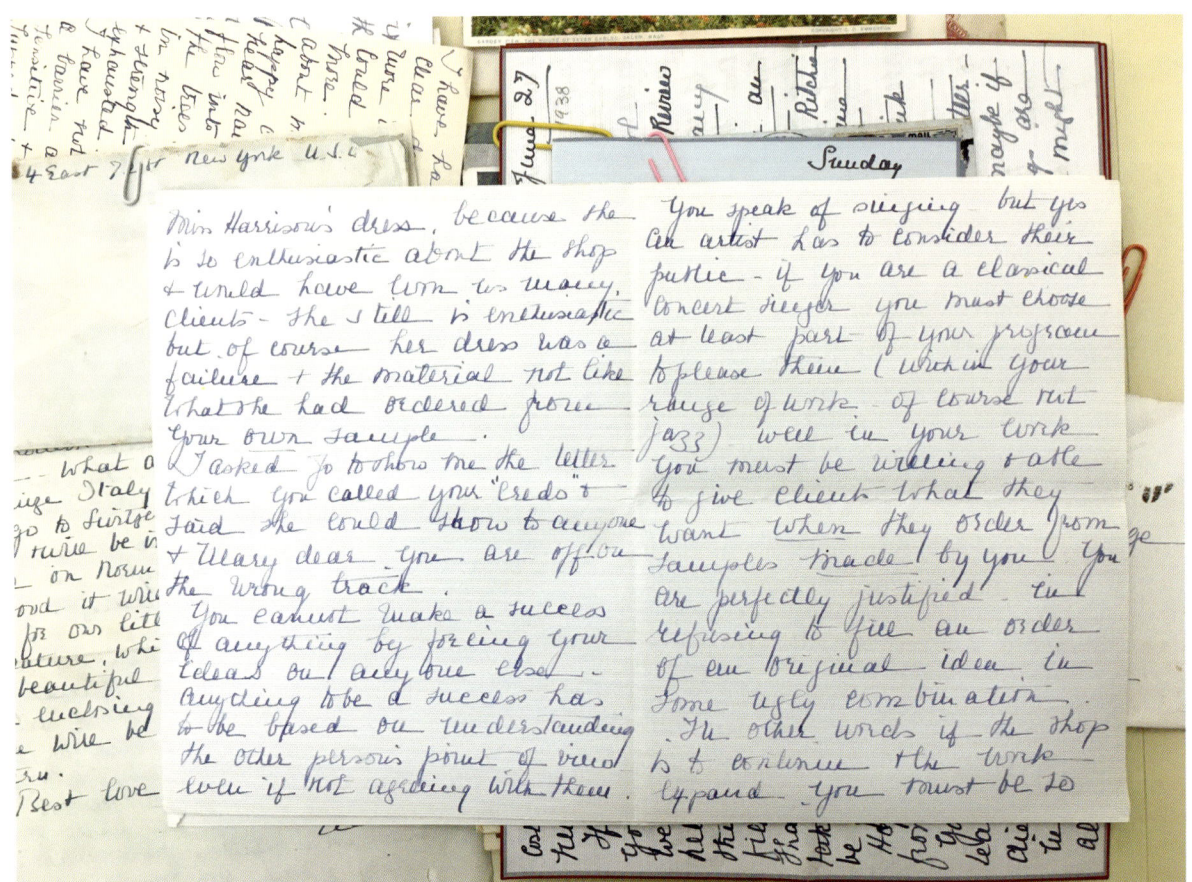

Eleanor Steele Reese letters to Mary Crovatt Hambidge. Kenan Research Center at the Atlanta History Center, box 52, folder 3

noted that "Mrs. E. P. Reese of Idaho has been contributing $1000 per month to the Foundation."[7] By the mid-1940s Mary was running a large operation—the farm, the weavers, the shop—and supervising supplies, equipment, salaries, travel, shipping, the kitchen, guests, and other responsibilities. To address Mary's occasional anxieties about having enough money, Eleanor wrote encouraging letters: "Don't worry about my being able to continue. I know that as long as I use my income to help others, there will always be plenty."[8] While the shop managers kept records and noted expenses, Eleanor's continuous contributions allowed Mary to focus on matters beyond securing day-to-day income. As Mary aged, she became less interested in finances and more antagonistic toward the idea of acquiring wealth for wealth's sake.

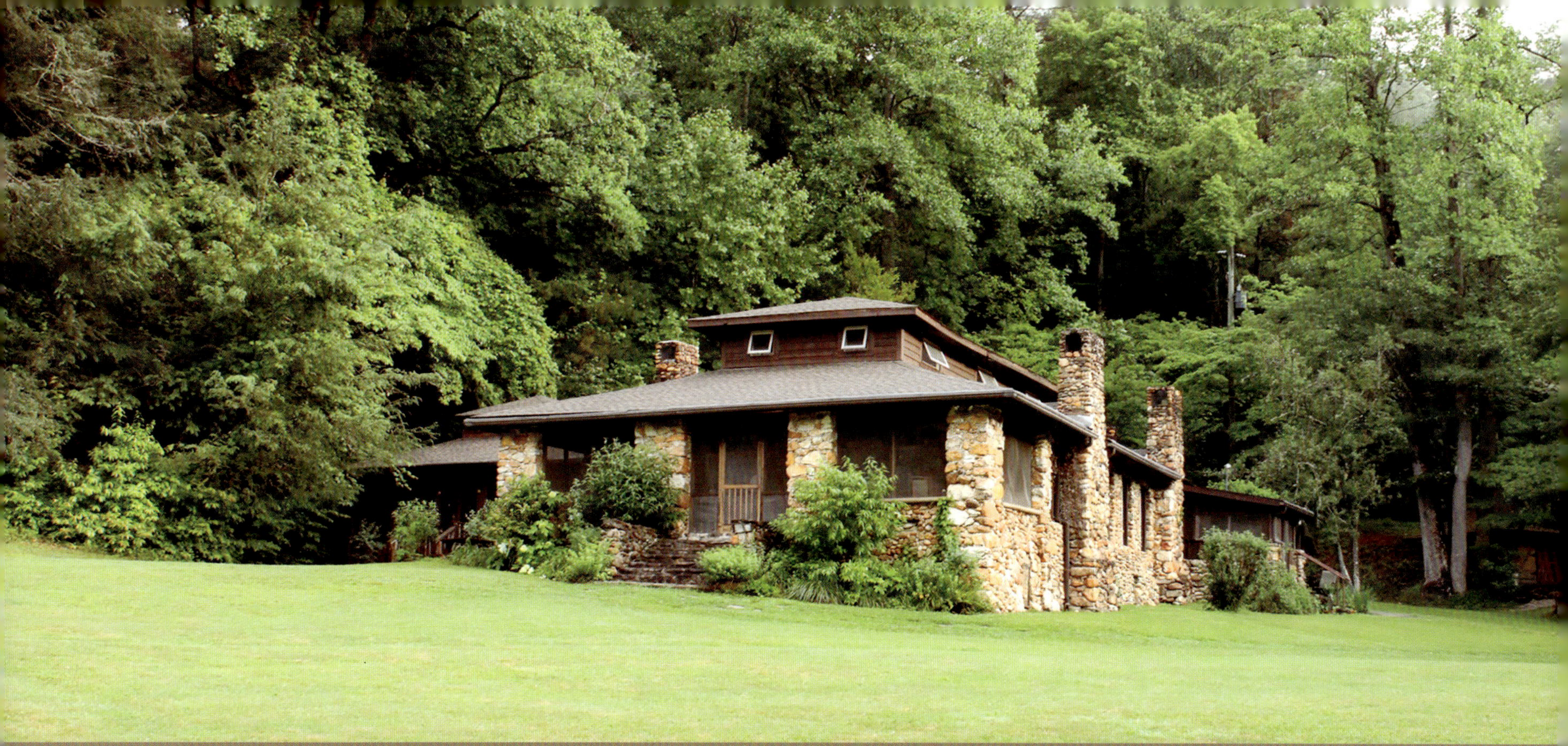

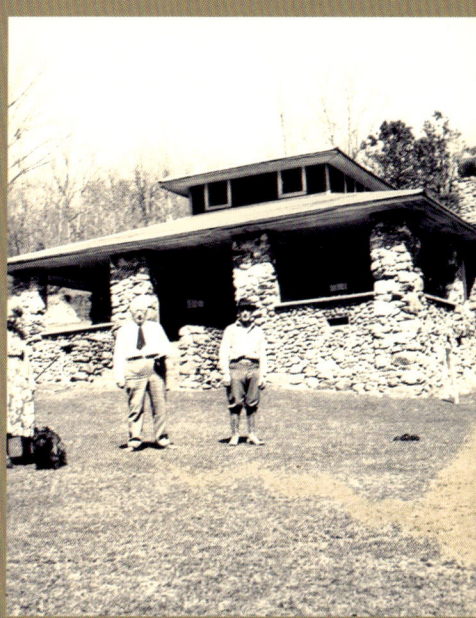

Rock House, Hambidge Center, n.d. Courtesy of the
Hambidge Center for Creative Arts and Sciences

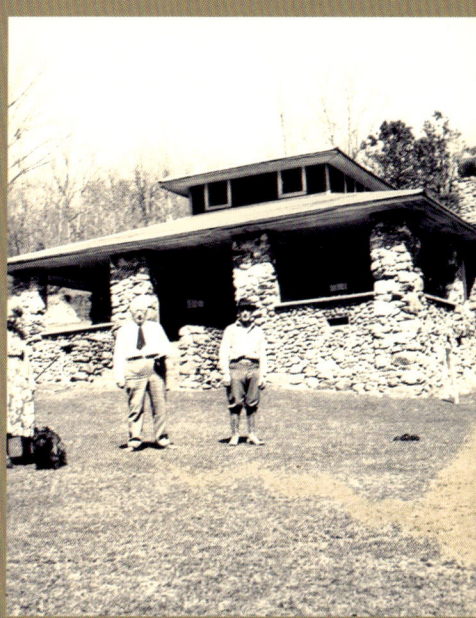

Rock House, Hambidge Center, c. 1930s.
Courtesy of the Hambidge Center for Creative
Arts and Sciences

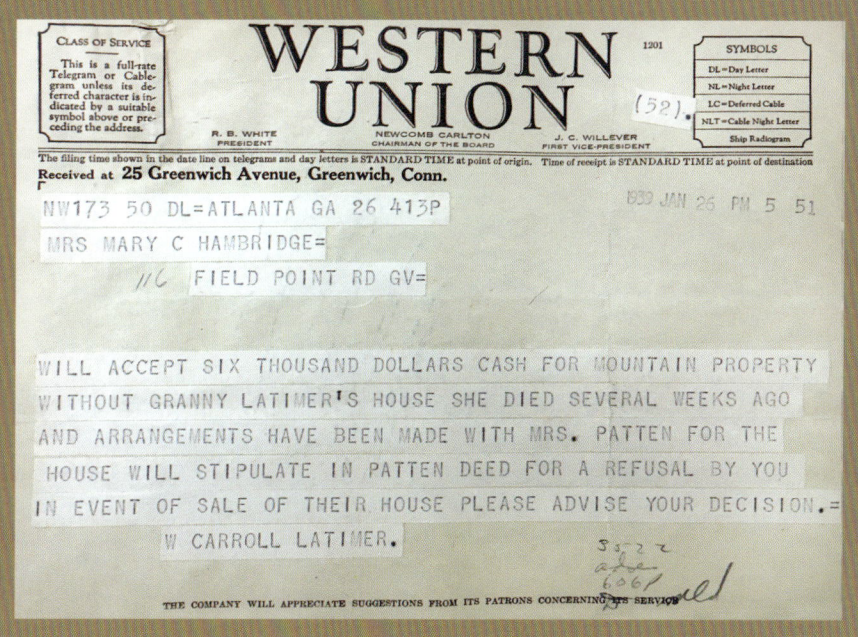

Western Union note of sale of the Latimer property to
Mary C. Hambidge, 1939. Kenan Research Center at the
Atlanta History Center, box 43, folder 6

The Weavers of Rabun

Mary was among many reformers in the early decades of the twentieth century who believed that they could contribute to the economic health of rural Appalachia by reviving traditional handcrafts.[9] These reformers, primarily enterprising women in association with churches or philanthropic sororities, supported traditional weaving as it was practiced by homesteaders as a way to enrich Appalachian women while maintaining their traditional family roles. For example, when the weaving program at Berea College in Kentucky was established in 1911, the goals, according to President William Frost, were not to "introduce forms of weaving which are new and foreign to the people here but to encourage and develop the forms which have been handed down by tradition from the old English and Scottish sources."[10] Lucy Morgan, who studied weaving at Berea, founded the Penland Weavers and Potters and the Penland School of Handicrafts in 1923 and 1929, respectively. With support from the Episcopal Church, she sought to "bring about a revival of hand-weaving . . . [and] provide our neighbor mothers with a means of adding to their generally meager incomes without having to leave their homes."[11] As Philis Alvic explained in her book *Weavers of the Southern Highlands*, the quest to build settlement schools, home-based "fireside" industries, technical institutions, colleges, and craft guilds during this period led to what is now referred to as the Appalachian craft revival.[12] Weaving was central to all of these activities because it was considered a timeless and worthwhile craft, especially for women. The enterprises provided instruction, workspaces, promotional and marketing opportunities, and a sense of community. Dozens of them were established in the region: Berea College in Kentucky; Biltmore Industries and the Southern Highland Craft Guild in North Carolina; Berry College in northwestern Georgia; and Tallulah Falls Industrial School and Rabun Gap–Nacoochee School, both near the Hambidge property in Georgia.[13]

Mary Hambidge shared some of the goals of these craft institutions in her resolute commitment to traditional handweaving practices. She recruited women who knew how to card, spin, dye, and weave raw sheep wool on handlooms from start to finish; and she recruited young women to learn these skills from their elders. Many of the young women came from Tallulah Falls School, which Mary considered "one of the finest, if not the finest, craft school in the South."[14] Mary paid women spinners to work from home, and she paid part- and full-time weavers to work on site at the newly constructed Weave Shed.[15] However, Mary's creation, the Weavers of Rabun,

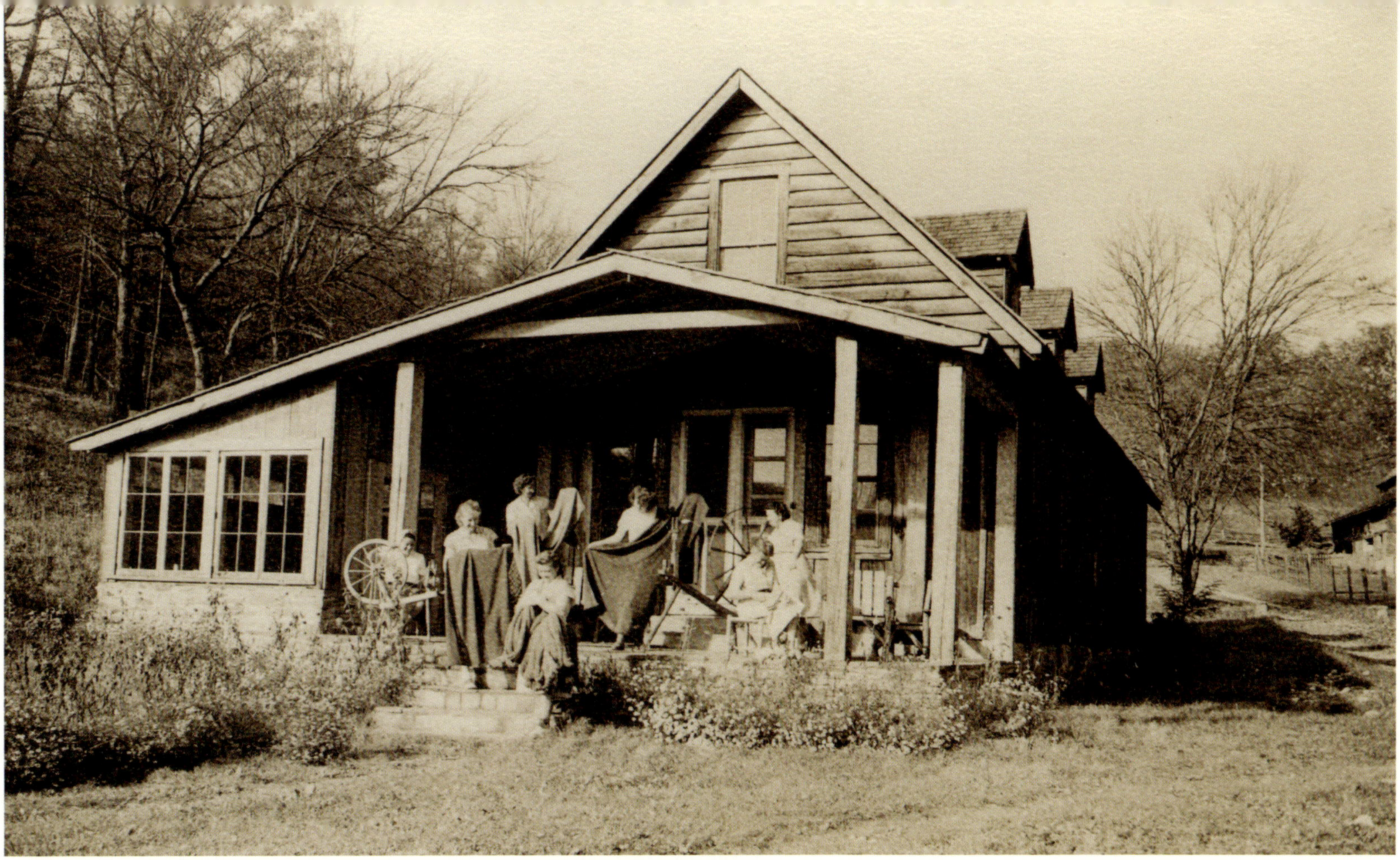

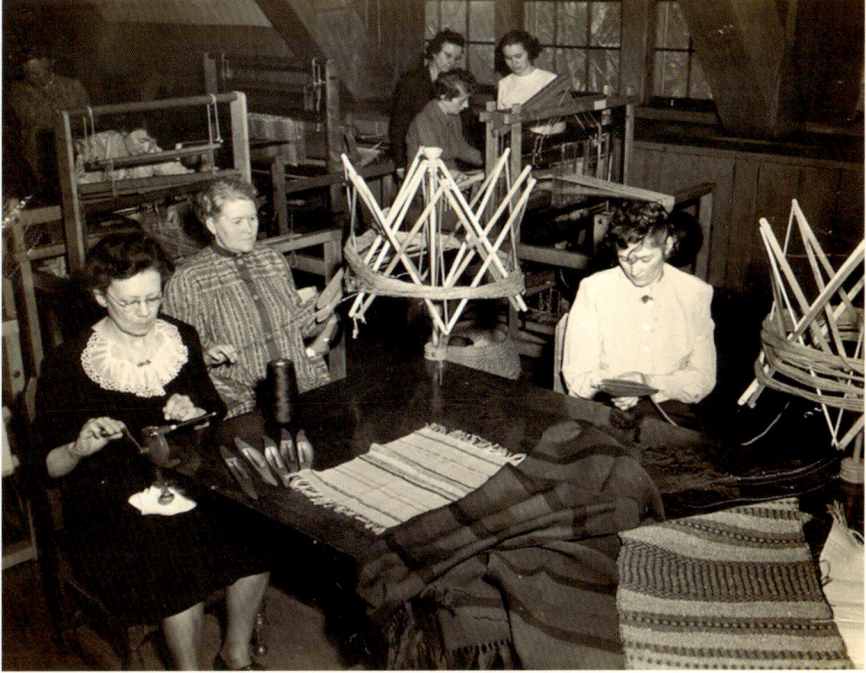

Weave Shed, Hambidge
Center, c. 1940s. Courtesy
of the Hambidge Center for
Creative Arts and Sciences

Weave Shed interior, c. 1940s.
Courtesy of the Hambidge Center
for Creative Arts and Sciences

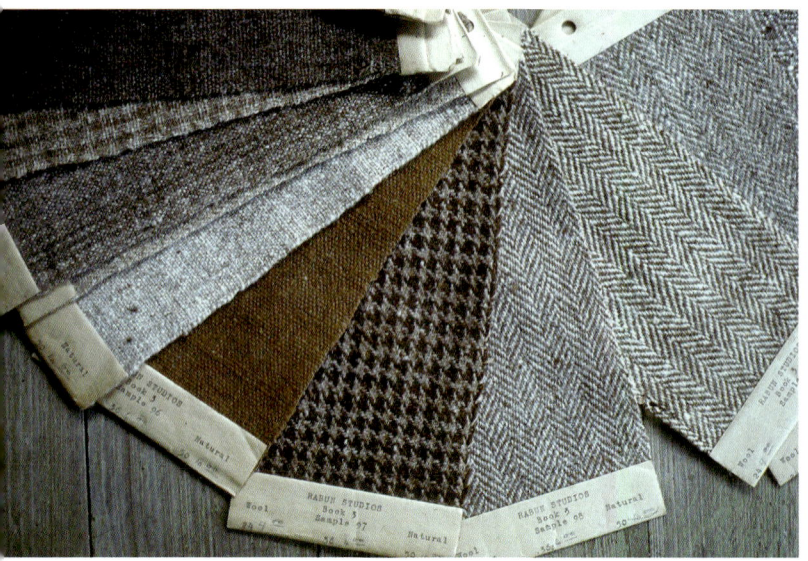

Weavers of Rabun sample
book 3, naturals. Courtesy
of Philis Alvic

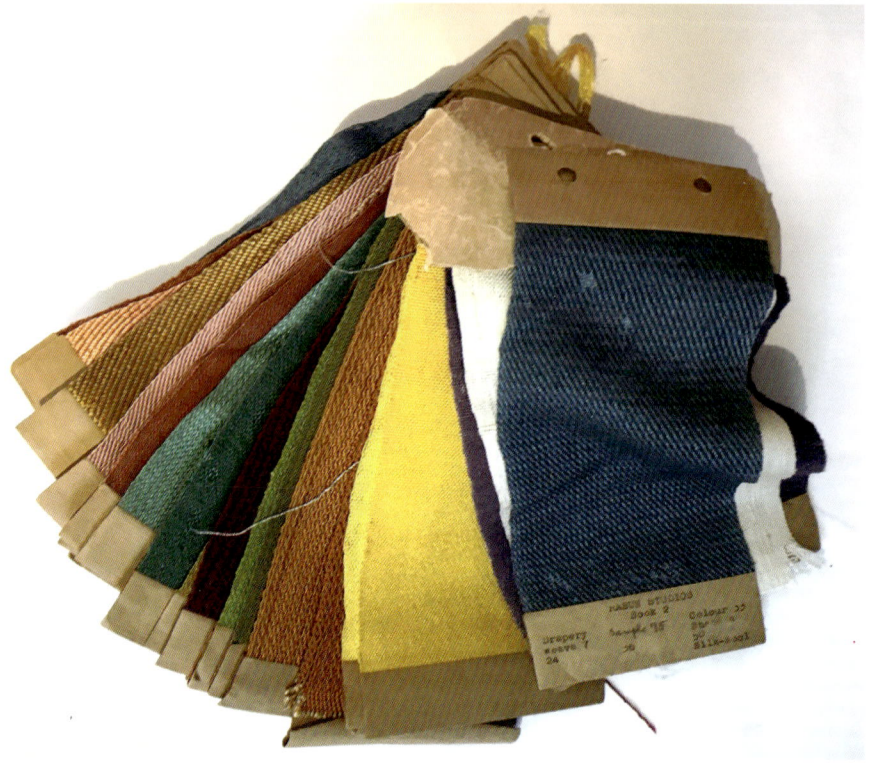

Weavers of Rabun sample book 2, silk-wool.
Photograph by the author, courtesy of the Hambidge
Center for Creative Arts and Sciences

was an anomaly in the Appalachian craft revival movement because it was privately sponsored and more independent than those relying on institutional support. The women she worked with didn't weave from traditional overshot patterns to make coverlets, placemats, and bookmarks from patterns, or "recipes," passed down from previous generations.[16] Instead, they focused on creating brilliantly dyed and woven silk or wool yardage, stoles, and throws, which clients could custom order from sample books organized by hue and fiber. An early pamphlet titled *The Weavers of Rabun* explained Mary's philosophy:

> We are not repeating the old fashioned weaving of the Mountaineers. Our work is modern and based upon nature. We are attempting to bring out the simple beauty and quality inherent in nature's raw materials. . . . This work is the continuation of experiments in the crafts begun by Jay Hambidge during his investigation of the fundamental design forms underlying natural law. It

The Weavers of Rabun pamphlet text:

M.S.A.C. 89-46

THE WEAVERS OF RABUN
BETTY'S CREEK
RABUN GAP, GA.

The basic idea of the work represented by the RABUN STUDIOS is that all art expression is built upon the crafts, which are by their nature, necessary organically to the life of a people.

In this work we are attempting at present to develop the basic art of weaving, but upon a fundamental principle which we expect to apply to all the crafts.

Our work shops are situated in the heart of the Blue Ridge Mountains of Georgia. We are not repeating the old fashioned weaving of the Mountaineers. Our work is modern and based upon nature. We are attempting to bring out the simple beauty and quality inherent in nature's raw materials.

The wool threads are carded and spun by hand by the older mountain men and women who still understand the art of carding and spinning. They do this in their own cabins during the long winter months when work in the fields is finished. The weaving is done in our own work shops by young girls from the various industrial schools of the South.

Our wool fabrics are created throughout by hand. The raw wool is bought in America, from the sheeps' backs and is as soft and fine as that imported from Europe. The fleeces vary in colour, ranging from cool whites to warm yellows, from light tans to black browns. To keep these natural shades we do not mix all the fleeces together but spin each colour separately.

The silk and linen fabrics are made of necessity from imported raw materials. Much of the silk is bought in the gum and boiled off in our own work shops. It is the purest quality, unspoiled by bleaching or weighting. Some of the silk threads are spun by our own spinners.

We do all the dyeing ourselves by hand, according to our own special colour process, using only the finest dyes, fast to light or to washing. All the fabrics are washed in the open air and sunshine.

Our materials are exclusive and individual because they are made by the warp, not by the bolt. Each warp is prepared for one length of material only. No two warps are made alike, unless specially ordered. Warps may be ordered in any of our colours, in any length and in any width up to fifty inches, for dresses, draperies, upholstery, or other purposes.

Hand spun yarns for weaving or knitting may be ordered in single or double ply thread, in white or natural shades.

Our weaving is functional—that is a piece is woven for the purpose or function for which it is to be used. Draperies and dress materials are woven to drape beautifully, upholstery strong for stretching and suit materials to tailor well.

A characteristic of our fabrics is that the natural warp end is left as a fringe, held in by an edge, laid in by hand on the loom. We take orders for special laid in designs.

This work is the continuation of experiments in the crafts begun by Jay Hambidge during his investigation of the fundamental design forms underlying natural law. It is based entirely upon the principle of proportion in nature and in Greek art, discovered and called by him "Dynamic Symmetry." All our designs and colour schemes are therefore new and original, not reproductions of the past.

Our work is created by human beings, not produced by machines. The workers are never hurried. Our objects are—to bring out the natural beauty of the raw materials by a simple, honest, hand process—to produce quality, not quantity—to give a living wage and a creative outlet to the worker and work of individuality to the individual. We believe that the future happiness of America lies in the development of its own natural resources, in training the hands of its people to use these resources and in educating the minds of its people to form them into beauty.

MARY CROVATT HAMBIDGE

RABUN STUDIOS
810 MADISON AVENUE
NEW YORK CITY

An early pamphlet, *The Weavers of Rabun*. Courtesy of Tennessee State Library and Archives

is based entirely upon the principle of proportion in nature and in Greek art, discovered and called by him "Dynamic Symmetry." All our designs and colour schemes are therefore new and original, not reproductions of the past. Our work is created by human beings, not produced by machines. Our workers are never hurried. Our objects are—to bring out the natural beauty of the raw materials by a simple, honest, hand process—to produce quality, not quantity—to give a living wage and a creative outlet to the worker and work of individuality to the individual.[17]

In his 1959 book, *Sketches of Rabun County History, 1819–1948*, Andrew Ritchie, founder of the Rabun Gap Industrial School (1905), now the Rabun Gap–Nacoochee School, described the Weavers of Rabun:

Mrs. Hambidge is not interested in making money. Her whole aim is educational. It is to preserve and propagate the principles of her art and in doing so to make it a home and fire-side industry among the mountain women.

Education to her means a well-rounded life, making an art of all the simple duties connected with it. . . . Mrs. Hambidge takes the mountain girls and teaches them how to do the weaving and to turn out the product in the form of the designs which she gives them. . . . As many as two dozen women at a time, in the surrounding mountain region, have been taught to card and spin by her in their homes. Two or three of the older women who work for her, have known how to card and spin from girlhood and they are now teaching the younger women. The whole aim of Mrs. Hambidge is to revive and perpetuate this art, not for those who learn it to make any more money than is necessary to live on, but mainly for them to have this kind of life and to be the kind of people that it makes out of them.[18]

Not having to worry about making money left Mary free to follow some of the goals of the Appalachian settlement schools while forging new territory by uniting traditional craft methods with intensely hued color schemes and laid-in geometric weft patterns, which appealed to contemporary tastes. She envisioned the Jay Hambidge Art Foundation as a place where this unification could take place through work in handcrafts "based upon nature" because she believed that "all art expression is built upon the crafts, which are by their nature, necessary organically to the life of a people."[19]

In her 1950 address to the University of Georgia's University Women's Club, "Creative Life in the Home," Mary stressed the importance of handcrafts in contributing to a healthy and productive life, especially for women:

If the home were made a creative and cultural center, [a woman] would then achieve the highest and fullest expression of her true self. . . . Men and women should have workshops in their homes. . . . It is in the self-discipline of making work a pleasure that it becomes more perfect. . . . The Handcrafts are vitally needed today because they alone can bring about the balance that has been thrown off by industry and over production through mechanism. I am not offering the Handcrafts as the ultimate hope of salvation. They are only instruments to be used and they can be misused, just as the machine has been misused, without a law of balance and perfection to direct them. But at this point in our development, they can be the means of bringing about the vitally needed balance in our practical living. . . . Somebody always pays for careless work—usually the innocent. Therefore bad work is selfish and immoral.[20]

Mary led a rigorous life at the Betty's Creek property. She was involved in most aspects of the operation: she ordered weaving supplies and dyes, seeds, grains, farming equipment, and livestock; she hired, housed, and fed staff; she supervised construction projects such as a dye shed, the weaving shed,

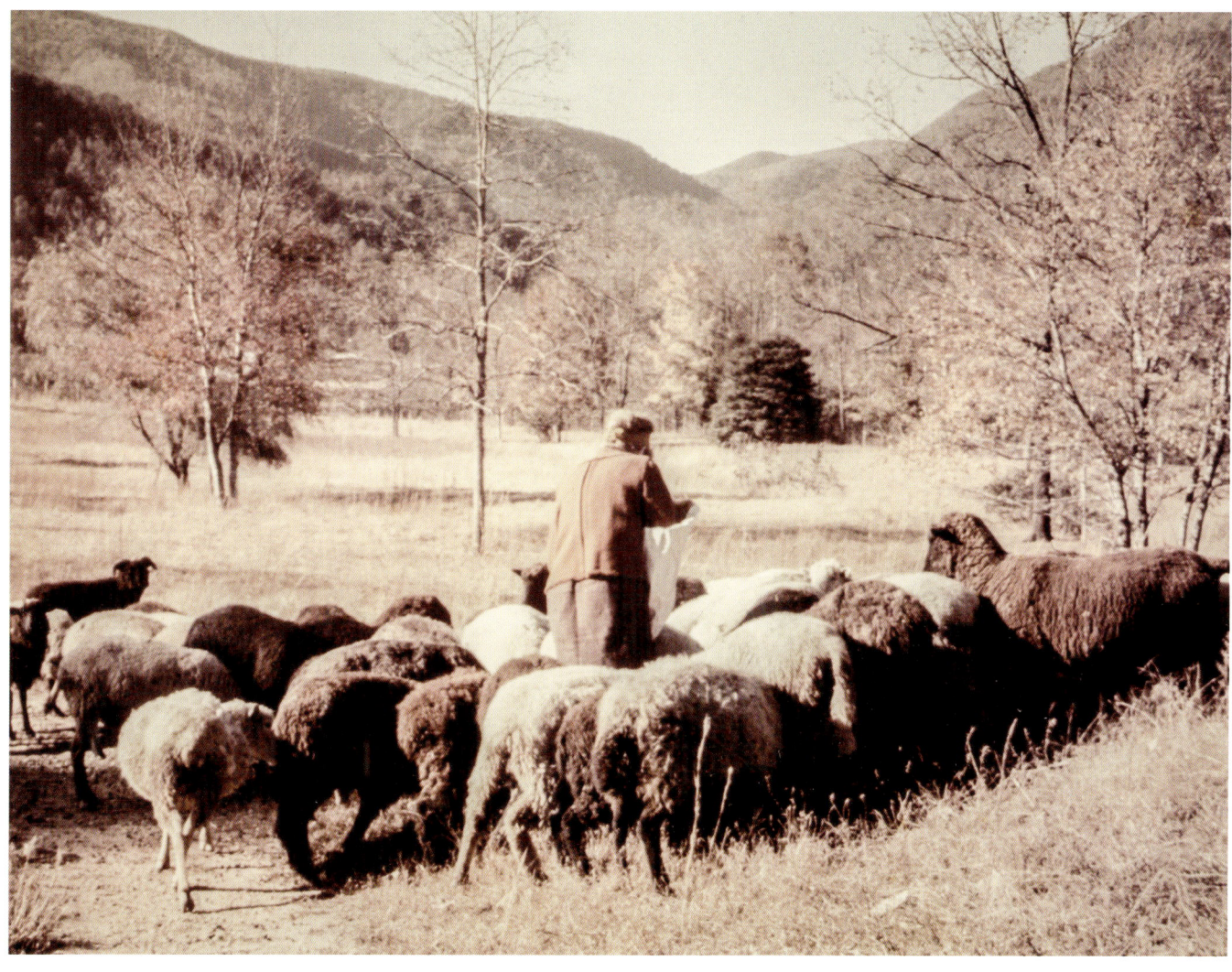

Mary Crovatt
Hambidge and
sheep, n.d. Courtesy
of the Hambidge
Center for Creative
Arts and Sciences

and a gristmill (built in 1944); she entertained visitors; she gave demonstrations and weaving presentations that emphasized the value of handweaving; and she envisioned forming a school of crafts based on Greek ideals. Mary was an early practitioner of the healthy farm-to-table lifestyle. Invoices show orders or inquiries for vitamins, wheat, beans, olives, and dates. Her appointment calendars listed daily chores, including washing, weaving, cleaning, fixing looms, ordering, cooking, and dyeing.[21] For Mary Hambidge, Dynamic Symmetry meant living a balanced and self-sustaining life.

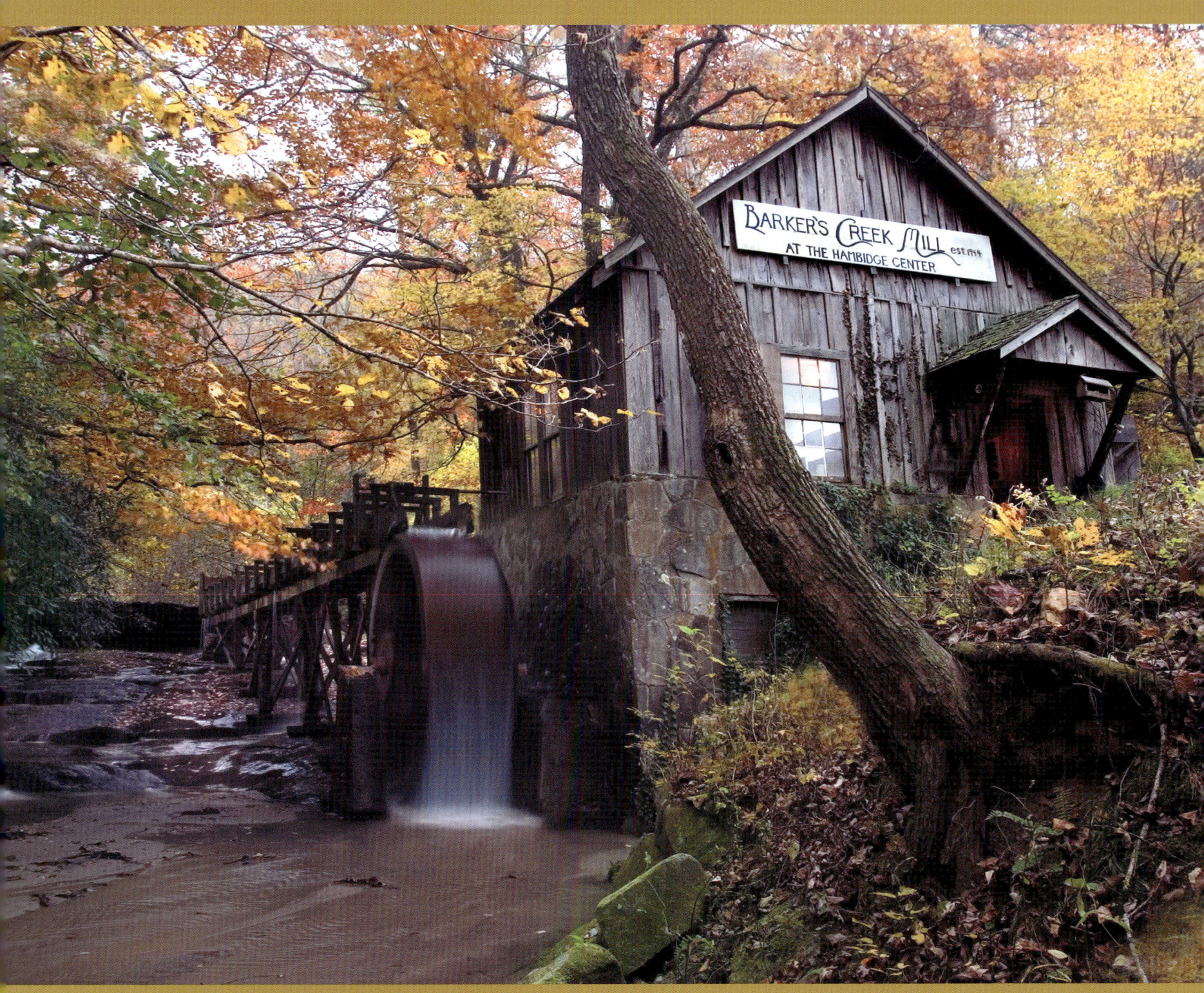

Barker's Creek Mill at the Hambidge Center.
Photograph by Peter McIntosh, courtesy of the
Hambidge Center for Creative Arts and Sciences

From the beginning, Mary sought out kindred souls to live with her and contribute to her vision; for example, Eva Palmer Sikelianos lived at the property from 1941 to 1944.[22] She connected with regional weaving centers and enjoyed a wide network of friends and acquaintances. As early as 1937 she had visited the weaving program that Anni Albers directed at Black Mountain College. In a 1938 letter, Albers inquired if Mary might be interested in buying a loom modeled on those of Biltmore Industries; she also enclosed two drafts of open-work weavings and asked Mary to send samples of her work: "I enjoyed your visit here very much and would be very grateful if you could send us some samples of your homespun wools, silks and linens. We are looking forward to driving over to Rabun Gap in the spring."[23] Interestingly, Mary Hambidge and Anni Albers came to represent opposite poles of the handweaving spectrum in midcentury America: Mary was aligned more closely with the Arts and Crafts focus on handcraft, while Anni embraced the practicality and efficiency of designing for machine production and using nontraditional materials, such as cellophane and synthetic fibers. Both, however, believed in emphasizing the inherent qualities of their chosen materials and structural processes, a modernist practice of maintaining the truth of materials. Albers perceived Mary's enterprise from a

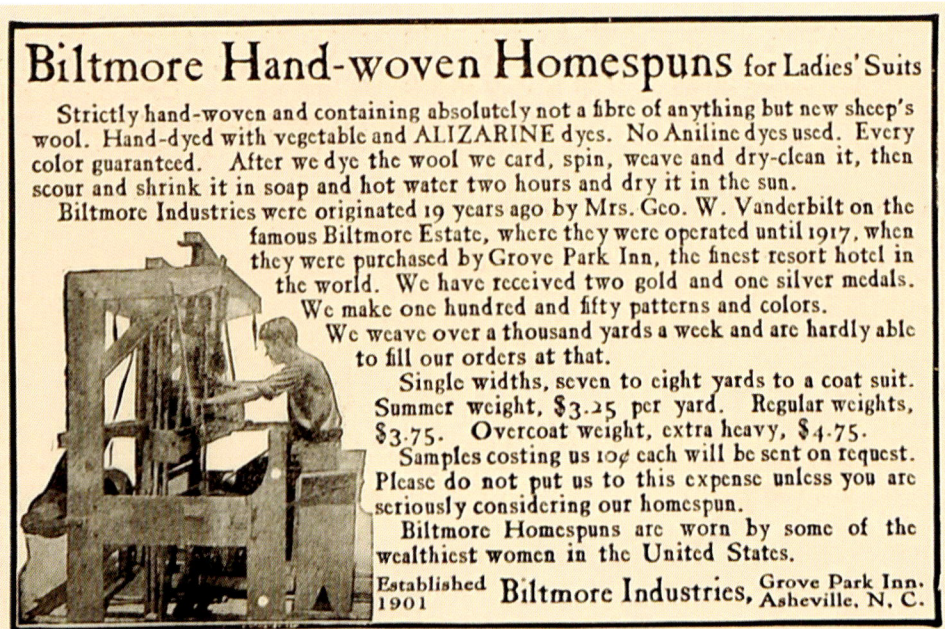

Biltmore Industries advertisement, 1919

Bauhaus perspective focused on efficiency and innovation, yet with a respect for handwork and craft. In a 1938 letter to Black Mountain College founder Theodore Dreier, Anni wrote:

> back from our trip to north georgia, to mrs. hambidge, the wife of the dynamic symmetrie man. she weaves and is a little crazy. but it was nice allthesame. . . . i saw today spinning and carding by hand for the first time and tried too to do it my self. we were with real mountaineers, an old woman chewing tobacco. i like machines and heard so much talk about the beauty of handwork. if you do a lot of it, it is just boring and just as boring as working with machines. only handwork as artwork has sense, so i still and always more believe.[24]

Albers seems to have viewed the Hambidge woven work not as modern art or as artistic products like her own unique, signed, and titled "pictorial weavings," but rather as finely constructed handwoven cloth, a difference that points to the increasingly diverse approaches to weaving and fiber in midcentury America.[25]

Several factors contributed to the success and longevity of the Weavers of Rabun operation. First and foremost was the Reese stipend, which permitted Mary to provide salaries, purchase supplies, and travel between Georgia and New York. In addition, despite being an outsider, Mary was able to create and maintain productive working relationships with the local population. Indeed, Faye Thompson, who wove the original sample books, worked as the weaving studio manager for twenty-two years (1937–1960), starting when she was eighteen, and weaver Dean Beasley worked there for thirty-one years.[26] At the same time, Mary was able to develop and maintain a significant network of influential people in the art and business worlds, including Hall Clovis, who managed the New York shop, sourced craft items for sale, and procured clients.[27] Finally, Mary, with practical advice from Reese, kept as much quality control as she could over the weaving, the dyeing, and the designs, based on her distinct aesthetic.[28]

Weavers of Rabun textiles were renowned for their spectacular hues. Mary did all of the dyeing herself, developing a color palette that was based on the principle of dynamic balance and that reflected colors found in nature. Sample books were organized according to "earth harmonies," "tree harmonies," and "sky harmonies," with two shades for each color.[29] Jay had earlier devised a color chart using mathematical ratios of dye amounts to produce particular hues; Mary may have used his chart or developed her own formulas with commercial dyes. As Philis Alvic wrote, Mary "mixed dyes the way a

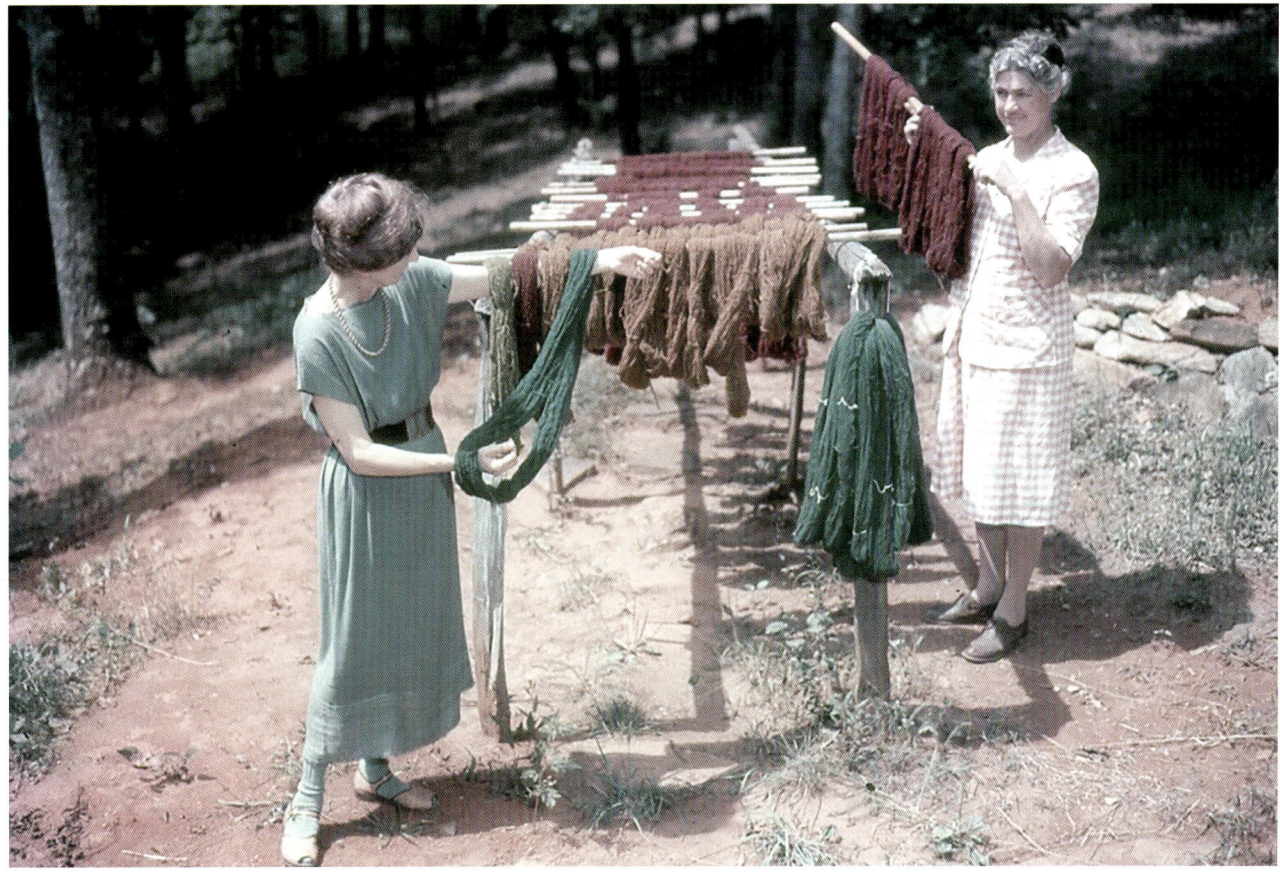

Mary Crovatt Hambidge inspecting dyed yarn, n.d. Courtesy of the Hambidge Center for Creative Arts and Sciences

good cook concocts a recipe—with a little of this and a pinch of that, letting her long experience guide the way."[30] Mary was often described as having the color equivalent of perfect pitch. Her friend and fellow weaver Frances Forbes Ison wrote that Mary "can glance at a roadside flower and days later dye a skein of thread exactly to match. In her dyeing she displays the cool greens of spring and summer, browns and silvers of winter, flames of autumn, and zinnia brightness. She has made famous the Georgia clay colors for upholstery, and the smoke-mist-blue of the Blue Ridge for silks."[31] The Weavers of Rabun also incorporated undyed sheep wool in hues ranging from white to brown to gray. Mary sourced most of the wool regionally and also maintained her own flock of sheep. The silk came from Texas, among other sources.[32]

Most of the woven work was produced using a plain weave in solid colors. Often the warp and weft threads were of different hues, which created

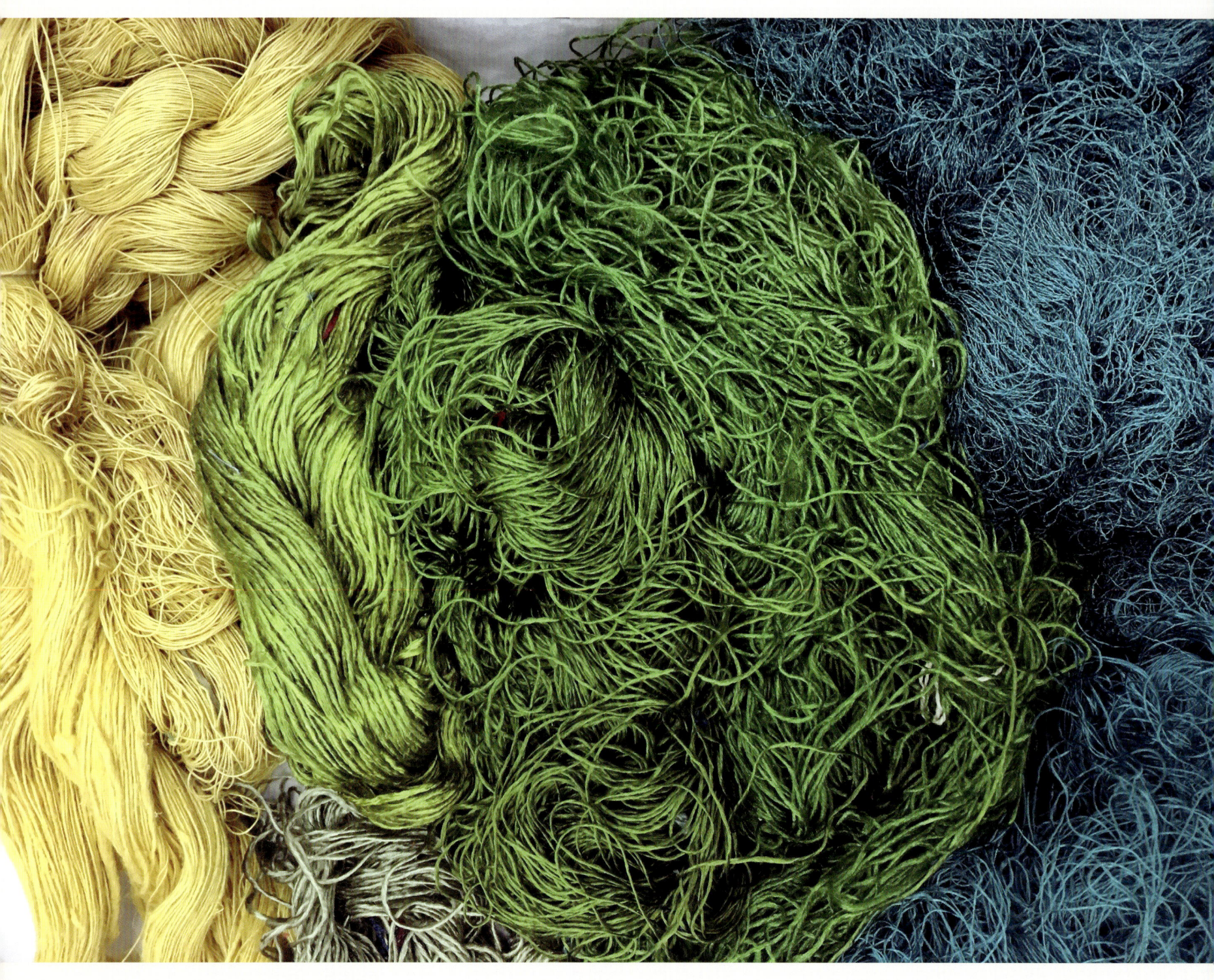

Weavers of Rabun yarn, "cool greens of
spring and summer." Kenan Research Center
at the Atlanta History Center, 1998.233

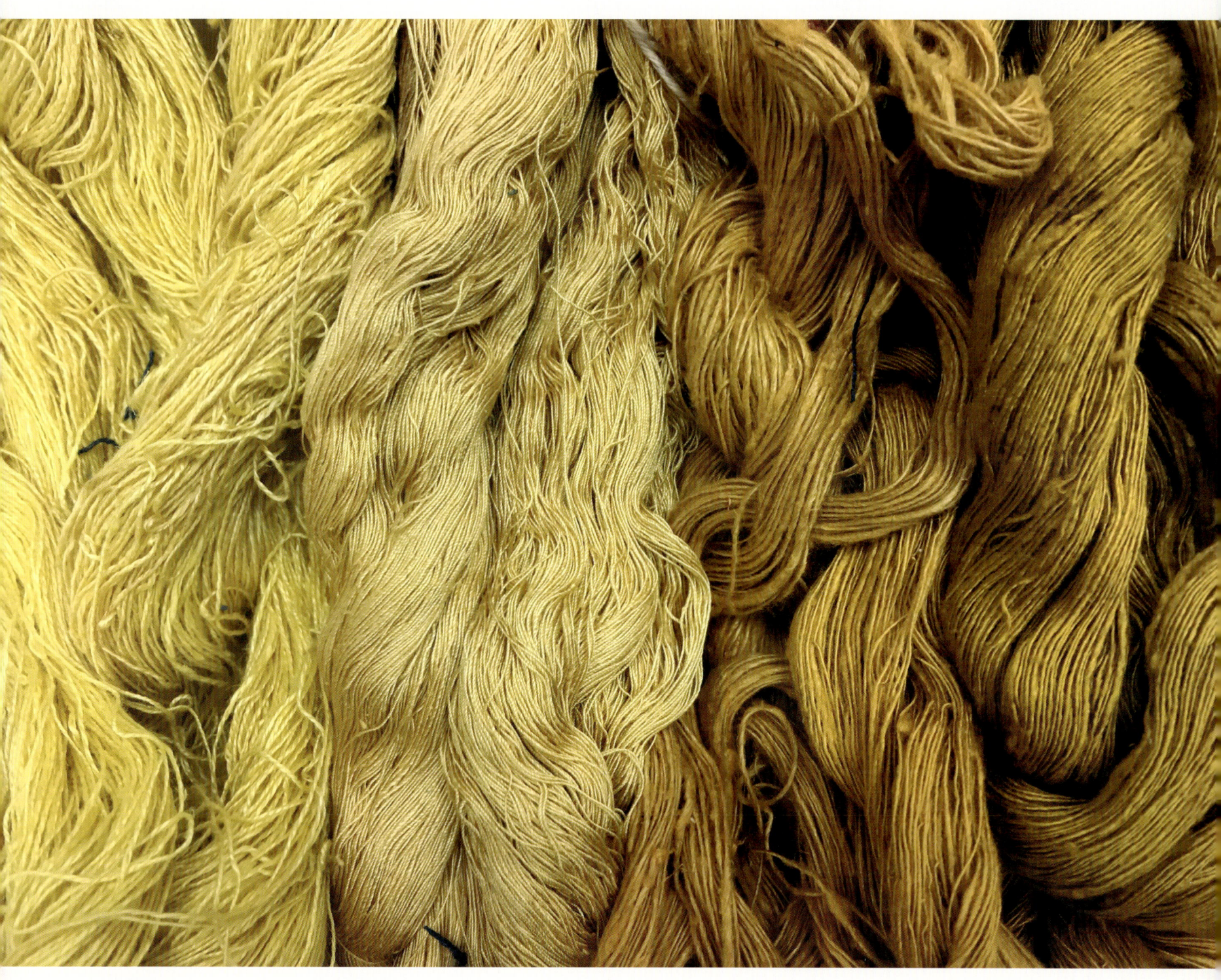

Weavers of Rabun yarn, "flames of autumn." Kenan Research Center at the Atlanta History Center, 1998.233

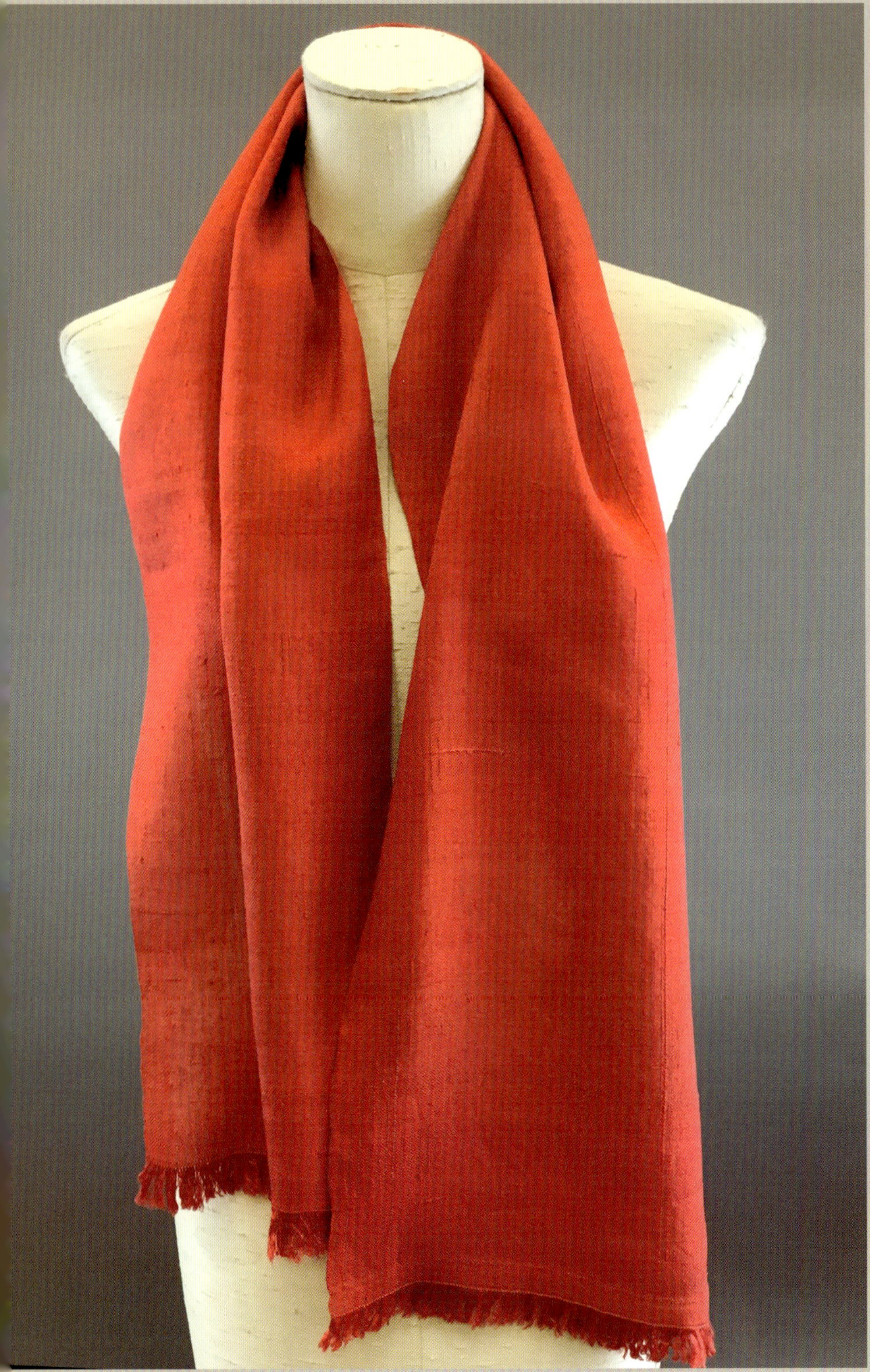

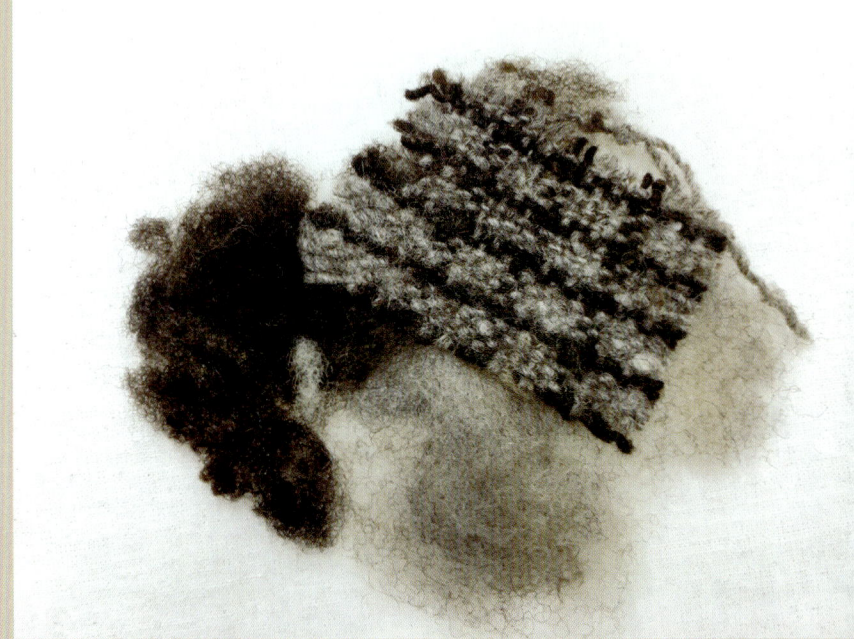

Weavers of Rabun
undyed sheep wool.
Kenan Research Center
at the Atlanta History
Center, 1998.233

Weavers of Rabun silk scarf,
"zinnia brightness." Kenan
Research Center at the Atlanta
History Center, 1998.233

rich, oscillating tones. The feel, or hand, of the cloth ranged from light and silky to thick and nubby, depending on fiber and weave. Supplementary weft patterns were usually reserved for scarves and for Mary's personal wardrobe. Sample books provided clients with the opportunity to choose from a myriad of colors, fibers, and weave textures for their custom orders.[33] By the 1950s the custom orders became too much for Mary to coordinate, and she eventually decreased this component of the operation.[34]

Rabun Studios

Rabun Studios was among several chic shops and galleries in midcentury New York City that marketed studio crafts and custom textiles to sophisticated audiences.[35] These shops included Bonniers, Georg Jensen, Form and Function, and Textiles and Objects, and in Cambridge, Massachusetts, Design Research.[36] The Weavers of Rabun textiles featured at Rabun Studios appealed to interior designers, architects, couturiers and tailors, and those seeking unique American-made handcrafts; the woven fabrics were tagged with either "Rabun Studios / New York" or "Rabun Studios / Rabun Gap Georgia" labels. The textiles were broadly appealing because they traversed two worlds: they were high quality and handmade with an authentic rural pedigree *and* could be adapted to modern urban life. According to one early *New York Times* reviewer, Rabun Studios textiles could be used "whether a room is traditional or modern . . . and are individual enough to serve as a focal point in a room's decoration."[37] The dazzling colors and sumptuous textures of the cloth could serve as backgrounds for decorative furnishings or be fashioned into suits, stoles, or dresses. Through her New York connections, Mary submitted work to the 1937 Paris International Exposition of Art and Technology in Modern Life and won a gold medal for handwoven textiles.

Rabun Studios became the store's official name in July 1938 with the leasing of 810 Madison Avenue. Before that, the shop operated at 843 Madison Avenue, and before that shared space at 810 Madison Avenue and a temporary exhibition space at 851 Madison Avenue. In 1955, when the shop relocated to 31 East 67th Street, advertisements featured the description "Rabun Studios, American Arts and Crafts"; it offered an expanded inventory that included high-quality studio crafts.[38]

Mary typically closed the Georgia weaving operation in the winter months and stayed in Greenwich and New York to check on the boutique, where she

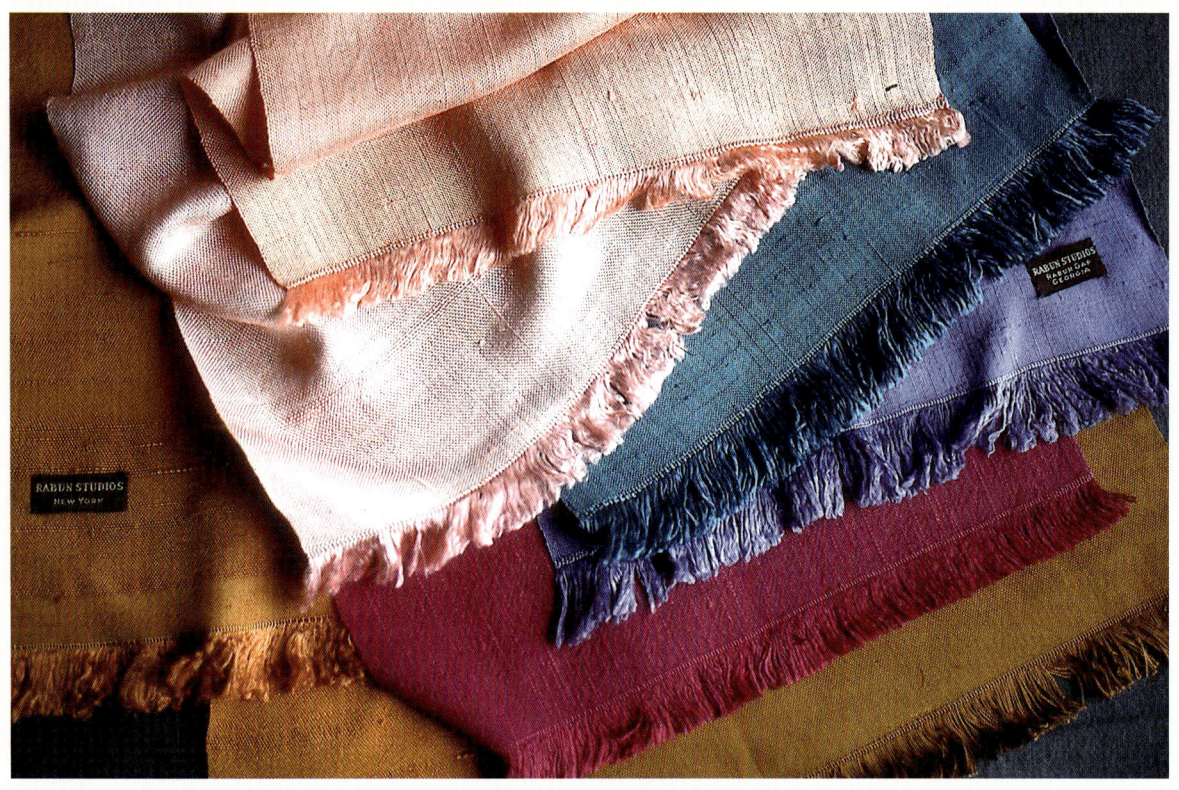

"Rabun Studios / New York"
and "Rabun Studios / Rabun Gap
Georgia" labels on scarves.
Courtesy of Philis Alvic

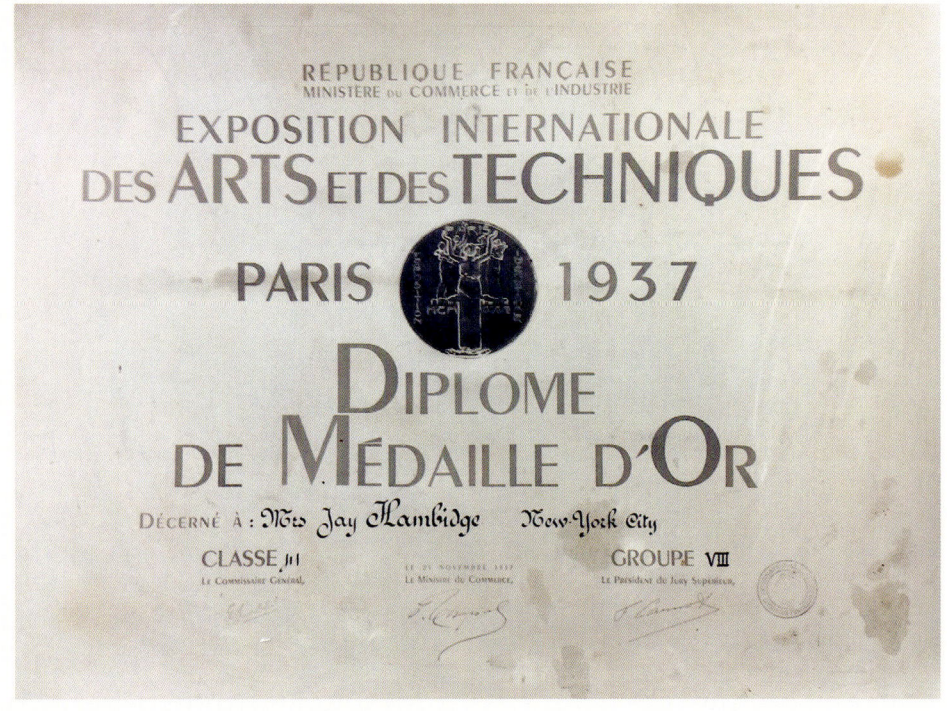

RÉPUBLIQUE FRANÇAISE
MINISTÈRE du COMMERCE et de l'INDUSTRIE

EXPOSITION INTERNATIONALE
DES ARTS ET DES TECHNIQUES

PARIS 1937

DIPLOME
DE MÉDAILLE D'OR

Décerné à : Mrs Jay Hambidge   New York City

CLASSE 111   GROUPE VIII

Paris Exposition award, 1937.
Kenan Research Center at the
Atlanta History Center, box 51

frequently gave weaving demonstrations. The shop was first managed by Josephine Kirpal and Roy Mundy with oversight and monthly funds supplied by Eleanor Reese and Hall Clovis.[39] Clovis and his partner, Charles Lee, formally took over management in the mid-1940s and were responsible for procuring the studio crafts component of the shop, with Kirpal serving as the on-site manager. In 1945, Kirpal was paid $200 per month, an amount she requested Reese to raise.[40]

Reviews in the *New Yorker* magazine and Rabun Studios advertisements in the *New York Times* and *Craft Horizons* provide an idea of the types and quality of merchandise that could be seen and purchased there. Textiles included yardage, blankets, stoles, scarves, and ties; the yardage, which could be ordered from sample books, was the most important part of the textile division. Reviewers in the *New Yorker* in September and November 1949 praised both the textiles and the crafts at Rabun Studios. From the September 17 issue: "Some of the most delightful examples [of ceramics] are to be found at the Rabun Studios 810 Madison Avenue, an admirable shop dedicated to American handicraft. Unlike most such enterprises, which appear to be on the embarrassing verge of breaking into folk dances, this place is one of great elegance."[41]

From the November 26 issue:

The silverware made by Harry Osaki . . . shows such beauty of design and soundness of execution that it can hardly fail to give the keenest pleasure. . . . We suggest that you investigate the shop's collection of hand-woven textiles, made from hand-carded, hand-spun wool by women who live in the mountains of northern Georgia. Unless you know more about sheep than we do, you will be astonished at the varied colors of the materials that are woven, one is told, from undyed wool. Dark brown, beige, gray, white, and pale yellow are the colors God has given these Southern lambs, with, obviously, an eye to the production of as handsome coverlets as you ever saw. Some of the wool, though, has been dyed and then loomed in a variety of weaves in vivid or subtle color combinations.[42]

The shop had a number of noteworthy customers and commissions. In 1945 the Weavers of Rabun were selected to provide the drapery and upholstery fabric for the staterooms of President Harry Truman's yacht, the USS *Williamsburg*. The weavers produced 250 yards of 15 separate pieces for that commission, totaling $2,358.75.[43] In 1947 Yale University Press purchased 65 yards of fabric to cover reprints of books by Jay Hambidge, and in 1949 the Madison Avenue Presbyterian Church selected Weavers of Rabun cloth for its new chapel.[44] Architect Philip Johnson, the director of the Department of Architecture at the Museum of Modern Art in New York, placed two orders for textiles in 1948 and 1953 for his newly designed modernist residence in New Canaan, Connecticut.[45] Celebrity customers included Mrs. Jules Levey, who ordered thirty yards of fifty-inch-wide cloth for Goldwyn Studio of Hollywood; fashion writer Diana Vreeland; actor Edward G. Robinson; and artist Georgia O'Keeffe, who purchased a blanket in 1948. Later, in 1956, O'Keeffe sent Mary some Peruvian alpaca wool with a request to have "a piece of fine material made from it for me" for suiting, along with a white wool scarf.[46]

Rabun Studios crafts and Weavers of Rabun textiles became part of the golden age of midcentury modernist studio craft, and both were featured in Museum of Modern Art (MoMA) exhibitions. This reflected the popular desire for quality handmade crafts, and clever marketing by the museum to create a culture around the concept of "good design," which presented household objects as aesthetically pleasing works.[47] Among the American studio crafts featured at the shop were silverware by Harry Osaki, ceramics by Minnie Negoro and LaGardo Tackett, and jewelry by Ronald Pearson, all of which were included in MoMA *Good Design* exhibitions during the 1950s. The shop also featured furniture by renowned designer George Nakashima.[48]

During the postwar 1940s and 1950s, MoMA assembled a number of design exhibitions for European audiences, which were intended to highlight American design innovation and serve as a form of cultural diplomacy. One of those exhibitions, organized by curator Edgar Kaufmann Jr., was *American Design for Home and Decorative Use*, which traveled to cities in six countries, including Finland and Italy, between 1953 and 1955, and included 312 objects. Rabun Studios contributed 16 works: 9 ceramic pieces, an Osaki silver place setting, and 6 textiles (2 stoles, 2 scarves, and 2 lengths of yardage).[49]

The other exhibition at MoMA featuring Weavers of Rabun textiles was the monumental 1956 *Textiles USA*, a juried selection of 200 examples of contemporary American apparel, industrial, and home furnishing textiles, for which Anni Albers served as one of the jurors. The Weavers of Rabun were represented by a length of deep burgundy plain-weave yardage described as "Wool suiting, hand-woven of hand-spun and -dyed yarn. Designed by Mary C. Hambidge, 1956. Weavers of Rabun, Rabun Gap, Georgia"; there was a photograph of a swatch in the exhibition catalog.[50] Albers no doubt appreciated the skillfully woven and dyed cloth as an example of good structural design without the need for ornamentation. Mary's friend George Christy

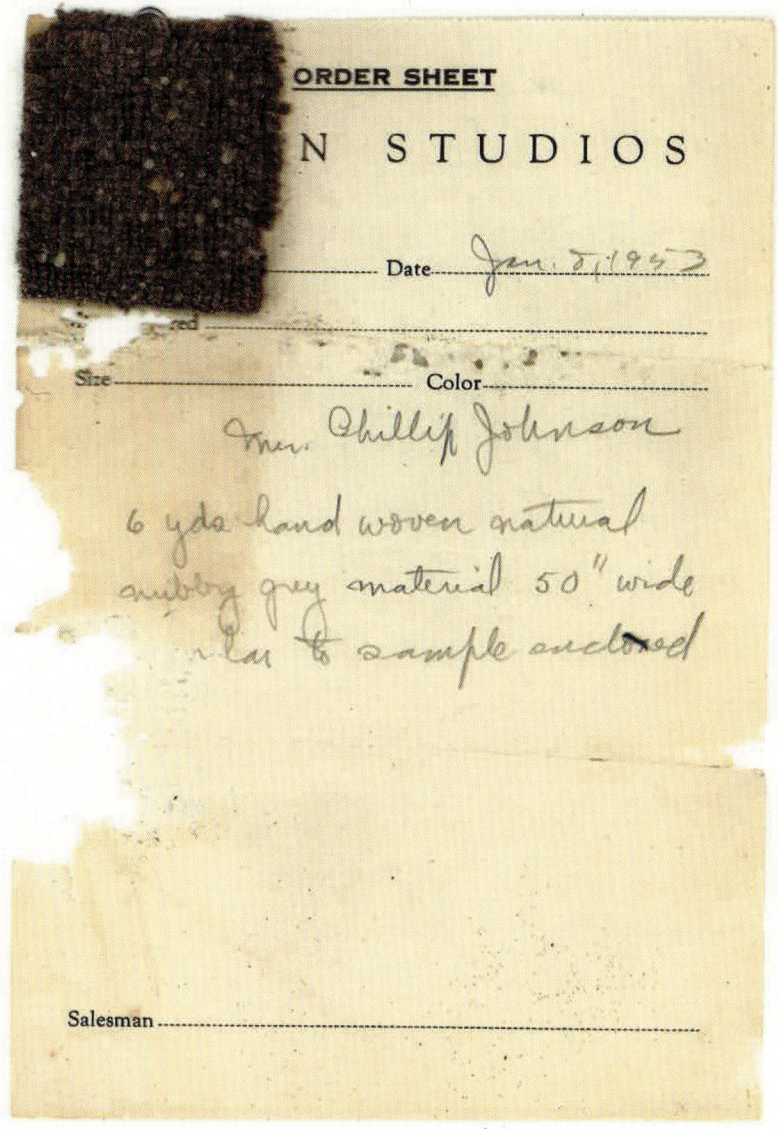

Rabun Studios, *Williamsburg*
order sheet. Courtesy of the
Hambidge Center for Creative
Arts and Sciences

Rabun Studios, Philip Johnson
order sheet. Courtesy of the
Hambidge Center for Creative Arts
and Sciences

ORDER SHEET

R A B U N   S T U D I O S

Order No. _____ Date __Oct. 4, 1947._____

Item Desired _____

Size _____ Color _____

Mrs Vreeland – President of Harpers
Bazaar.

4½ yards of orange wool for
jacket. (Make more for stock
if you can.) 35 inches wide.

Salesman _____

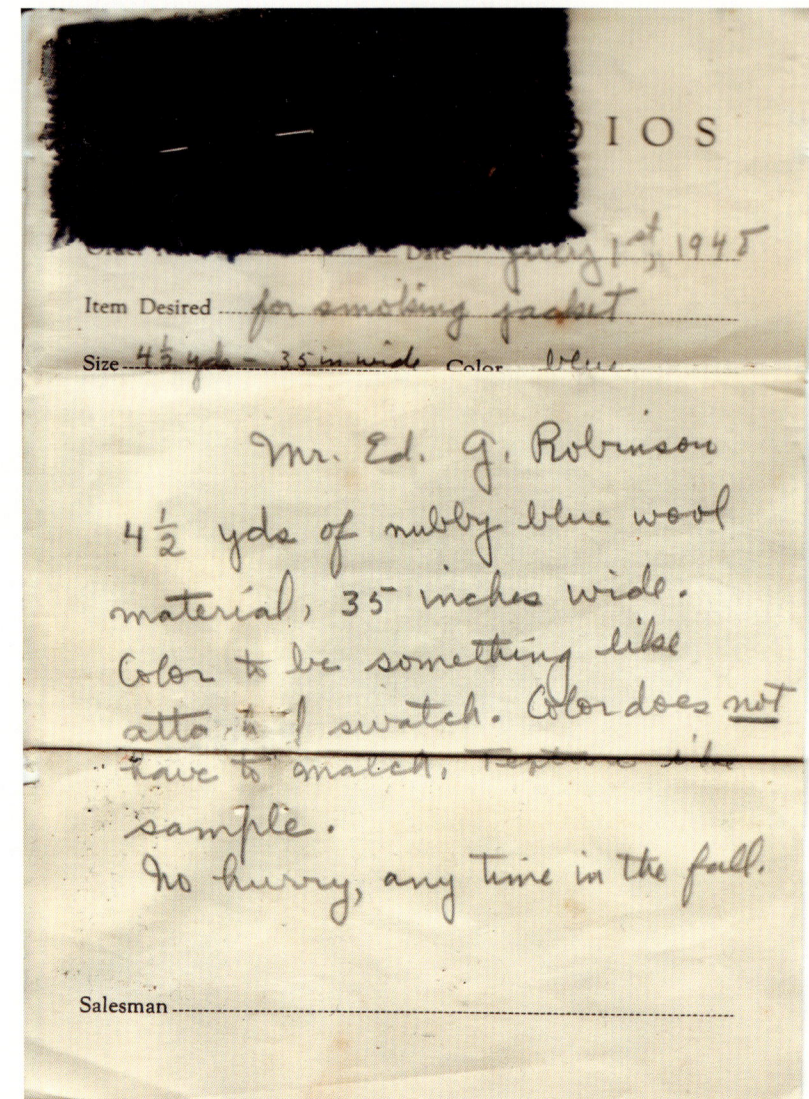

...D I O S

Order No. _____ Date __July 1st, 1945__

Item Desired __for smoking jacket_____

Size __4½ yds – 35 in wide__ Color __blue__

Mr. Ed. G. Robinson

4½ yds of nubby blue wool
material, 35 inches wide.
Color to be something like
atto⅓ of swatch. Color does __not__
have to match. Texture like
sample.
No hurry, any time in the fall.

Salesman _____

Rabun Studios, Diana Vreeland
order sheet. Courtesy of the
Hambidge Center for Creative
Arts and Sciences

Rabun Studios, Edward G. Robinson
order sheet. Courtesy of the Hambidge
Center for Creative Arts and Sciences

Abiquiu, N.M.
Oct- 56

Dear Mrs. Hambidge:
I was in Peru for three months this
past spring and seeing `the millions of
indians all in hand woven clothing made
me think of you.
What I send you is alpaca wool. If
I got some of the black or white would
you have a piece of very fine material
made from it for me ~ and how much
wool should I get ?
What they make of it
in Peru is not very fine but is very useful
I hope all is well with you. My life
now in New Mexico is very good
Sincerely
Georgia O'Keeffe

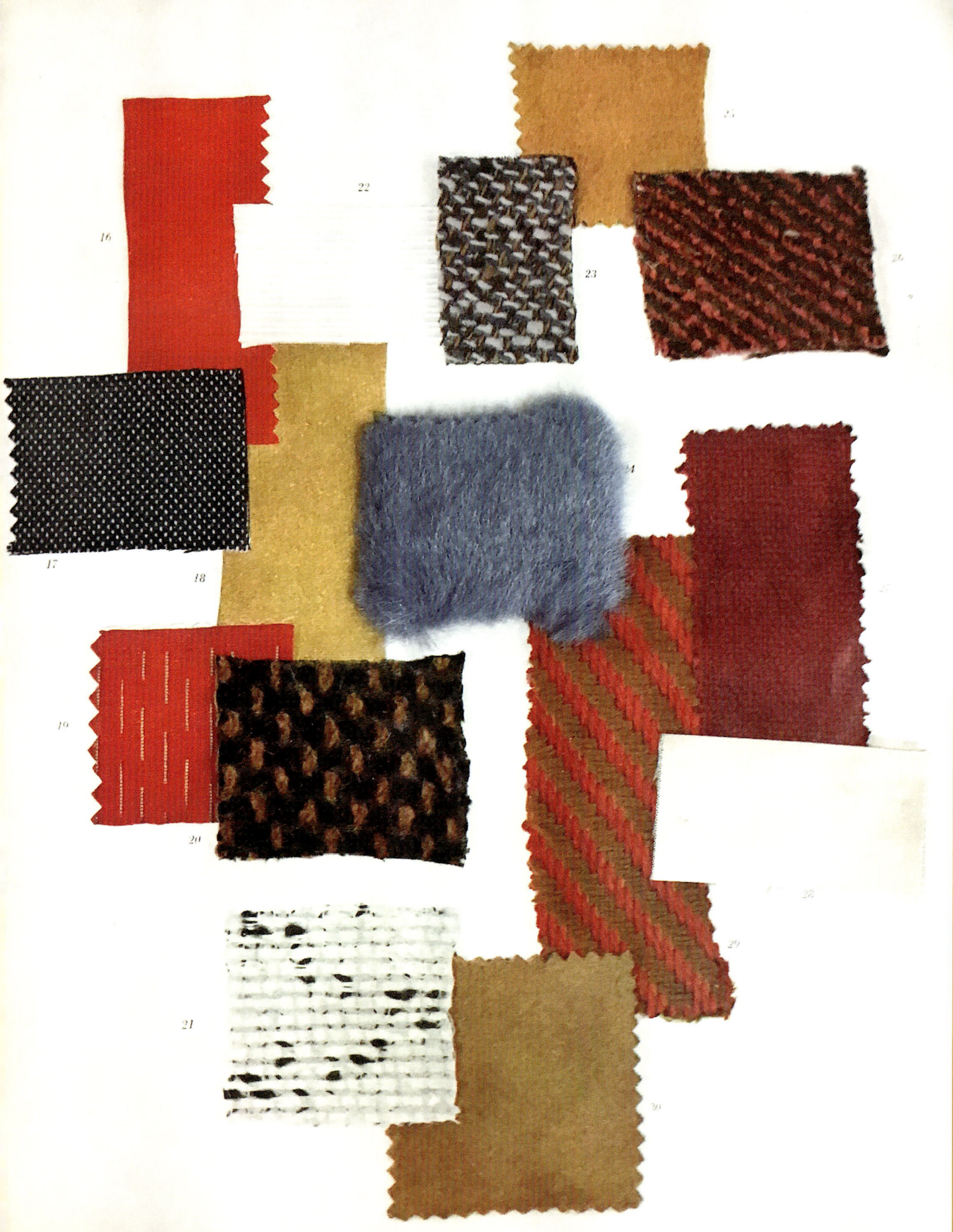

Mary Crovatt
Hambidge and
Weavers of Rabun,
Textiles USA
exhibition, MoMA.
American Fabrics,
no. 38 (Fall 1956):
14–15

saw the exhibition and praised her work: "Let me tell you right here and now how magnificent your red suiting fabric is in the *Textiles USA* show. 99% of the fabrics are cheap, sleazy machine-made things that lack life. Your fabric sings! It was the only fabric that really attracted the eye with its LIFE! And I hope this exhibit shows to the people the tawdriness of all this machine-made stuff."[51] This comment points to the clash of designers at midcentury: those embracing the machine and working with industry, and those, like Mary, utterly opposed to it. Her textile won an award of merit in the handwoven division.[52]

Weavers of Rabun textiles were featured in 1958 in a large, 150-piece exhibition, *The Weavers of Rabun*, in the rotunda of the Arts and Industries Building of the Smithsonian Institution. The official press release described the exhibition this way: "Beautiful hand-spun yarns dyed in brilliant colors of the hillside flowers and fall foliage and woven into exquisite fabrics will be shown together with the spinning wheels and the treadle loom on which they are made by the mountain weavers of Rabun County, Georgia." Careful to note that the textiles were high design and not hobby crafts, the announcement continued, "Although the workshops are located in the heart of the Blue Ridge Mountains of north Georgia, the work is based on fundamental designs of nature rather than on traditional patterns."[53] Preparing for the exhibition, Mary had a number of suggestions for the display and text panels, including requests for statements criticizing industrialization and its detrimental effect on the creative spirit. In response, Grace Rogers, the curator in charge, wrote, "I question that the creative spirit of our people has reached a hopeless state. . . . We must encourage this creative spirit but only with words of praise for it and not with words of criticism against 'machines.'"[54]

End of an Era

The Smithsonian exhibition can be seen as one of the significant moments in 1958 that precipitated a change in the life of Mary Hambidge, then seventy-three years old, and the Weavers of Rabun. Mary's rage against industrial progress alienated her from a number of developments in American art and design—and also from her immediate neighbors on Betty's Creek Road in Rabun Gap. Her anger was personal too: in 1957 the state of Georgia had begun to widen and pave Betty's Creek Road, which Mary objected to vociferously, writing to her senators and governor about the "Roman racetrack the Barbarians are forcing upon our little valley."[55] Her neighbors, however, had found her holdout stance unacceptable, going so far as to present her with a petition of eighty or ninety signatures that concluded: "We feel you are not a desirable neighbor."[56] Furthermore, in 1958 Lees Carpet opened a plant in Rabun Gap, which depleted Mary's workforce.[57] These issues made it more difficult to find, train, and retain weavers, leading to a decline in production and an inability to fill orders.

In a 1958 letter, Josephine Kirpal noted to Eleanor Reese that the lease on Rabun Studios was to expire that August, that Hall Clovis had lost interest in the shop and wanted to hold a removal sale, and that Mary "seems to be giving up."[58] This set of conditions led Reese to decide to stop funding the shop. Although the Rabun Studios name was officially canceled on June 17, 1958, Kirpal continued to operate under the Rabun Studios moniker while changing the inventory to more gift items; Mary finally had to take legal action to stop Kirpal from using the Rabun Studios name.[59]

The late 1950s was also a time when American museums began to designate and display textiles in separate categories depending on whether they were industrially designed, handcrafted, or part of the new fiber art movement; the museums, including MoMA, began to focus on more contemporary uses of fiber and textiles in the latter category. By then manufactured woven and printed textiles were readily available in department stores and showrooms, decreasing the need for custom handwoven orders. Regional enterprises, such as the Weavers of Rabun, were overshadowed by newly established textile divisions and stylish showrooms at national manufacturers, such as Knoll Textiles (1947) and Herman Miller (1953); new academic programs, such as Cranbrook Academy of Art; and advertising campaigns for new synthetic fibers, which appealed to postwar consumer tastes. These trends in American textiles were driven by midcentury modernist powerhouse designers, such as Alexander Girard, Florence Knoll, Jack Lenor Larsen, Marianne Strengell, Dorothy Liebes, Anni Albers, and Boris Kroll, who advocated for and succeeded in merging high design with machine production. They could even manufacture woven and printed textiles that appeared to be handmade.[60] Homespun and handcrafted textiles from the Weavers of Rabun were no longer valued as luxury items in the face of quality manufactured textiles, which offered easier accessibility and a wider variety of choices.

Despite plans by Brooks Wigginton, the father of *Foxfire* founder Eliot Wigginton, in 1952 to draft a foundation prospectus and create a board of directors, the Jay Hambidge Art Foundation never found significant footing as an active art residency program while Mary was alive, although courses were offered intermittently, including summer sessions at the Jay Hambidge School of Dynamic Symmetry and Weaving in 1941 and 1942.[61] According to Mary's friend and frequent resident Frank Coleman, who also sought to solidify a mission statement and future for the foundation, the Hambidge Foundation papers still were not organized as of 1970.[62]

Mary maintained an active life during the 1960s: weaving, entertaining visitors, writing poetry and long typed letters, and serving as a mentor to a younger generation of people interested in traditional crafts, folklore, oral histories, and back-to-nature living. Those interests became the basis of the *Foxfire* publications, which began in 1966 as a series of essays by students at the Rabun Gap–Nacoochee School, where Eliot Wigginton was teaching. Today, the Foxfire Museum and Heritage Center preserves the traditions of southern Appalachian culture through education and exhibitions.

Thanks to the leadership of Mary Nikas Beery, who became the foundation's director after Mary's death, the Hambidge Center for Creative Arts and Sciences, as it was renamed in 1974, was established and became a vibrant residential art program. By the 1980s many classes were offered on a variety of subjects, including Dynamic Symmetry in Clothing Design: Mary Hambidge's Approach to Garment Design, taught by Karin Schaller; and Weaving—Beginning and Intermediate, taught by Tommye McClure Scanlin. The 1985 program, for example, included nature walks, classes, lectures, a dance weekend, and musical performances, a type of program that Mary had dreamed about.

As the residency and art offerings grew, the legacies of Jay Hambidge and Mary Crovatt Hambidge began to be studied and their work exhibited with more frequency. In 1984 the Hambidge Center reissued *Apprentice in Creation: The Way Is Beauty*, a compilation of Mary's writings assembled by her friend Aspasia Voulis, which brought additional attention to the many facets of Mary's life. Her poem "I am My Destiny, I am the Weaver" is a fitting self-portrait:

I am the Weaver of Eternity—
I am Eternity.
I am the Earth
And the Earth is my Warp.
I am the Light
And the Light is my Woof
And forever I am weaving
The Great Fabric of Eternity.

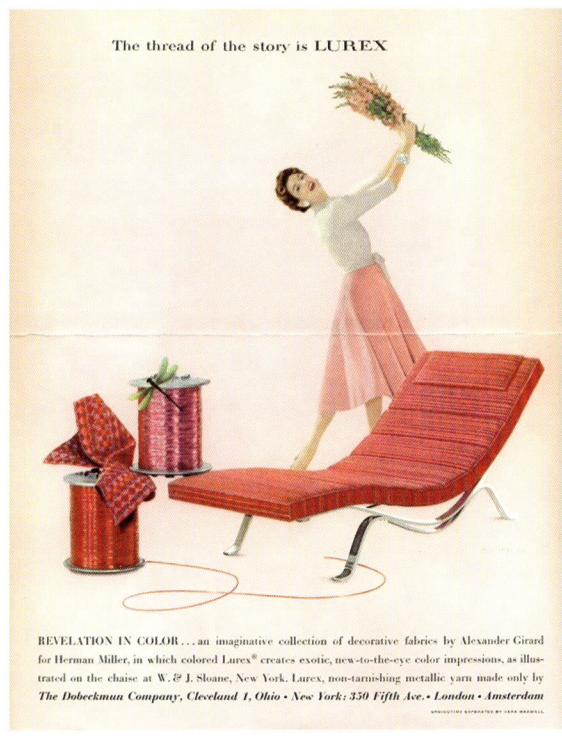

DuPont advertisement for Lurex, *House and Garden*, May 1955

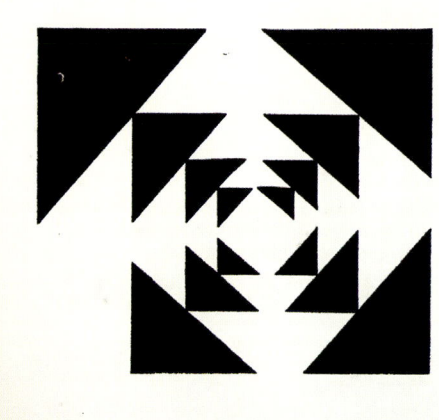

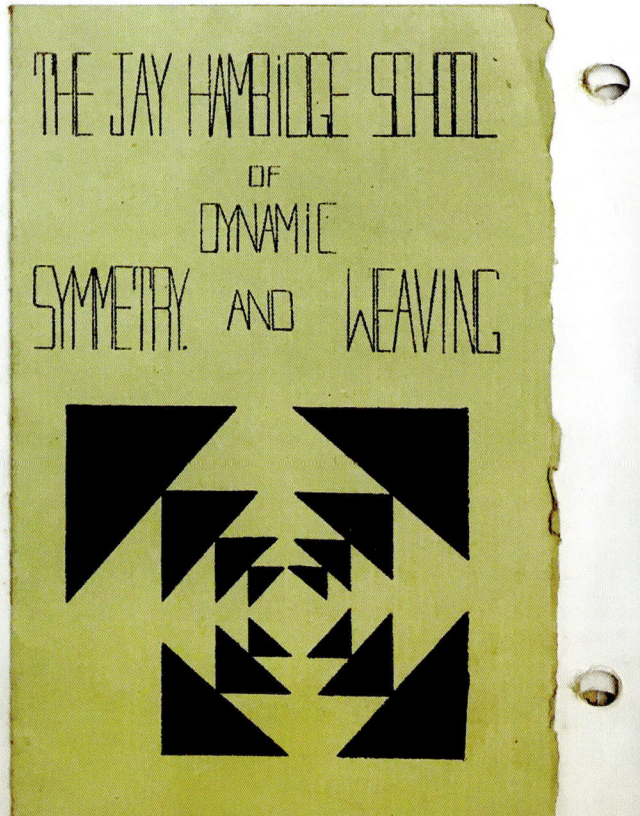

Jay Hambidge
School of Dynamic
Symmetry and
Weaving pamphlets
1941–1942. Kenan
Research Center at
the Atlanta History
Center, 0s.4.91

From my being I spread out the Earth
And establish my Warp.
From my being I shoot forth my rays
And create my Woof.
And the Warp is my Warmth
And the Woof is my Light
And the fabric is my Life
That I weave.

I am the Great Horizontal—
I am the Earth and the measured.
I am the Great Perpendicular—
I am the Light and the Measureless.
I am the two
And the two are One.
I am the Warp and I am the Woof—
I am the Weaver.

   M. C. H.[63]

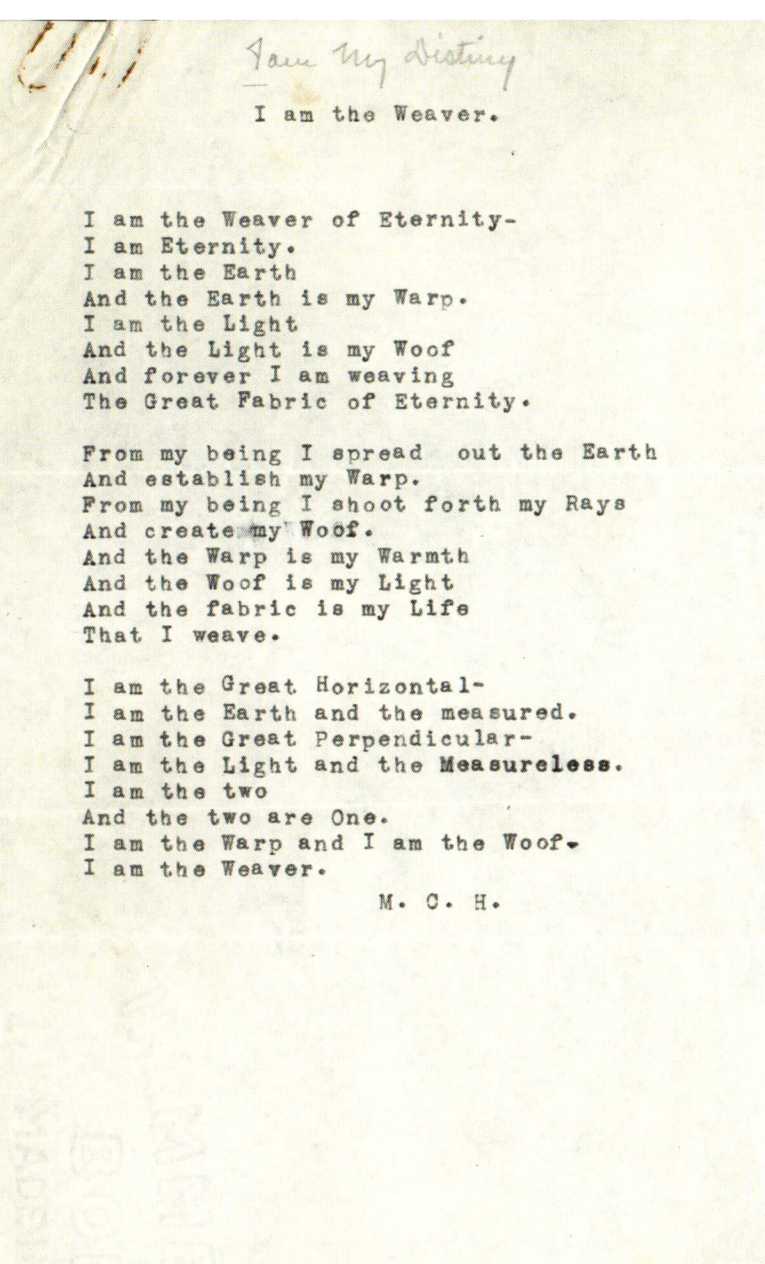

Mary Crovatt Hambidge,
"I am My Destiny, I am the
Weaver." Kenan Research
Center at the Atlanta History
Center, box 17, folder 8

CHAPTER 5

Tommye McClure Scanlin

Memories of Hambidge Center Experiences

Workshops and Residencies

The Hambidge Center has played a vital role in my life as an artist for decades. I work in the medium of handwoven tapestry, with images inspired by the landscape of the southern reaches of the Appalachian Mountains, where I live and the Hambidge Center is located. This chapter is a reminiscence of my long history with the Hambidge Center, and how my experiences there have shaped my artistic career.

I first learned about the Hambidge Center in the early 1970s as a new faculty member at North Georgia College (NGC), now the University of North Georgia in Dahlonega. Bob Owens, the head of the Fine Arts Department at NGC, was active in art and craft communities of northeastern Georgia. In particular, he was instrumental in the development of Georgia Mountain Arts Products, a craft cooperative with a sales gallery called the Co-op in Tallulah Falls, not many miles from the Hambidge Center.

At some point through his involvement with the Co-op Owens met Mary Hambidge. After one visit with her, knowing I was a fledgling weaver, Owens encouraged me to become acquainted with her. I was intrigued and wanted to know more about her, the history of the Weavers of Rabun, and the center that he was describing. As it turned out, Mary died in 1973 before I had the chance to meet her, something I've regretted many times in the years since. Even so, I continued to think about the Hambidge Center and the creative possibilities it held, and I dreamed of someday becoming involved there. In the 1980s those wishes began to take shape.

Remembering Workshops at the Hambidge Center in the 1980s

Mary Creety Nikas Beery, who became the executive director of the Hambidge Center after Mary's death, reached out to educational and artistic institutions for assistance in keeping the foundation alive. She encouraged collaboration between NGC and the Hambidge Center, which developed into an academic and community relationship that continued for a few years.

In 1985, Beery planned a program to celebrate the hundredth anniversary of Mary Hambidge's birth, offering over two dozen events presented from March through October. Notable among the offerings were an Intensive Journal Retreat led by Sister Annette T. Covatta, a journaling consultant;

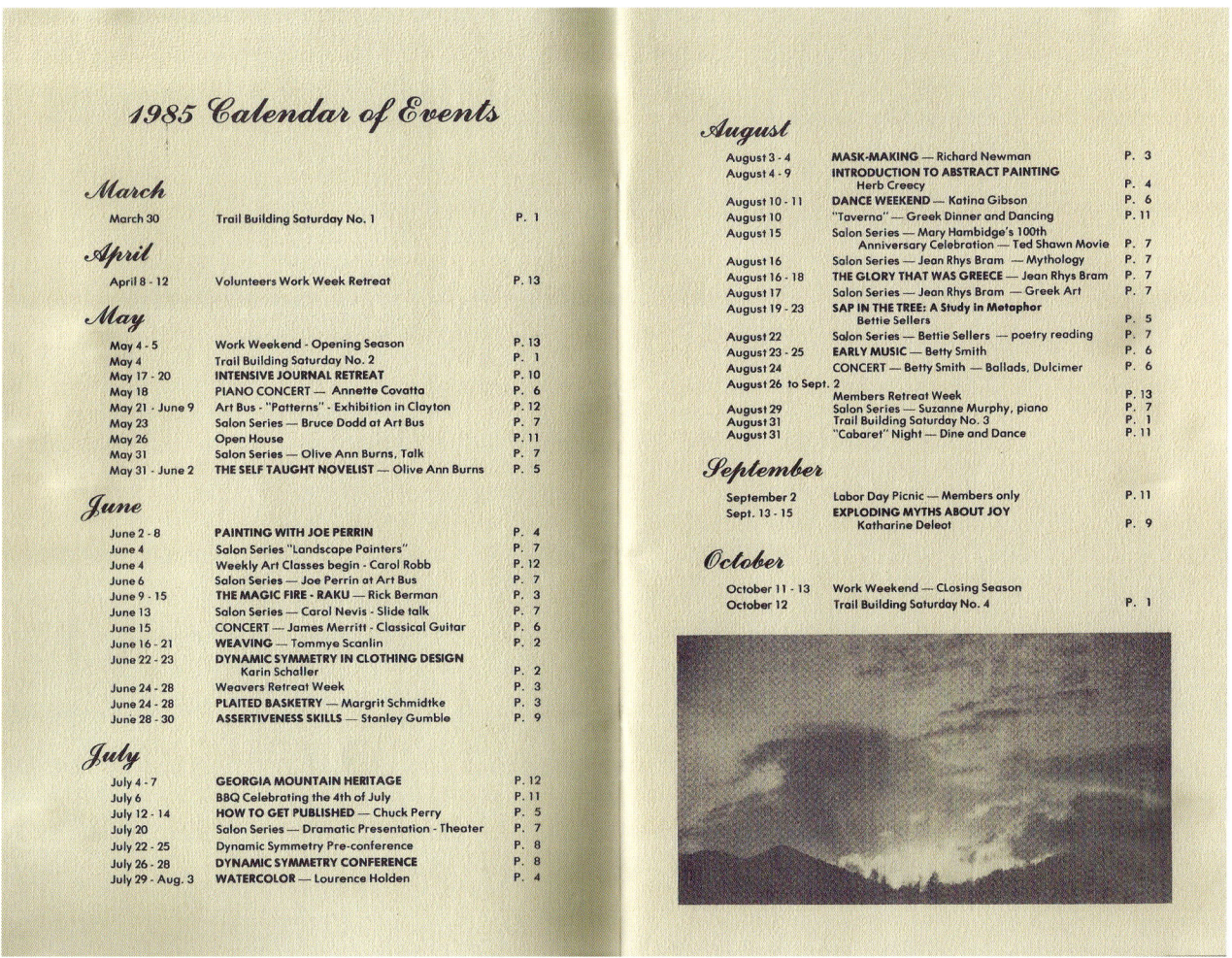

1985 Calendar of Events

March

March 30	Trail Building Saturday No. 1	P. 1

April

April 8 - 12	Volunteers Work Week Retreat	P. 13

May

May 4 - 5	Work Weekend - Opening Season	P. 13
May 4	Trail Building Saturday No. 2	P. 1
May 17 - 20	INTENSIVE JOURNAL RETREAT	P. 10
May 18	PIANO CONCERT — Annette Covatta	P. 6
May 21 - June 9	Art Bus - "Patterns" - Exhibition in Clayton	P. 12
May 23	Salon Series — Bruce Dodd at Art Bus	P. 7
May 26	Open House	P. 11
May 31	Salon Series — Olive Ann Burns, Talk	P. 7
May 31 - June 2	THE SELF TAUGHT NOVELIST — Olive Ann Burns	P. 5

June

June 2 - 8	PAINTING WITH JOE PERRIN	P. 4
June 4	Salon Series "Landscape Painters"	P. 7
June 4	Weekly Art Classes begin - Carol Robb	P. 12
June 6	Salon Series — Joe Perrin at Art Bus	P. 7
June 9 - 15	THE MAGIC FIRE - RAKU — Rick Berman	P. 3
June 13	Salon Series — Carol Nevis - Slide talk	P. 7
June 15	CONCERT — James Merritt - Classical Guitar	P. 6
June 16 - 21	WEAVING — Tommye Scanlin	P. 2
June 22 - 23	DYNAMIC SYMMETRY IN CLOTHING DESIGN Karin Schaller	P. 2
June 24 - 28	Weavers Retreat Week	P. 3
June 24 - 28	PLAITED BASKETRY — Margrit Schmidtke	P. 3
June 28 - 30	ASSERTIVENESS SKILLS — Stanley Gumble	P. 9

July

July 4 - 7	GEORGIA MOUNTAIN HERITAGE	P. 12
July 6	BBQ Celebrating the 4th of July	P. 11
July 12 - 14	HOW TO GET PUBLISHED — Chuck Perry	P. 5
July 20	Salon Series — Dramatic Presentation - Theater	P. 7
July 22 - 25	Dynamic Symmetry Pre-conference	P. 8
July 26 - 28	DYNAMIC SYMMETRY CONFERENCE	P. 8
July 29 - Aug. 3	WATERCOLOR — Lourence Holden	P. 4

August

August 3 - 4	MASK-MAKING — Richard Newman	P. 3
August 4 - 9	INTRODUCTION TO ABSTRACT PAINTING Herb Creecy	P. 4
August 10 - 11	DANCE WEEKEND — Katina Gibson	P. 6
August 10	"Taverna" — Greek Dinner and Dancing	P. 11
August 15	Salon Series — Mary Hambidge's 100th Anniversary Celebration — Ted Shawn Movie	P. 7
August 16	Salon Series — Jean Rhys Bram — Mythology	P. 7
August 16 - 18	THE GLORY THAT WAS GREECE — Jean Rhys Bram	P. 7
August 17	Salon Series — Jean Rhys Bram — Greek Art	P. 7
August 19 - 23	SAP IN THE TREE: A Study in Metaphor Bettie Sellers	P. 5
August 22	Salon Series — Bettie Sellers — poetry reading	P. 7
August 23 - 25	EARLY MUSIC — Betty Smith	P. 6
August 24	CONCERT — Betty Smith — Ballads, Dulcimer	P. 6
August 26 to Sept. 2	Members Retreat Week	P. 13
August 29	Salon Series — Suzanne Murphy, piano	P. 7
August 31	Trail Building Saturday No. 3	P. 1
August 31	"Cabaret" Night — Dine and Dance	P. 11

September

September 2	Labor Day Picnic — Members only	P. 11
Sept. 13 - 15	EXPLODING MYTHS ABOUT JOY Katharine Deleot	P. 9

October

October 11 - 13	Work Weekend — CLosing Season	
October 12	Trail Building Saturday No. 4	P. 1

Calendar of events at the Hambidge Center, 1985. Digital scan courtesy of Tommye McClure Scanlin, courtesy of the Hambidge Center for Creative Arts and Sciences

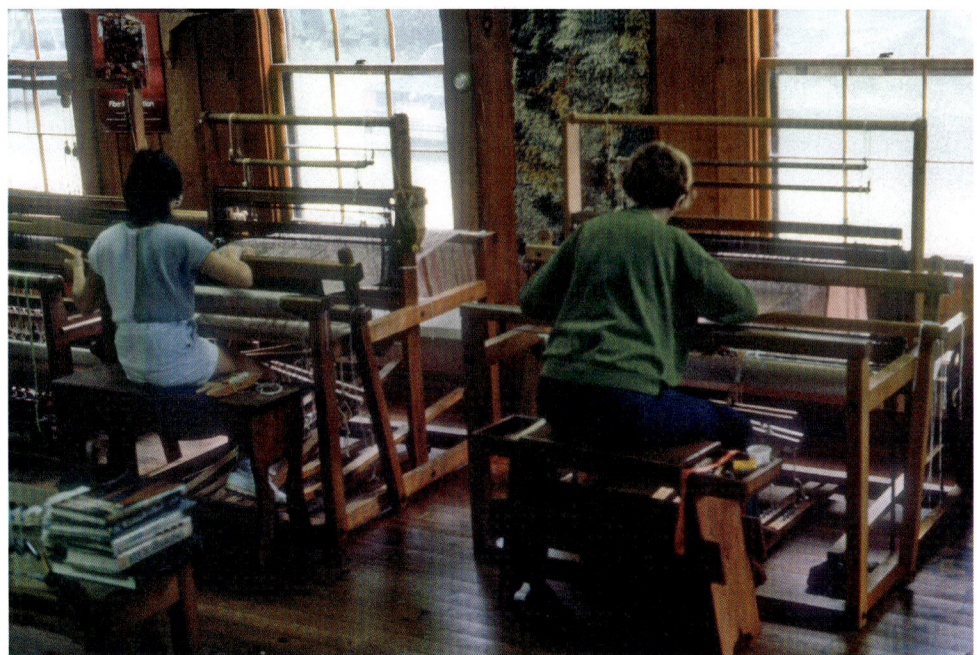

Two students weaving on Hambidge Center looms during Scanlin's 1985 workshop. Photograph by Tommye McClure Scanlin

The Self Taught Novelist, a seminar on writing conducted by Olive Ann Burns, the author of *Cold Sassy Tree*; Early Music: Dulcimer, Autoharp, and Ballads, a three-session workshop led by Betty Smith, a noted authority on Appalachian, English, Scottish, and southern ballads; The Magic Fire—Raku Pottery with Rick Berman, a well-known ceramicist; Watercolor: Form and Process in Nature taught by Laurence Holden, an artist and poet; Dynamic Symmetry in Clothing Design: Mary Hambidge's Approach to Personal Garment Design with Karin Schaller, an artist, weaver, and author; and a Dynamic Symmetry conference described as "a first gathering of people from various disciplines who have an interest in Dynamic Symmetry."[1]

The workshop I led in the summer of 1985 was Weaving—Beginning and Intermediate, which was held in a small building called the Weave Shed, where much of the fabric woven by the Weavers of Rabun had been created. Many of the looms from that time were still in place, and during the week the students and I each wove at least one project using the historic looms. It was nostalgic to be working with the old equipment, but it was also somewhat frustrating. The looms had not often been used in the preceding years, and at first we struggled to make them function well. In spite of that, each of

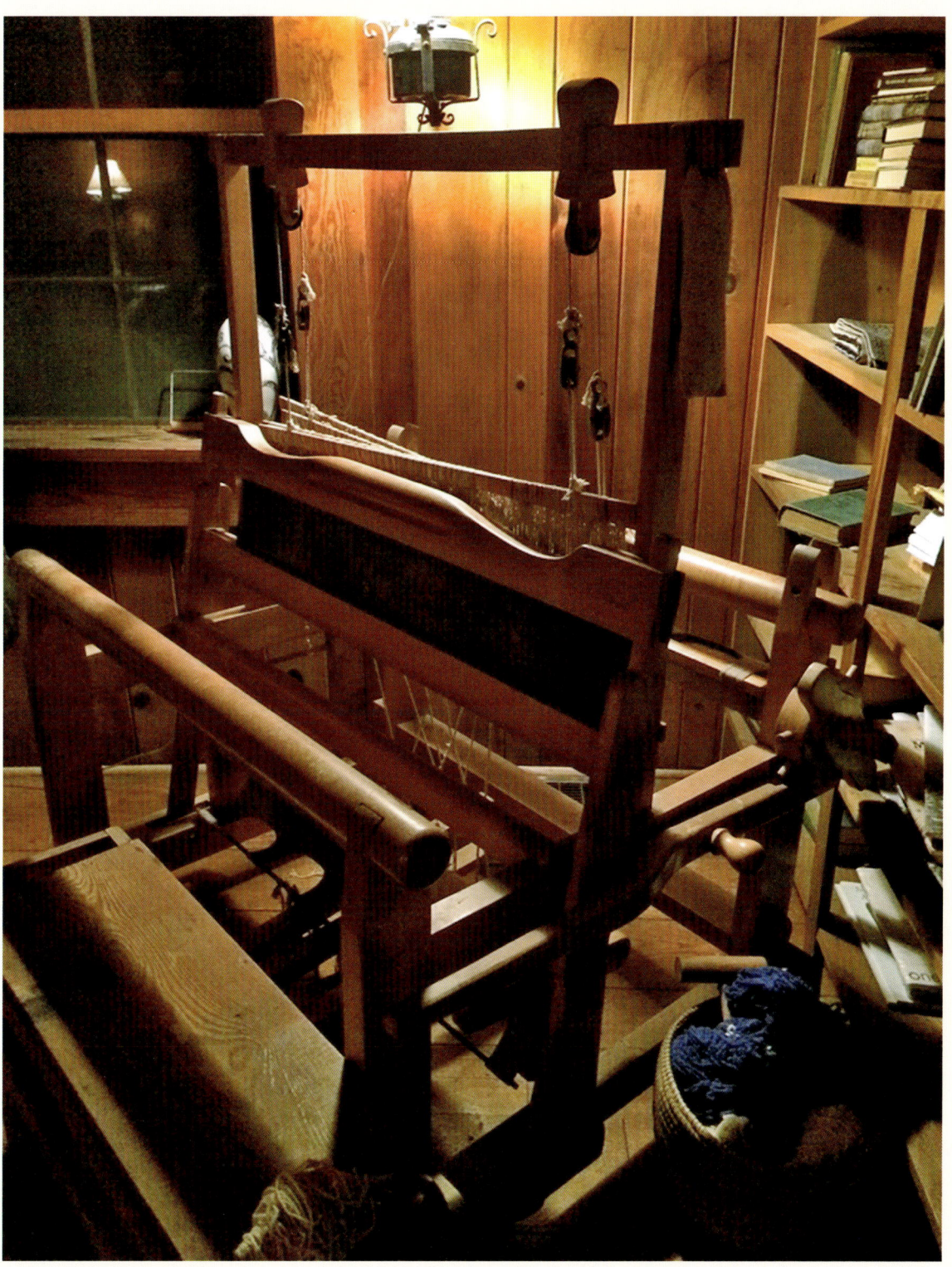

Mary Hambidge's loom,
Hambidge Center, 2016.
Photograph by Tommye
McClure Scanlin

us felt the threads of connection with Mary Hambidge and the women who worked with her through the years producing many yards of handwoven fabrics in that beautiful weaving room.

I returned twice more to the Hambidge Center during the 1980s to conduct weaving workshops before the old looms were dismantled and moved into storage in the attic of the Weave Shed. In recent years, the building has been used as a gallery where exhibits curated by Hambidge Fellows and others are held. The loom originally used by Mary Hambidge is still at the center and as of 2021 was on display in the Weave Shed.

Tapestry Workshops in the 1990s

In the mid-1990s I initiated and facilitated three tapestry workshops, which were held at the center under the guidance of Executive Director Judith Barber. Five internationally known tapestry artists were invited to present week-long sessions, which took place in 1994, 1995, and 1996; students traveled from all regions of the country to participate.

Jean Pierre Larochette and his artist wife, Yael Lurie, conducted the first workshop during April 4–8, 1994.[2] Larochette was a cofounder of the San Francisco Tapestry Workshop, one of the few professional tapestry studios in the United States in the later twentieth century.[3] A press release from the Hambidge Center prior to the event stated: "[The center's] current role is that of an artists' residency program, but since that program does not go into full operation until May 1, it will be an ideal setting for the workshop. It is an ideal place for weavers, given its long history in the arts and crafts."[4]

During April 10–14, 1995, Marcel Marois, a member of the Royal Canadian Academy of Arts and a participant in the Tenth and Thirteenth International Biennials of Tapestry in Lausanne, gave tapestry instruction.[5] Participants for his class came from Georgia, North Carolina, Florida, Minnesota, Virginia, and Washington state.

Archie Brennan and Susan Martin Maffei led the third of the tapestry workshops at the Hambidge Center in the spring of 1996.[6] Brennan had been the director of the Dovecot Tapestry Workshop in Edinburgh, Scotland, in the 1960s, and in the 1970s he had advised in the establishment of the Victorian Tapestry Workshop (now the Australian Tapestry Workshop). By the 1990s, he was living in New York City, and he and his partner and fellow artist, Maffei, were traveling extensively to teach short classes. Once again, the workshop was filled with students from around the country.

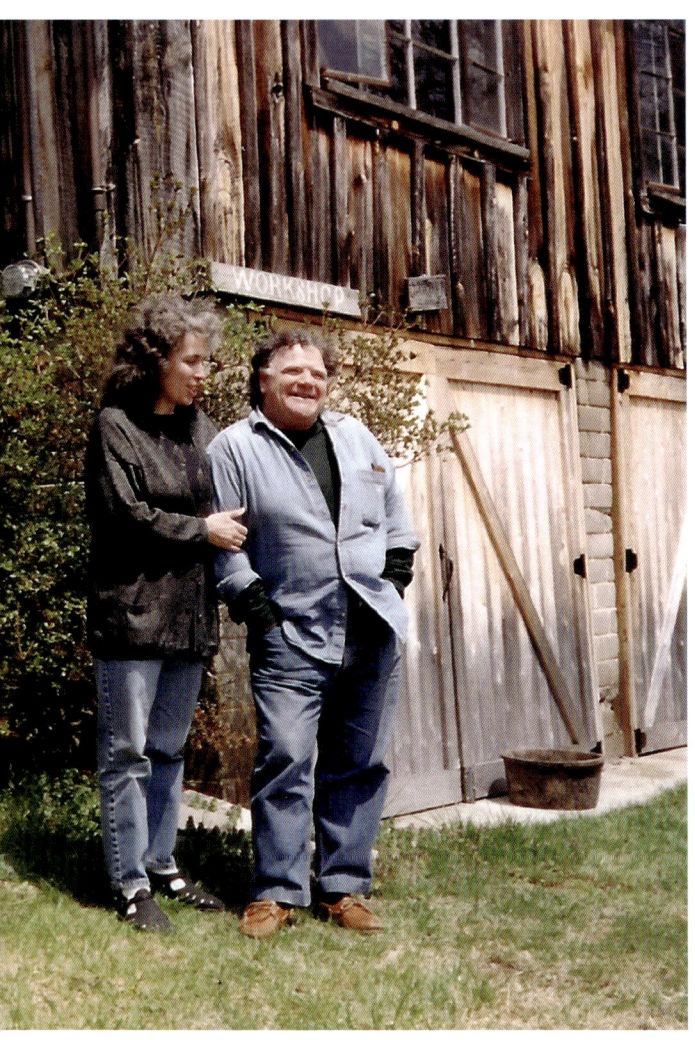

Archie Brennan and Susan Martin Maffei at the Hambidge Center, 1996. Photograph by Tommye McClure Scanlin

Pat Williams, who attended both the Larochette-Lurie and the Brennan-Maffei workshops, said: "Both were life-changing for me in that I was introduced to an aspiration for fine quality craftsmanship and an increased respect and deep love of the medium."[7]

The three week-long tapestry workshops held in the mid-1990s were outstanding. However, by the late 1990s, the residency program became of foremost importance at the center. The season available for Fellows became longer, and only a few workshops were scheduled from the late 1980s through the early 2000s. However, by the 2010s more were being offered, with some being taught by Fellows during their residency.

In the 2020s, the prospects for participation beyond the residency program are expanding because of a planned addition at the center called the Antinori Village. The village will be located along Betty's Creek Road near the existing Antinori Pottery Studio, with announced goals that include establishing new revenue-generating workshops with accommodations available for participants. Programming opportunities will include themed collaborative residencies in a variety of topics, as well as occasions for small group and leadership retreats. The plans for creating a new setting so that more people can experience the beautiful surroundings of the northern Georgia mountains while learning the history of the Hambidge Center are exciting.

Artist Residency Memories

I've had the good fortune to be able to have many weeks of retreat at the Hambidge Center since my first residency in 1994. Leading workshops there in the mid-1980s had given me a deep affection for the beautiful surroundings, and I hoped to become a Hambidge Fellow one day.

I had been a faculty member of the Fine Arts Department at NGC for over two decades when I finally applied for a residency. Although I was making artwork constantly, early on I found myself jumping from one medium to another, searching for the *what*, *why*, and *how* of a meaningful studio practice. It seemed that most two-dimensional media didn't completely satisfy my seeking, and over time it became clear that fiber techniques held the most appeal for me. Weaving had made an impact on Mary Hambidge's life. Why not on mine as well?

Like Mary, I delved into dyeing my own yarn, which I wove into fabrics of all kinds, from functional scarves to wall hangings. Also like Mary, sometimes I added imagery to the weavings through various methods, including inlay techniques similar to those found in her fabrics. In my sketches and paintings, I continued to be attracted to nature and especially focused on details. I embarked on explorations of a wide range of fiber art methods, finding satisfaction in both the potential for image creation and the technical challenges of various weaving techniques.

By 1988 I determined that tapestry weaving was the direction I would pursue. For me, tapestry held the key: combining my love of image making with a desire to use fiber as a medium. I had chosen a method but still searched for insight into the *why* of it all. What would my tapestries be about, and why should those ideas be explored? I felt hindered in that search for concept and meaning, however, because I had little time to concentrate on my personal artwork due to the workload demands at the college.

I realized that an intense immersion experience in which to both explore and focus my thoughts would be beneficial, and in 1994 I applied for a residency at the Hambidge Center. The weeks I spent in Foxfire Studio that summer were a fulfillment of a long-held dream to be a Hambidge Fellow. I read, drew, painted, and even wove a small tapestry during my stay. As it turned out, the most surprising result of the retreat was the outpouring of writing that happened.

My writing helped me articulate and then reexamine many issues troubling me at the time, including directions for my creative yearnings and struggles with personal issues. "Seeking epiphany" is one of twenty-two poems I wrote then:

Seeking epiphany
in the red of a maple leaf—
rain soaked and shining—
on the path.
Path of beyond here
Path to the near
Yet the near is far,
strange and new—
Essential nature of that leaf
and that noticing—
an epiphany of sorts.

Since 1994 I've returned to Hambidge many times, sometimes for only a few days but more often for a couple of weeks and, on one occasion, for a month. No matter how often I've gone back, my first residency at the center

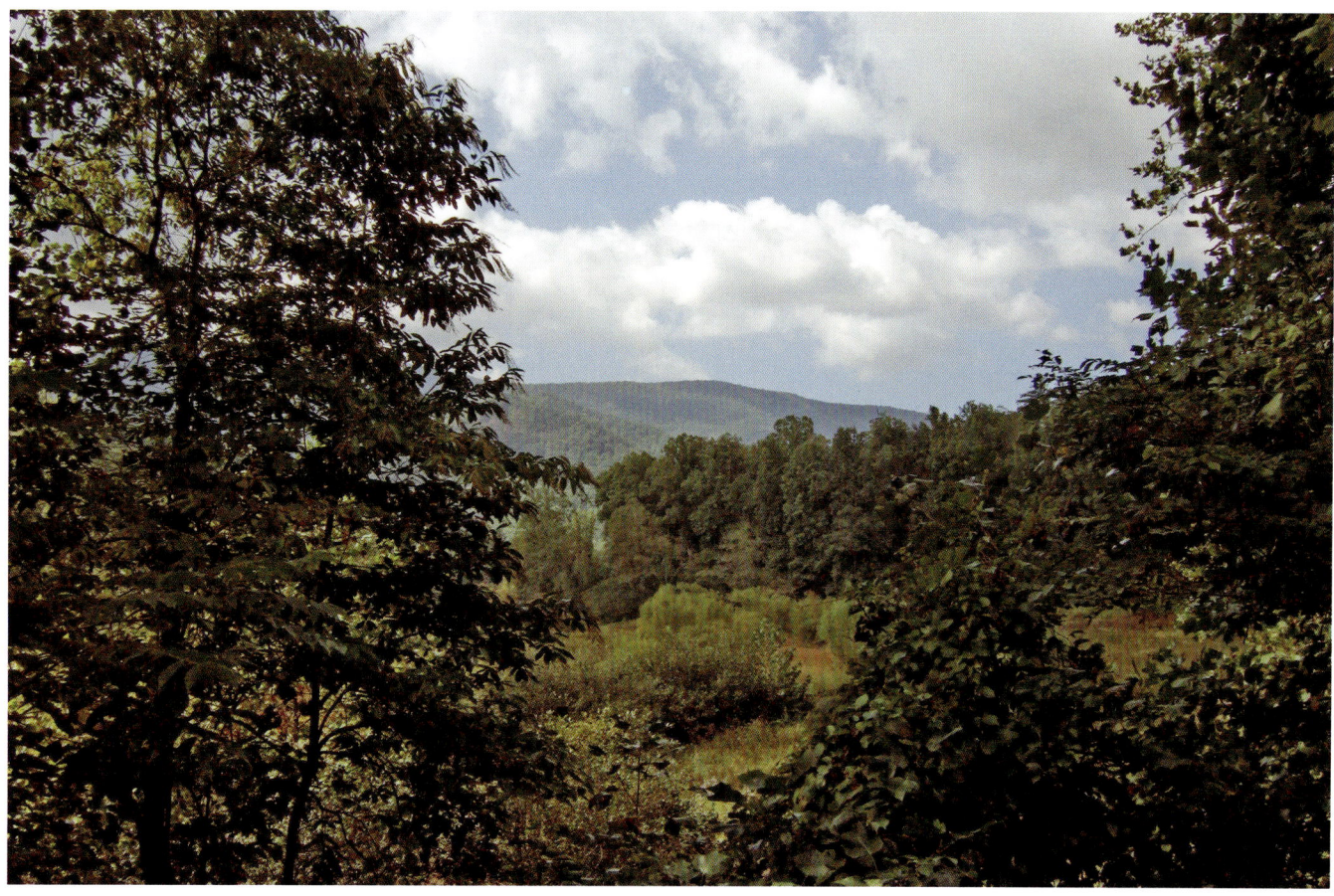

Fields and mountains near the Hambidge Center, c. 2010. Photograph by Tommye McClure Scanlin

remains a special memory. I know that the experience helped confirm my commitment to learning and growing as a tapestry artist.

Several times I've gone to a residency with no particular plan in mind. Instead, the days unfolded with ideas and images coming as they may. Often, I have woven tapestries based on the visual explorations begun at the center. For instance, during one stay I became fascinated with the details of the many stones and bricks found on the property, and small tapestries resulted from those studies.

In early December 2016 I was able to arrange a short residency so that I could do visual research to aid the completion of a tapestry that was under way. It had begun as an abstraction of leaf litter, but in October and November of that year, wildfires swept through many acres of the southeastern Appalachian Mountains, and I knew the concept and design for the

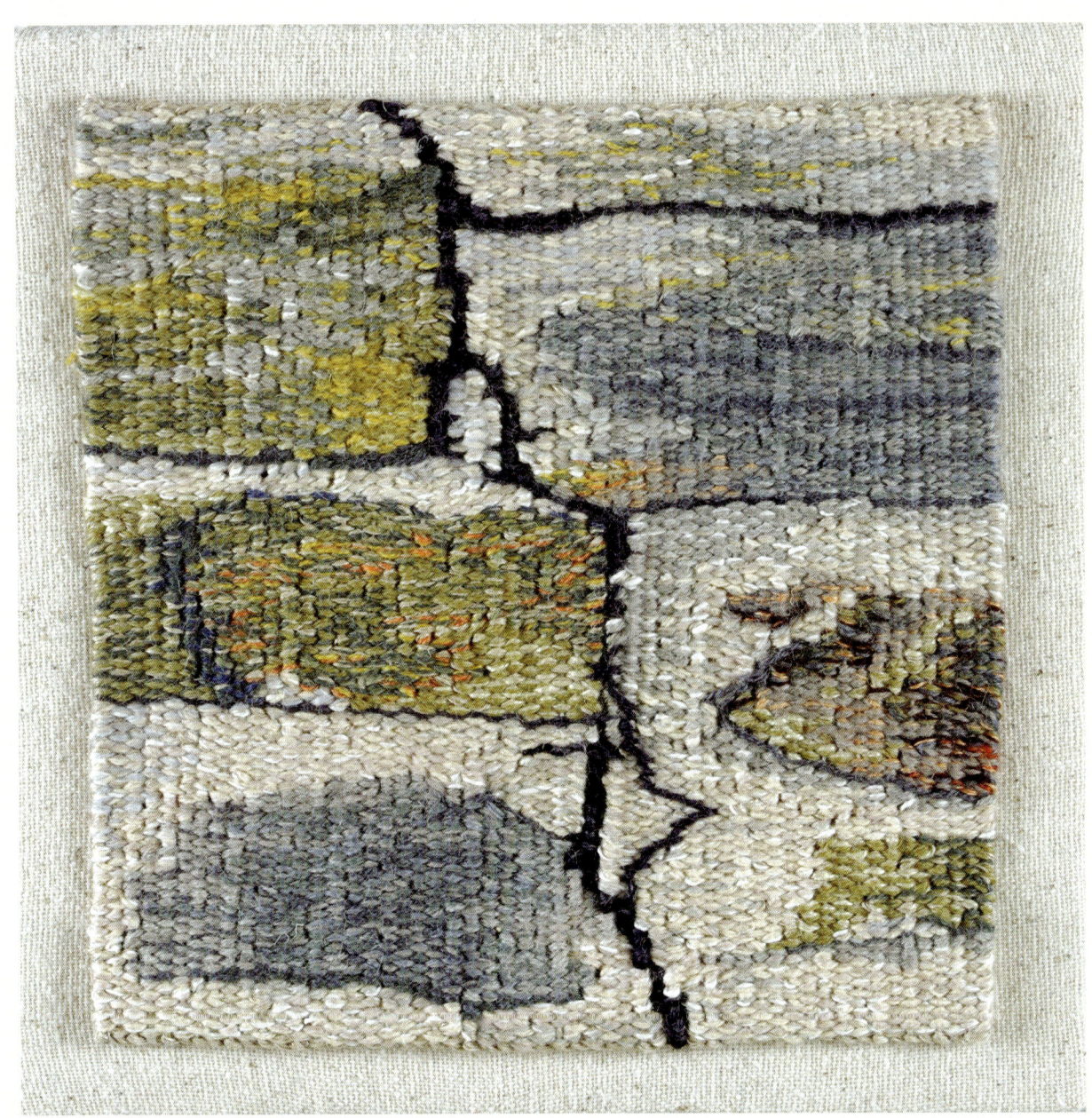

Tommye McClure Scanlin,
Hambidge House Foundation
Stones, 2016, tapestry, 6 × 6 in.
Photograph by Tim Barnwell

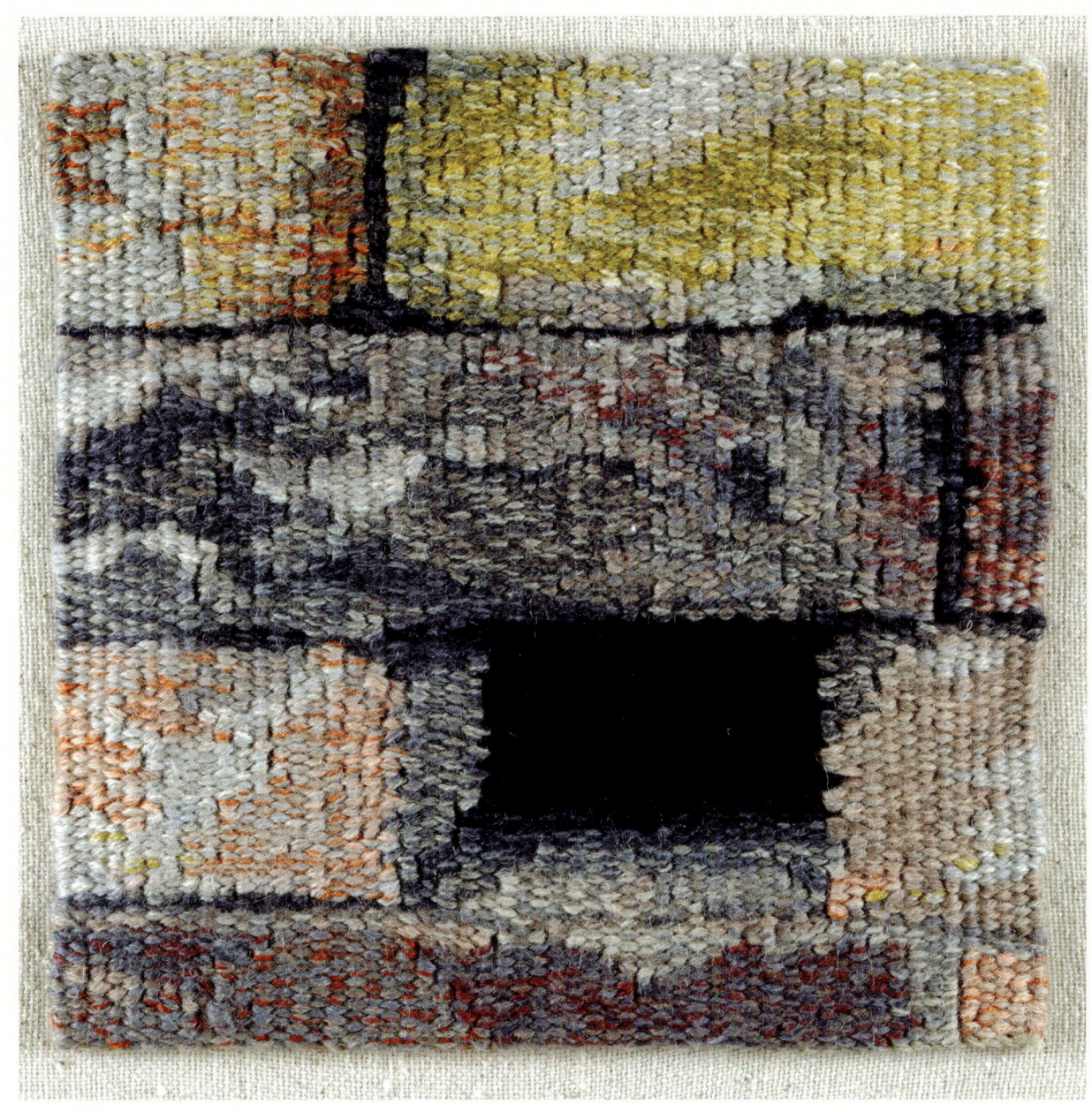

Tommye McClure Scanlin,
Hambidge Kiln Bricks, 2016,
tapestry, 6 × 6 in. Photograph
by Tim Barnwell

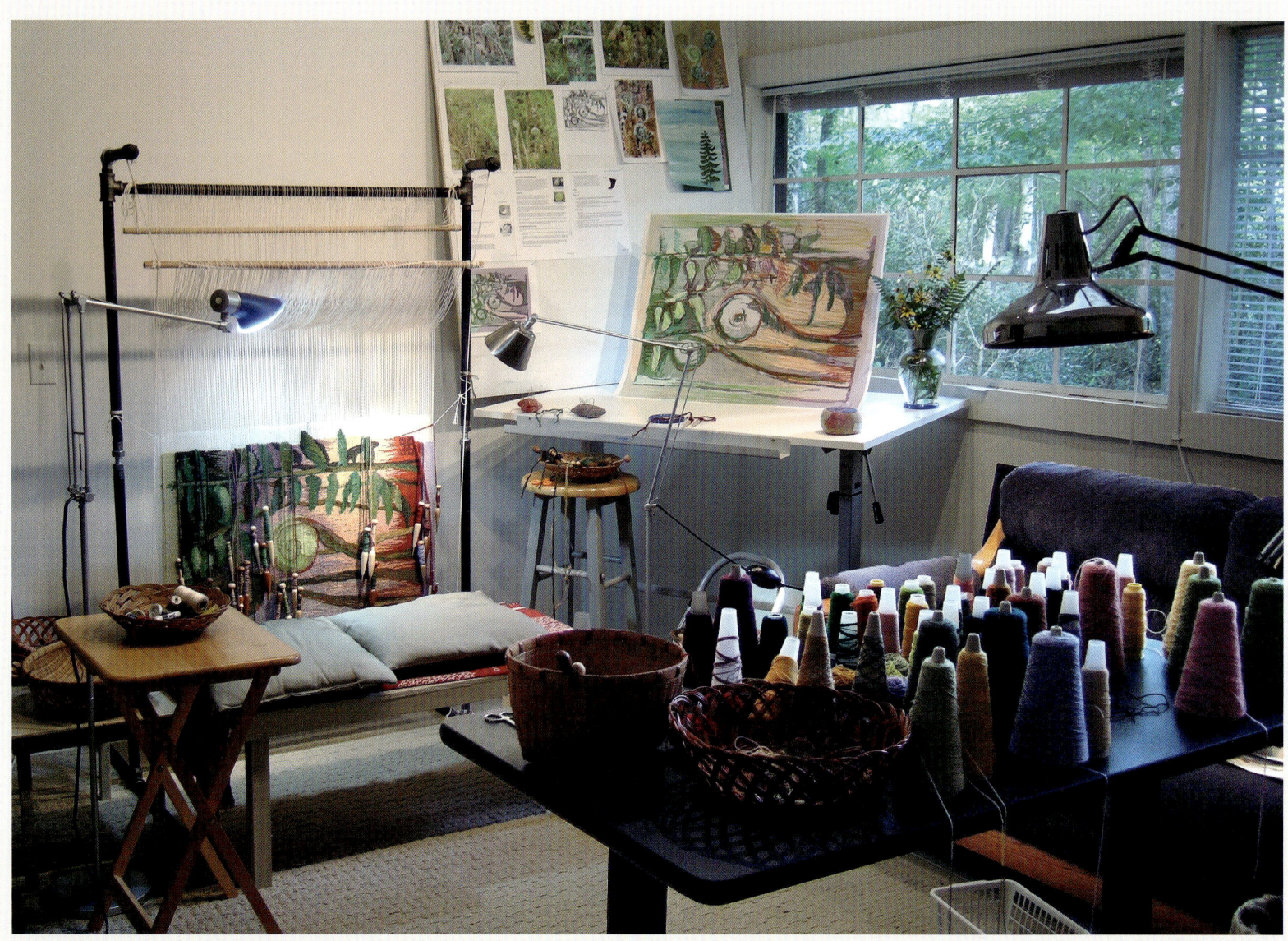

Tommye Scanlin's loom with tapestry in
progress at Cove Studio, 2008. Photograph
by Tommye McClure Scanlin

tapestry should be changed. More appropriate would be a piece about the devastation created when drought caused the dried leaves of the forest floor to become a tinderbox. In fact, some of the fires had come close to the center, and for their safety, Fellows were temporarily moved to other locations until the danger was past.

During that residency, I made and then used as reference photographs of burned areas near the Hambidge property, creating drawings with charcoal from charred tree limbs, enhanced with earth pigment colors. Based on those visual studies, the design was transformed. The resulting tapestry was titled *Phoenix*.

One aspect of a residency at the Hambidge Center is the opportunity to meet others who are also on a creative journey. For instance, Jennifer Garza-Cuen was working on a photographic series called *Imag[in]ing America* when we happened to overlap in our residencies during 2015.[8] About her first encounters there, Garza-Cuen said:

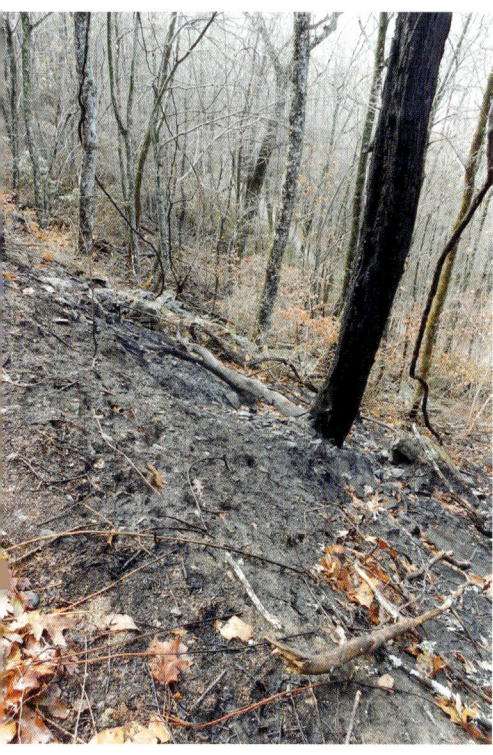

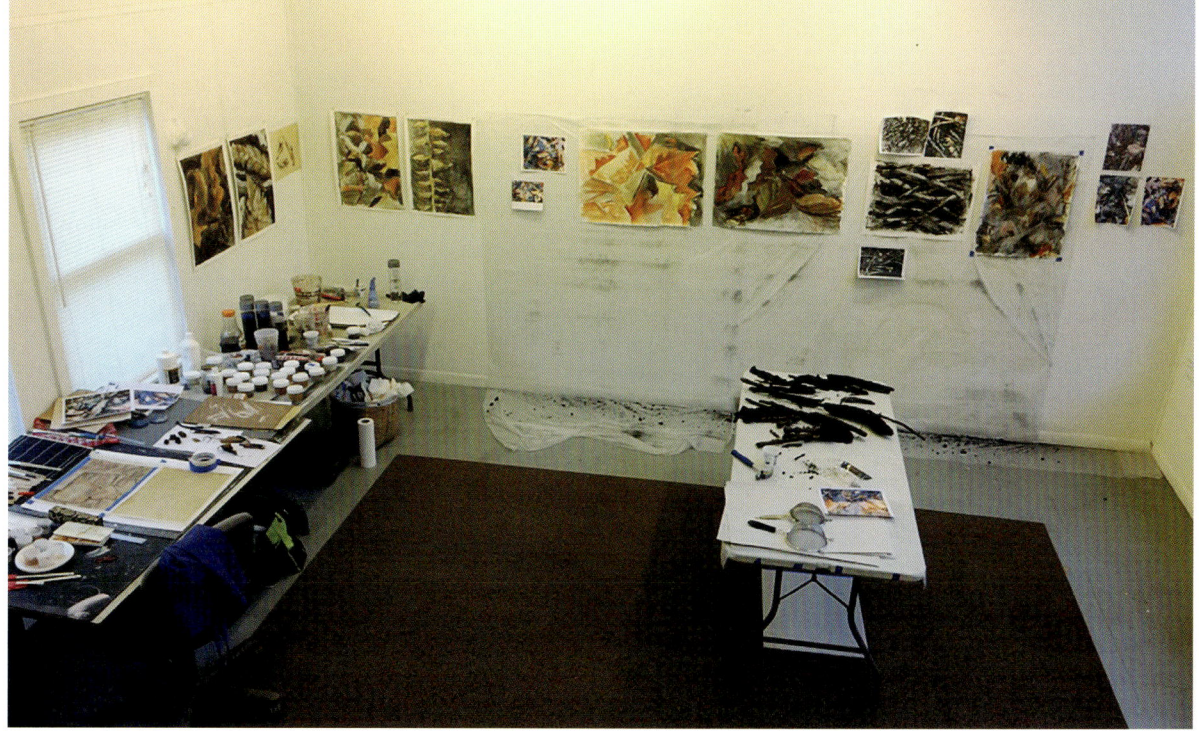

Controlled burn area near the Hambidge Center along Patterson Gap Road, 2016. Photograph by Tommye McClure Scanlin

Paintings and drawings in progress at Fisher Studio, earth pigment and charcoal from charred tree limbs, 2016. Photograph by Tommye McClure Scanlin

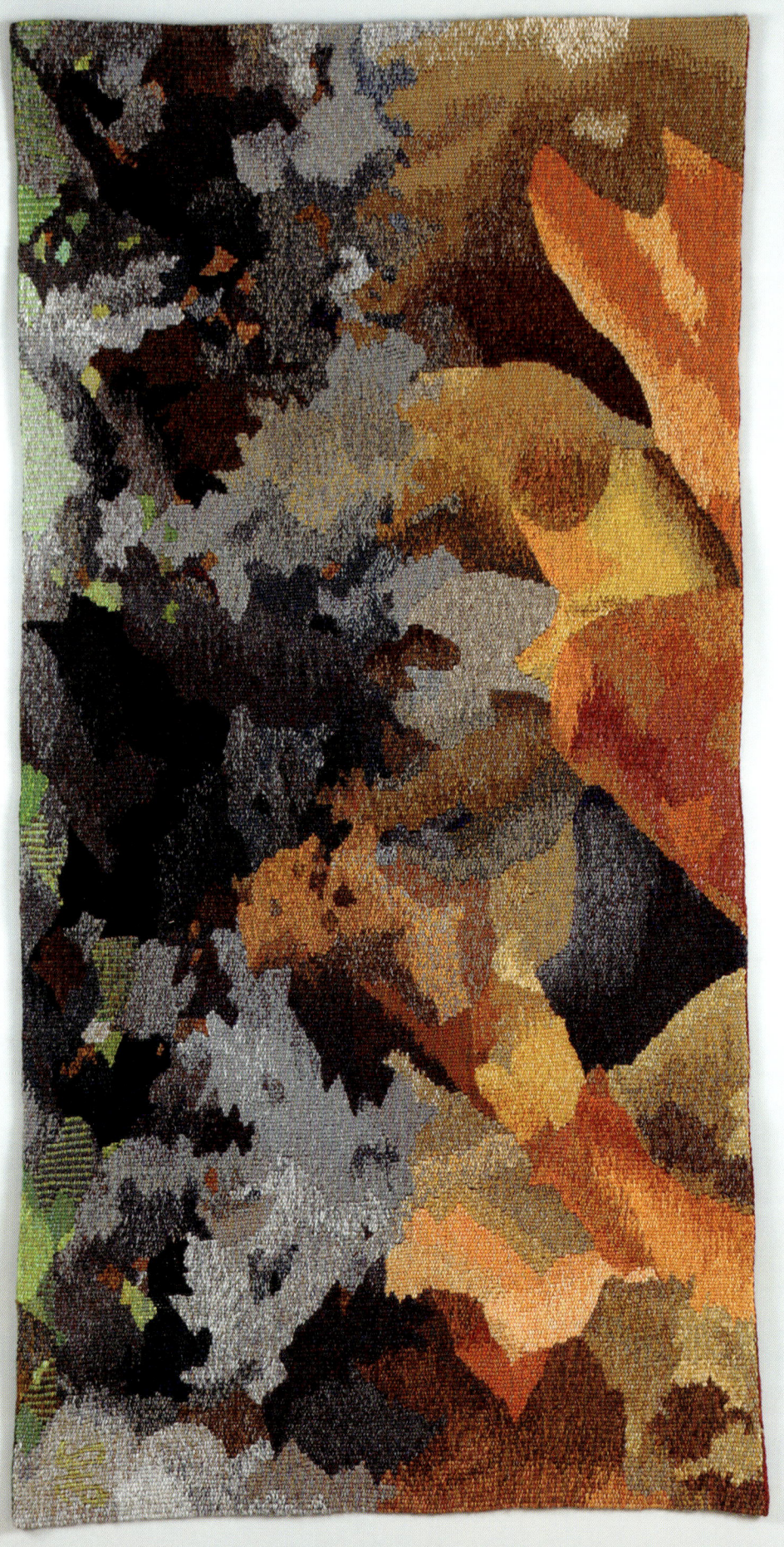

Tommye McClure Scanlin, *Phoenix*, 2017, tapestry, 60 × 30 × 1 in. Photograph by Tim Barnwell

I remember arriving at Hambidge late on a November evening in 2015. Virginia Ammons (program manager at the time) welcomed me and Andrew Fitzgibbons (building and grounds supervisor) accompanied me up a winding dirt and gravel road to Son House. He was so warmhearted and kind, he brought me firewood and said to contact him if I needed anything. I remember the long pause before I thanked him and said goodbye. I was processing a mixture of fear and excitement. The fear and excitement of being so alone and seemingly isolated in a "cabin" in the dark winter woods of northern Georgia. It felt like a shock. Then as the fear eased a deep sense of calm came over me, something primal that felt like memory, the kind of genetic memory that connects us to those that have come before and those that will follow. It was extraordinary, both profoundly grounding and exalting and I believe the images I produced there will always carry some of that in them.[9]

Garza-Cuen calls a portion of her photographic series *Rabun*, which has images both found and imagined/created. I became one of her subjects in *Untitled—Woman with Gun*.

Many individuals I've encountered at the Hambidge Center through the years have inspired and intrigued me. I'm grateful to have met each of them, even if only briefly. Every one of us who has had a Hambidge Center experience can attest to the importance of finding the time, space, and solitude to have a brief respite, a time-out from our daily lives.

At the Hambidge Center I first discovered the value of the respite to be found in an artist retreat. In subsequent years I've occasionally experienced another residency center also located in Rabun County—the Lillian E. Smith Center of Piedmont College.

The Lillian E. Smith Center was begun by the family of Lillian Smith as a way to recognize and honor her legacy. Smith was an outspoken advocate of social justice who was well known in the mid-twentieth century for her activism and writings. She was both praised and criticized for her frank analyses of how continuing racial inequities and attitudes were harmful for all people, not just in the South. Her books *Strange Fruit* and *Killers of the Dream* were widely praised by some and reviled by others.[10] In fact, *Strange Fruit* had the dubious distinction of being banned in Boston when it was published in 1944.[11]

Smith oversaw the Laurel Falls Girls' Camp near Clayton, Georgia, from 1925 to 1948. There, affluent young southern women took part in traditional activities like horseback riding, swimming, and arts and crafts. But they were also exposed to ideas that Smith hoped would cause them to

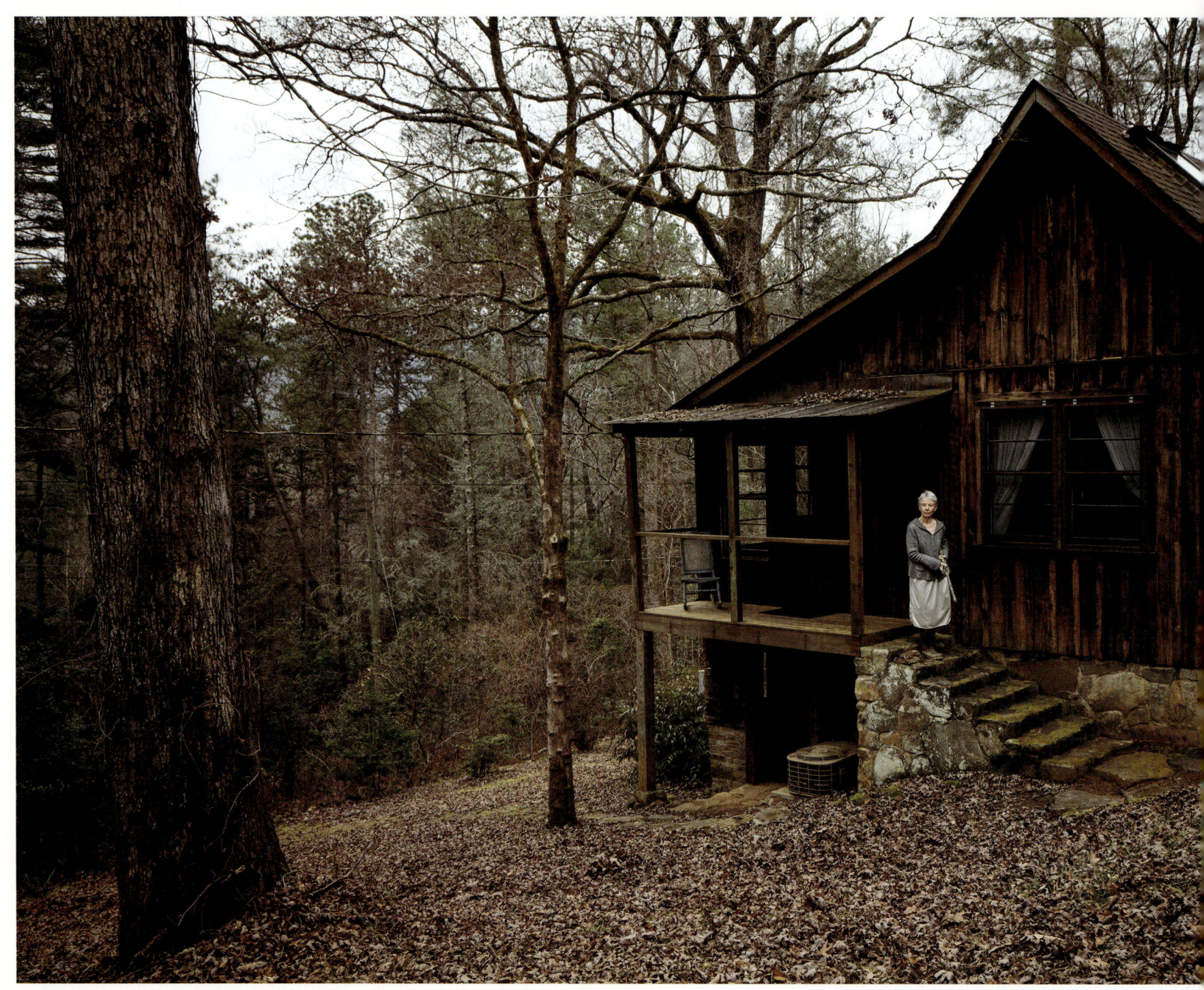

Jennifer Garza-Cuen, *Untitled—Woman with
Gun*, 2016, archival pigment print, 32 × 40 in.
Courtesy of Jennifer Garza-Cuen

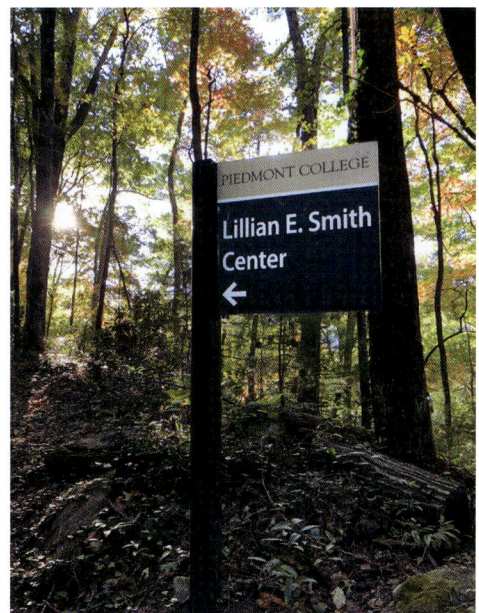

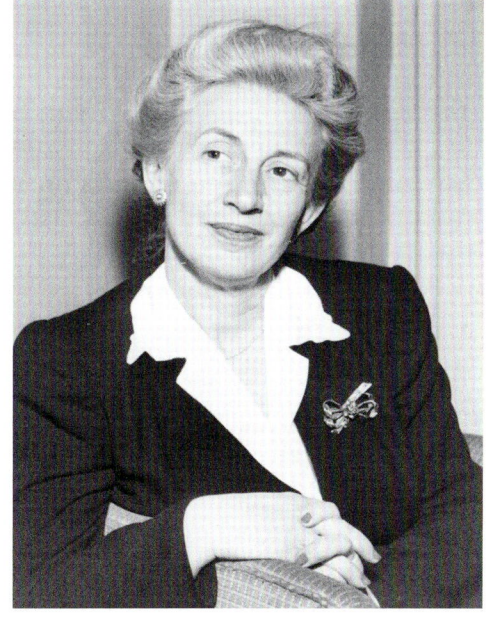

Entrance of the Lillian E. Smith
Center, Clayton, Georgia, 2019.
Photograph by Tommye McClure
Scanlin

C. M. Stieglitz, *Lillian Eugenia Smith*,
1944. World Telegraph photo, Prints and
Photographs Division, Library of Congress,
NYWTS-BIOG-Smith,LillianoWriter,
https://www.loc.gov/pictures/item
/94504357

think and feel differently about the realities of the world in which they were
growing up.[12]

In a 1947 letter to parents of campers, Smith wrote: "Our conversations
together have been unusually fine this year. More real give and take; more
good ideas from the girls; more thoughtful probing analyses of our mistakes
and the ways to grow out of them. All of our emphasis . . . is about growing;
not on 'right and wrong' which is so puzzling to children, but on growth, on
ideas rather than guilt."[13]

In 2001, Smith's family transformed the property of the former girls camp
into a residency program called the Lillian E. Smith Center. In 2015 own-
ership of the center was transferred to Piedmont University. To date, the
university has continued the residency program.[14]

Lillian Smith and Mary Hambidge lived in Rabun County during many
of the same years of the twentieth century. They likely knew of each other.
At least, it is documented that Smith was aware of Hambidge. In a column

for the *North Georgia Review*, a publication that Smith coedited with Paula Snelling, Smith had this to say: "Up Betty's Creek, about seven miles from Old Screamer Mountain, the Rabun Weavers (a project breathed into life and driven along by its creator, a little diesel engine of a woman named Mrs. Jay Hambidge) quietly continue along their Greek Way. They are a group of forty mountain women, skilled, expert craftswomen, who weave . . . designs based on those esthetic principles of dynamic symmetry once so familiar to old Greek and Egyptian artists."[15]

Although both Mary Hambidge and Lillian Smith were committed and passionate about their beliefs, their worldviews were quite different. Hambidge sought to celebrate artistic and creative freedom, colored by her inspirations from classical Greek ideals. Smith fought against the realities of the racial and social inequities of the times. It's remarkable that two equally strong and idealistic women would be found in a small county of northern Georgia in the same span of time. It's just as remarkable that part of the legacy of both are artist retreat centers that bear their names.[16]

I am grateful for the experiences I've had during each residency at the Hambidge Center and at the Lillian E. Smith Center. They have given me confirmation that the path I set upon many years ago seeking a creative life has been the right one for me. As Mary Hambidge wrote in *Apprentice in Creation*: "The urge to create and to develop in creation is natural, instinctive to man, drawing us ever forward towards becoming one with the Great Creator."[17]

CHAPTER 6

The Hambidge Center Today

Donna Mintz

An Artist's View from the Inside

The Hambidge Center in the twenty-first century describes its mission in straightforward terms. It provides a 600-acre sanctuary to empower "talented individuals to develop, explore, and express their creative voices . . . [offering the] time and space that inspires individuals working in a broad range of disciplines to create works of the highest caliber."[1] Its list of Fellows includes Grammy Award, James Beard Award, and Pulitzer Prize nominees and winners; poets laureate; Guggenheim and MacArthur Fellows; arts administrators; scientists; dancers and composers; sculptors and painters; and playwrights. Tucked away in a secluded mountain home, the Hambidge Center values inclusion and the diversity of its residents. In 2019 alone, the center awarded 188 residencies lasting from two weeks to six to creatives ranging in age from twenty-four to eighty-eight, representing thirty-one states and seven countries. These are the facts, some of them anyway, but it is not as easy or as straightforward to describe what happens at the center, what it feels like to be there, and why it matters. Like those 188 fortunate souls, I am among the more than 2,100 Fellows in the Hambidge Center's residency history, and I will try.

As a visual artist and a writer of literary nonfiction and art criticism, I have gone to the Hambidge Center for inspiration and the blessings of time, nature, solitude, and communion for almost fifteen years now. Enamored after my first residency in 2009, I began research into the lives and letters of Mary and Jay Hambidge, eager to know more about the woman who started this project ninety years ago and the man whose name she gave to her foundation. Theirs is a compelling story, which Virginia Gardner Troy has woven so well; this story, along with my devotion to the place, is why I was honored to be asked to write this chapter on what the center has become.

Like all love at first sight, mine for the Hambidge Center was a coup de foudre, a lightning strike. Most of what I know about it now I have accrued over time with repeated residencies and my efforts to help where I can. I have helped to archive the historic materials still in the center's possession and have read through or visited those already in the Atlanta History Center and the Hargrett Library at the University of Georgia. As an Atlantan living only two hours away from Rabun Gap, I have volunteered at many events both on the campus and in Atlanta. The Hambidge Center hosted forty-three of them in 2019—nature hikes and artist talks, workshops and shows in the Weave Shed Gallery, two anagama kiln firings, and the annual art auction and extravaganza, the center's major fundraiser and undertaking each year.

In 2014, I cowrote and coedited *The Hambidge Center: A Creative Sanctuary 80 Years in the Making*, celebrating its anniversary year. During those eighty years, the center grew from a sustainable farm dedicated to local tradition and craft into a weavers collective and later a place where artists, most of them friends of Mary, were welcomed for long respites. Despite the care, concern, and efforts of friends and supporters, the center went through lean years, especially after Mary's death in 1973, but the twenty-first century has brought plans for an even more impactful future, led by the tireless and innovative executive director, Jamie Badoud.

I interviewed Badoud after the site was threatened by wildfire in the late fall of 2016. Over eighty years, the center had suffered many an existential threat, but this may have been the worst. The fire was so close that a molten necklace of flames draped the ridge above the property. Everyone had to face the prospect of crippling devastation to Hambidge's historic buildings and natural beauty, a tragic and unimaginable loss. For Badoud, acceptance came *after* he had done all he could humanly do to protect everything, resulting in one of the fire's greatest lessons. What was most important, he believed, was not the tangible to be found in Hambidge's historic buildings and artifacts, and maybe not even in its natural beauty, though both are integral to the Hambidge experience. Fortunately, the fire was stopped, but what really mattered to Badoud was the knowledge that Hambidge would have been rebuilt had it not: "The fire would come and go but we would carry on." This has been the indomitable spirit of the Hambidge Center for all its years.

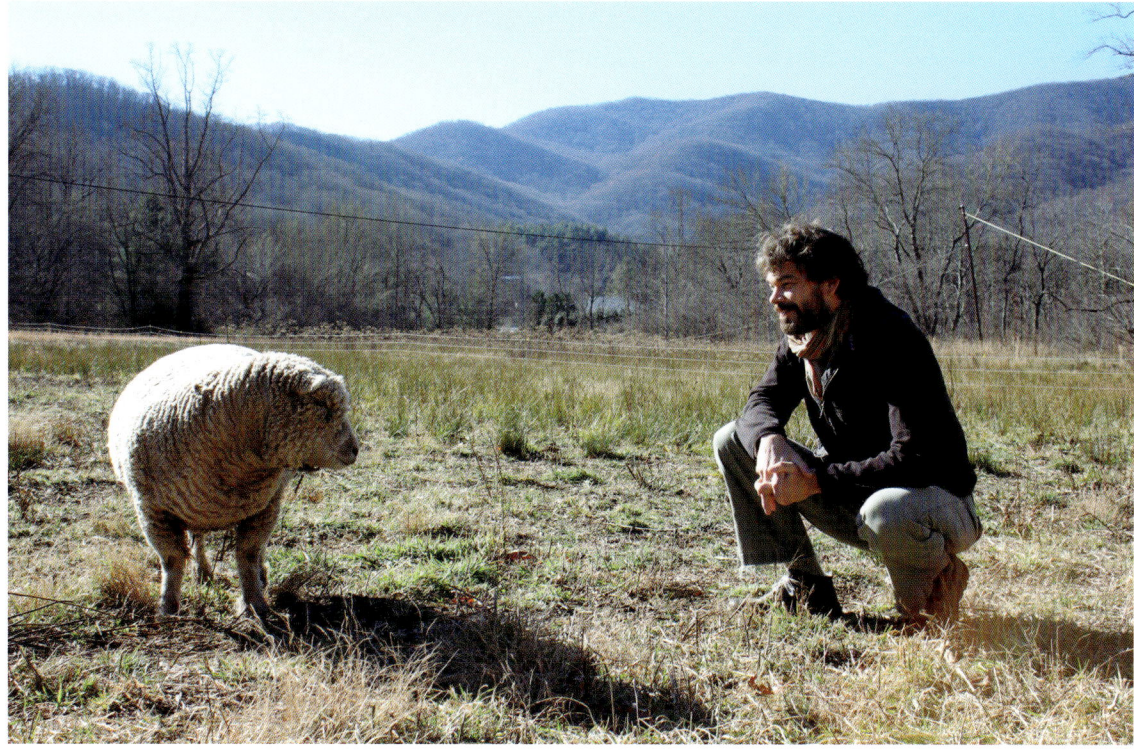

Jamie Badoud, executive director, in the sheep pasture at the Hambidge Center, n.d. Photo by Dayna Thacker, courtesy of the Hambidge Center for Creative Arts and Sciences

My residencies have varied depending on the season, the duration, my own projects at hand, and connections with the other seven or so artists in residence with me each time. What has been constant, though, is open time and boundless possibility, which can be either daunting or exhilarating, like any time you finally get what you wish for. Each day, yours for filling however you choose, stretches out like an empty road where prayerful attention is rewarded and creativity sparked if only you start walking it.

Place

Let me take you there. To know the Hambidge Center, you must begin with its unique location in the physical world. Writers, especially those we think of as southern writers, know the importance of capturing and conveying a sense of place—and the difficulty of adequately doing so. Almost everyone who goes to Hambidge notes the strong pull of this special place, but beyond the natural beauty and slow pace, few can say just where that attraction originates. Does our sense of any site emanate from something rooted in the land, the sum total of all that ever happened or all who lived there? Is it conferred on the land by the people who live and have lived there, or is it independent, intrinsic in the land itself? What are the elements that create the sense of a singular place?

Whatever the answers to these questions may be, the sum is ineffably greater than its parts. The Latin expression for the sense I am trying to conjure is genius loci, the presiding or protective spirit of a place. Think of Faulkner's great bear, the mysterious spirit that presided over Mississippi's immense woods in that central and eponymous chapter of *Go Down, Moses*. Or duende, the Spanish expression for the spirit of the earth: something that may not be described but can be evoked by the smell of orange blossoms on a breeze or the slant of afternoon light through pines. A sense of place, duende, or genius loci, whatever we call it, the spirit that presides at the Hambidge Center is woven into my every sense of the place. I am not unique; almost everyone who spends time there feels some form of what one composer who had recently completed his residency recorded: "A Hambidge residency is a magical experience. The beautiful setting in the southern Appalachians is itself inspiring. [It] encourages one's soul to manifest in the artist. And when the artist is in better touch with the soul . . . it is easier to tap into the wells and streams of creative energy."[2] Whatever this magic may be, I don't believe it began with Mary Hambidge's dream of an artist enclave and sustainable farm. Whatever the singular alchemy there, it originates in the land where the center resides.

First, some facts: the center is located on 600 pristine acres in the Blue Ridge Mountains of the southern Appalachians near Rabun Gap in Georgia's northeasternmost county. From your back door at the center, climb a hill— and you *will* climb a hill if you go there—and you can step into North Carolina. Now gentled by time, the mountains there are among the oldest, and once tallest, in the world. The Blue Ridge is one of the most biologically significant and diverse ecosystems of the United States, a biodiversity resulting from the fact that these mountains were the southernmost point of advance of the glaciers during the Pleistocene era, our most recent Ice Age, which ended about 11,000 years ago. The hills and mountains became a refuge for many northern species of plants and animals that were pushed there and remained when the ice receded. The Blue Ridge also is the northernmost border of many southern species. Both found sanctuary there for evolutionary development.

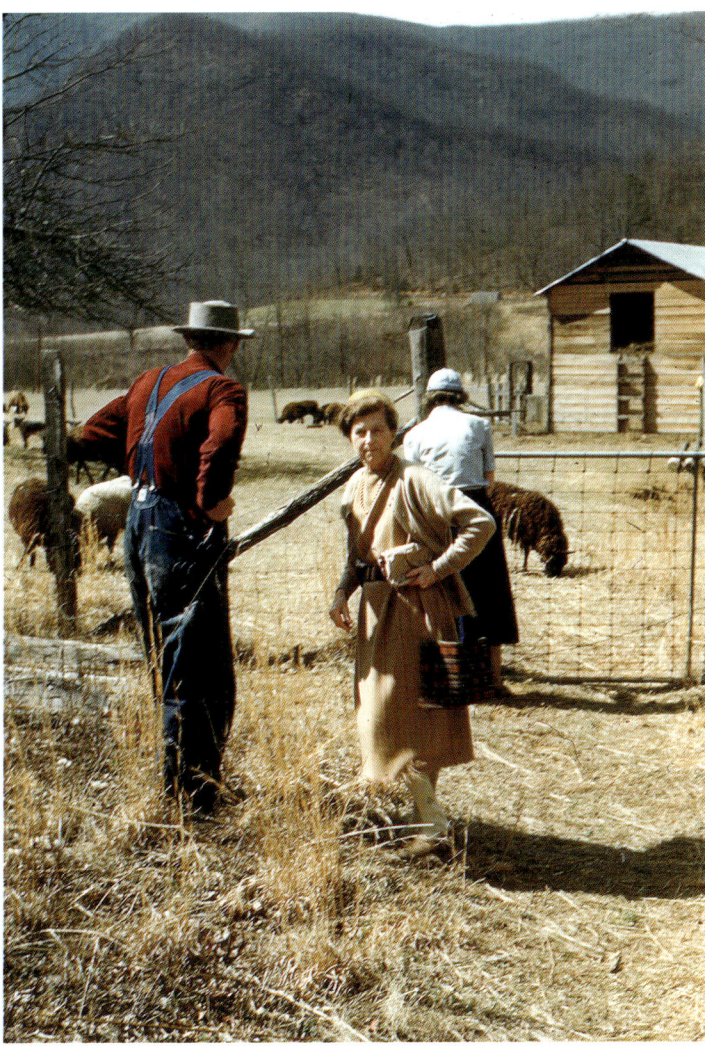

Mary Hambidge at the sheep pasture, n.d. Photo by Bob Shepherd, courtesy of the Hambidge Center for Creative Arts and Sciences

Most of the center undulates in gentle swells in the Betty's Creek valley, but at around five thousand feet, the highest peaks that surround it are home to spruce and fir, relics of the Ice Age. Their slopes are filled with mostly deciduous hardwoods, whose exhaled moisture gives a bluish sfumato to the landscape and this mountainous area its name: Blue Ridge. Lower down, the cove forests found in the cool, damp, and shadowed valleys comprise the most diverse forests in North America. Lush and mysterious, life begins there in the pungent, organic soil; the ancient ferns and mosses and rare

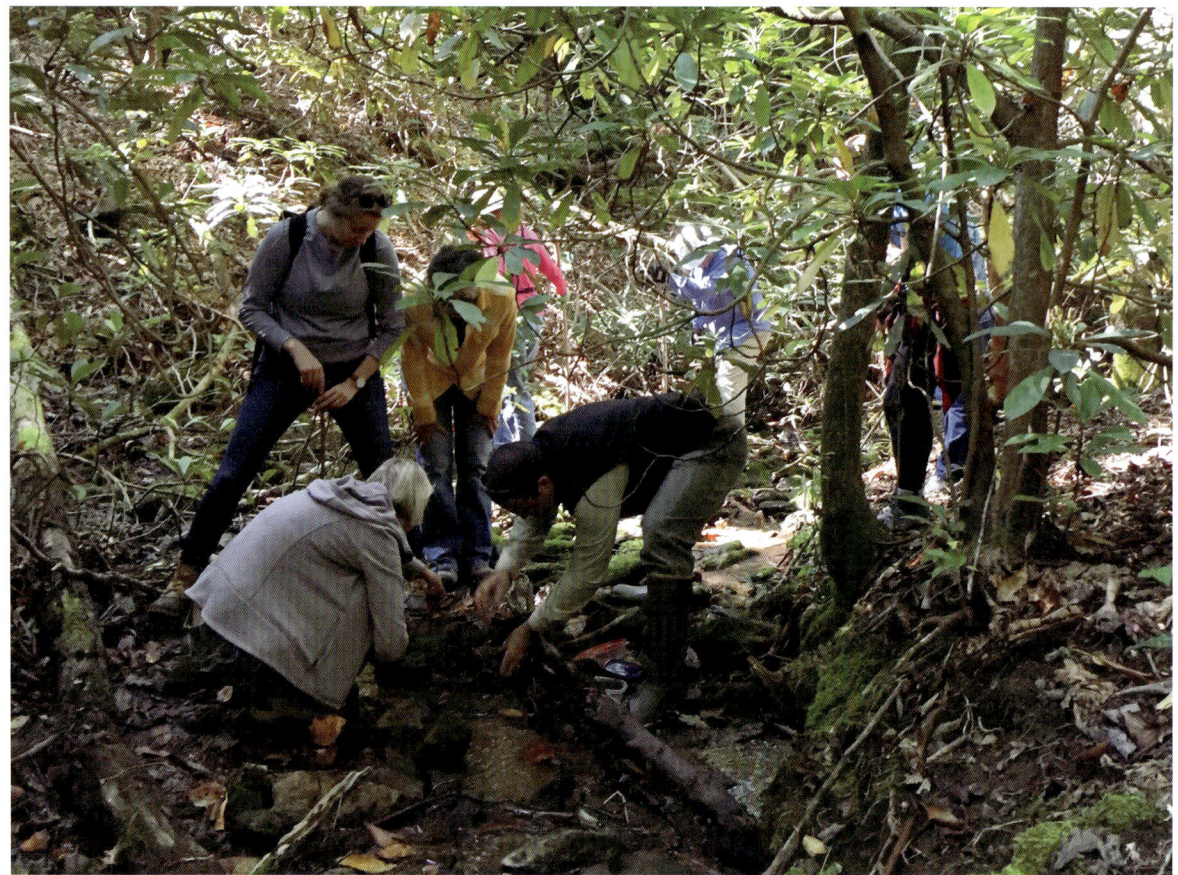

Looking for rare salamanders in a Hambidge Center stream, n.d. Photo by Dayna Thacker, courtesy of the Hambidge Center for Creative Arts and Sciences

trillium thrive in the spring. You hear life's imperative in the all-night sexual chorus of peepers in the pond as the days lengthen and in the katydids' seesaw on warm summer nights. There is a bounty of native plants and of bird life, both those that are native and the great waves of migrating birds that pass overhead. There are salamanders that exist there and nowhere else in the world. Seven miles of trails wind through this remarkable diversity of forests, meadows, streams, and waterfalls—all of which the center protects as the irreplaceable assets that they are. Why does all this matter if you are writing a play set in New York City or a novel set in Brazil? It matters because there you, too, are part of creation, and you know it.

The Hambidge Center has eighteen structures on the National Register of Historic Places. When Mary acquired the land in 1939, some of them were already there, including Lucinda's Rock House. Built of local stone and the first structure you see upon entering the campus from Betty's Creek Road, it stands as the enduring emblem of the Hambidge Center and is hearth and home to the artists in residence there. It was constructed in 1920 for private use and first rented and then purchased by Mary for her foundation.

Mary's Cabin, the log cabin former home of Mary Hambidge and current home of the deputy director, was built around 1915. Residents often spend their first evening at the center with an after-dinner visit to Mary's Cabin for local moonshine—legal, of course—and a screening of the wonderful documentary film by Hal Jacobs, *Mary Crovatt Hambidge: Whistler, Wanderer, Weaver, Utopian* (2017).

In 1940, Mary built the Weave Shed, now a gallery and shop that also houses the Hambidge office, for the weavers she employed as the Weavers of Rabun in the 1940s and 1950s. Most of the eight additional artist cabins/studios were added as the program grew after Mary's death in 1973.

In Residence

You are among the most fortunate if you have a place you love, where you can say, "Here is what counts. Here is what lasts." The Hambidge Center is that place for me. There is where I shed what I don't need, always surprised by just how much of that there is, and where I find what I *do* need. There, the fragments of my authentic self stitch back into one garment, which falls so lightly on my shoulders I don't feel myself wearing it.

There is the land I love—gently rolling green hills, dark and mysterious cove forests, with the mountains rising beyond, stark and gray in the winter and lushly blue-green in the summer. There is the dirt and gravel road that winds through the woods and leads to my cabin, or to dinner in the Rock House, golden light spilling at dusk from its windows. There, vegetarian meals are prepared four nights a week by the center's inimitable chef, Lori Speed, a seventh-generation Rabun Countian who knows the land and its offerings intimately. At dinner, conversation satisfies and enlightens and sometimes just comforts when you realize that you are not alone in your efforts—apart, but not alone. The energy is palpable as each resident in her own way tries to figure out for herself how to conceive and execute her own dream of an idea while the cross-pollination of ideas and experiences enhances the work of all.

There is a note of grace in Mary's Weave Shed and the fragrance of another time emanating from the chestnut boards cut from the ancient trees that used to tower over these forests before the blight took them all. Eight artist studios sit in constellation around Lucinda's Rock House, each rustic and tucked away from every other one, each home to one artist for periods of two weeks to six. Each has a studio, kitchen, bath, and bedroom, some with fireplaces and all offering solitude in nature.

Though unrestricted time to create is respected above all else, there are two fast rules at the Hambidge Center. First, go to dinner on the four nights it is served in the Rock House, and second, do not go unannounced or uninvited to another's studio. Solitude and, moreover, the expectation of solitude are sacrosanct, as is the communion that happens around the table in the Rock House dining room or on its generous screened porch. One artist described it this way: "A rich mix of visual artists, writers, and scholars breeds a cross-pollination that enriches one's own work in unexpected ways. The invaluable bonding among residents attests to [the center's] great ability to nurture creative freedom, space, and time."[3] Often, artists will have salons, studio tours, or potlucks on the nights dinner is not offered, or drive into Clayton for a good pizza. But just as often, artists go deep into the uninterrupted time and reemerge refreshed for next week's dinners with new work and new ideas. That's part of the beauty; your rhythm is your own, and often you discover one you didn't even know you possessed. This aspect is often difficult for non-artists and for those funding artists' residencies to absorb: that downtime *is* creative work time.

Many artists come with projects that they are mad to complete and begin to work feverishly and at once. Others take their time, slow down, disconnect (the center is proud of being wired for internet only in the gathering place of the Rock House, and there is no cell coverage), and reengage with self and ideas. There is a sense there of long time and its effects on both land and dwelling. Stay longer than a few days, and you feel a simultaneous loosening of time's grip and an awareness of your place in its flow. It's the so-called downtime that fuels the creative thought where art is conceived. New and inspired ways of thinking flower in the cracks of the between-time, and making something new requires those new and inspired ways of thinking.

It is easy to describe the tangible properties of a place like Hambidge, but less easy to describe the intangible gifts, such as inspiration, or to put into words just what that is or how it arrives. But I know what it feels like. I have often expressed it as the sense, after I have struggled and worked and failed and been made miserable by the shortcomings of those failures, that someone, somewhere, has decided that I've done enough work, paid my time,

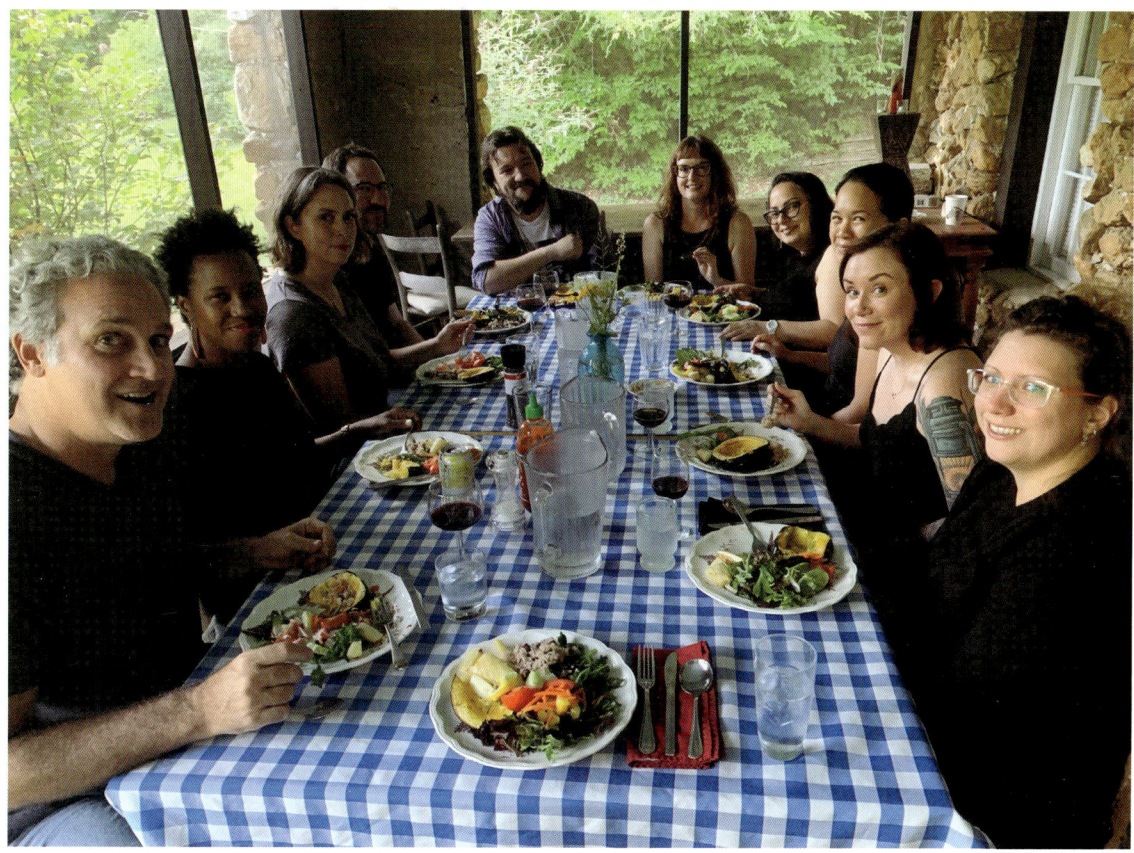

Dinner with Hambidge residents, n.d. Photo by Jamie Badoud, courtesy of the Hambidge Center for Creative Arts and Sciences

and finally I deserve a little help. In that moment, my head is cracked open, and the golden fairy dust of ease and understanding sifts in, and I see the thing—the painting, the tapestry, the book—as it was always meant to be. I may not have complete resolution, but the path is clear, and I know what to do next. I have had three such instances—a synchronous snowfall, a new way of seeing, and the perfect answer to a book's ending—that could have happened nowhere else.

When I first went to Hambidge in 2009, I wasn't yet a writer, but I had the feeling that I wanted to be. Having applied as a visual artist, I was assigned to Fisher Studio, one of the newer spaces designed to accommodate paint-ers, sculptors, and other visual artists. Fisher stands alone on a hill above the Rock House, reached by way of the dirt and gravel road. I walked this road back home after dinner beneath the stars, beyond the lighted windows of

Garden Studio, and into the darkness I treasured. Only a wooden sculpture of a bird—left beside the road by another artist as a touchstone in the dark—told me I was on the right path and halfway there.

Upstairs, the bedroom windows opened over the trees and onto a view of Owen Mountain to the east. On the first floor, the working floor, light streamed in through tall windows; one side faced deep, quiet woods, and the other overlooked an empty field. From the latter windows, a long view down the slope of Hambidge Center's property showed the great blue mountains beyond, which time and nature have seemingly formed into the shape of a reclining woman—the dip of a waist and flare of hip, twin peaks forming her breasts. I have always imagined that this must be the location of Twin Tops, the place Mary stayed when she first visited in 1927 and later when she came to live in Rabun County. I have thought how, once upon a time, she surely looked out from there over this land, not ever imagining that it would one day be hers—or maybe she did know. In Hal Jacobs's film, we learn that Mary believed that this place rejected or accepted its own. Maybe this land drew her. I know it drew me.

During that first stay at Fisher Studio, one spring midnight, though I hadn't intended to, I sat down in front of a darkened window and wrote my first story. It was a tale of first love and loss and death and snowfall. It was about two characters I knew well because they were based on my own life, but into my story that night crept that of two other lovers separated by time and loss. The idea came first as a whisper and then as a command. I knew what I had to do. I would write Mary's story. That night in Fisher Studio, it was as if Mary Hambidge had delivered the message herself. As her story began to entwine with mine and I realized this would be a story of two pairs of lovers and not one, I began to write a scene of young lovers on a snowy night. As I did, some kind of shift, a weighted silence, entered the room. It was not silence as the absence of something, but the presence of something else, more felt than heard.

Spring in Georgia, even northern Georgia, is a time of suddenly warm days and blooming things. It had been one of those blue days, but the room grew suddenly chilly, and I stood from my makeshift desk to fire up the heater. When I crossed the floor of my studio, I looked out the windows and into the woods beyond. Cherry blossoms were falling through the gray trees, or so I thought before I realized what I was really seeing. The "cherry blossoms" proved to be snow, a gentle, miraculous snowfall that would be gone by sunrise, and had I not been paying attention it would have come and gone without my notice. The snowfall, that fairy dust of inspiration, and my feeling of being compelled to write without understanding why were a sign bestowed, a message to *pay attention to the mystery*—which I have never forsaken.

Since that first residency when I was inspired to write about Mary, I have written many an essay or article and created many a painting there. In fact, I trace most of my work back to the Hambidge Center. Much of *Ex Astris*, my most recent body of work, was conceived and completed there. In my studio at home before bringing the work to Hambidge, I had begun large, shimmering golden works made with mosaics I cut from layers of collage I had built up from years of my own and others' writing. Letters received and other personal papers were all hidden beneath a last layer of gold leaf, but at Hambidge, against the dark, wooden walls where I made them, the works glowed with a holy quality I didn't impart or intend. Seeing them there lent the feeling of walking into a darkened church from a sunny street, having to adjust your eyes before the light of Byzantine mosaics or golden reliquaries harboring the bones of saints. Seeing the work that way, I knew what they were and what I had to do. I had been making my own reliquaries, containers for memory and place and even time itself, and at Hambidge I could now see that.

I have not finished that first snow story, although I think maybe I will one day. Instead, I have spent my time writing a different book about life and art and beauty and paying attention to it all. "As Stars at Noon" (its working title) is told through the lens of my experience of *Let Us Now Praise Famous Men* (1941), an unclassifiable work by author James Agee and photographer Walker Evans, a sprawling book disguised as a study of southern tenant farming in the Depression-era South, but in truth a prose poem echoing the very themes I was writing about. Even though I had just committed the ultimate act of my story, I wasn't sure how to end my book until deep one night in 2019 Hambidge's Foxfire Studio when, suddenly, I was certain. I was awakened from a dream by an animal cry I had never heard, the same one (I learned by researching) that Agee and an imagined Evans heard in the last pages of their book. In my dream, I had been having a graveside conversation with a man, and as I awoke I thought perhaps the cry I had heard was part of that dream. But then, beside the very real embers sighing in the very real fire dying in my fireplace, I heard it again, an urgent, plaintive, wild sound, a shrill and insistent cry from the woods behind the cabin. It was a fox—an unmistakable sound—and though I had read about it in the

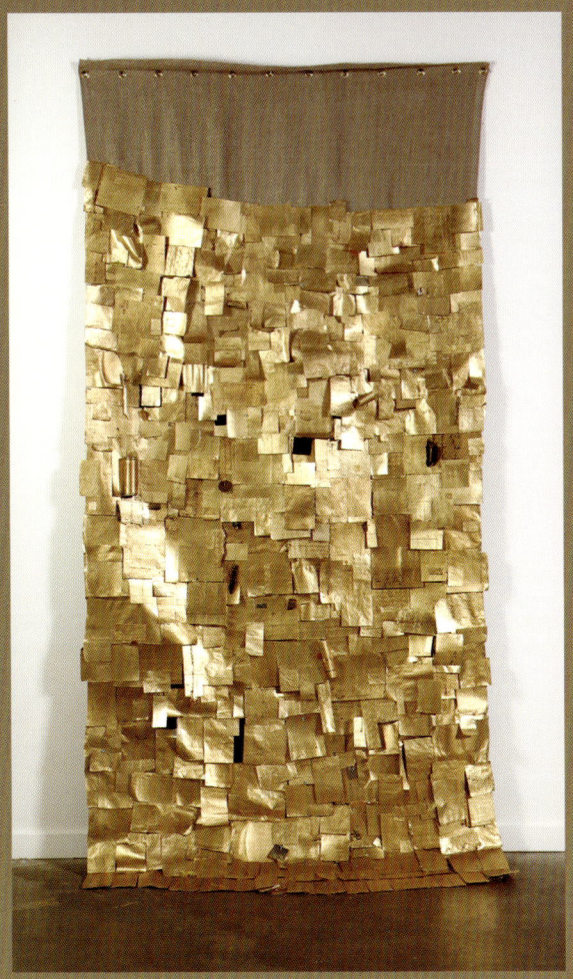

Donna Mintz, *Nothing Gold Can Stay*, 2019, composition gold leaf, found objects, cotton thread, 23ᴋ gold thread on linen, 118 × 56 in. Photograph by Mike Jensen, courtesy of Donna Mintz and Sandler Hudson Gallery

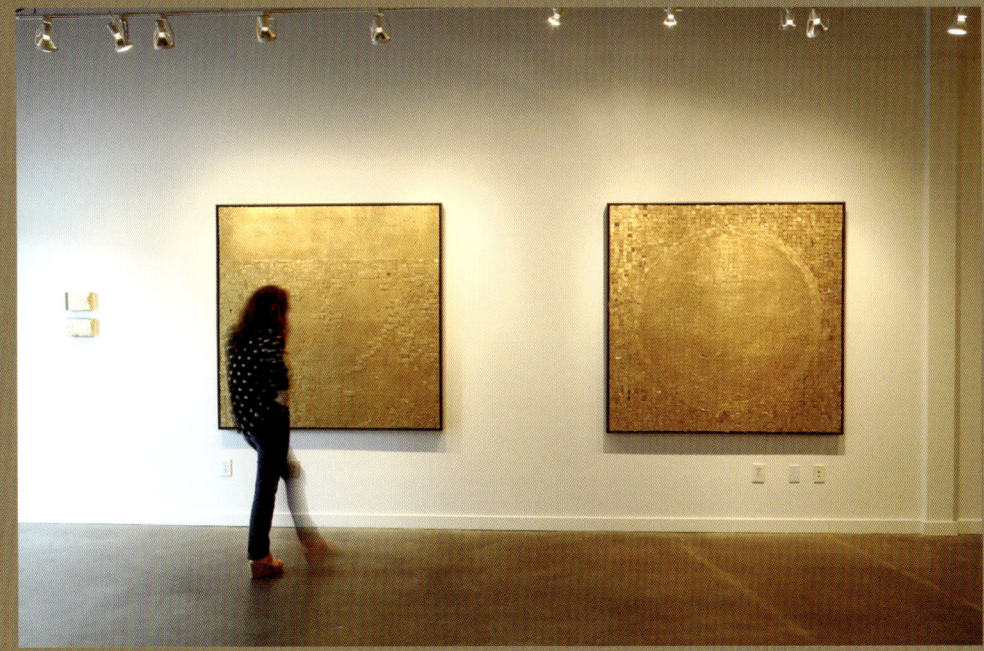

Left, Donna Mintz, *Reliquary for Blue Sky*, 2018; *right*, Donna Mintz, *Reliquary for All Those Words*, 2018–2019. Both works are oil, collage of found and personal papers, composition gold leaf, mineral pigment on canvas, 61.25 × 61.25 in. Photograph by Mike Jensen, courtesy of Donna Mintz and Sandler Hudson Gallery

closing pages of *Famous Men*, this was the first time I had ever heard it myself. Experiencing what Agee described as the "frightening joy of hearing the world talk to itself," I knew the world was talking to me as well.[4] Hearing the fox wasn't a coincidence; it was meant to be. *That's* what inspiration feels like: a validation and a certainty of direction, which artists so rarely feel, and it is always a gift, always a wonder. It's what happens at the Hambidge Center.

I am one person telling one true story, but everyone who goes there has a version of her own. The stories are legion, as varied as the ways of creativity itself, but you have seen the results. The paintings, the plays, the books, the music that has soothed or excited you—all may well have begun there. As time winds down on one's residency, everyone has the same lament, "I wish I could take Hambidge home with me." But that's just it, you can't. You have to go to Hambidge who, after all, always accepts her own. Writing this last sentence, I feel a frisson of recognition. *This* is what I was supposed to tell you.

There is a coda to the story of the Hambidge Center. The center temporarily closed to the public during the height of the pervasive COVID-19 pandemic. Staff members worked during the downtime to prepare for reopening under new safety guidelines. For the first time, the mandate to gather for dinner was suspended. Chef Lori prepared sack dinners for each resident and left them in the dining room for each to take back to their cabin or to sit at a distance in the covered, open-air pavilion beside the Rock House. Operations Manager Christine Jason sewed facial coverings, which were given to each artist on arrival and, for the foreseeable future, will be worn in all public spaces.

In better news, under the leadership and vision of Executive Director Jamie Badoud, the center has embarked on Hambidge 2.0, a transformative capital campaign designed to create a more sustainable future and to preserve Hambidge's legacy and dynamic role in the region's art community. There will be improvements to all existing studios and a new Antinori Village, which will offer eight new spaces incorporating Mary's dogtrot-style floor plan as inspiration. It is to be developed for multiple uses, allowing for public and private programming while preserving the traditional campus as a protected space, thus expanding the center's presence and reach.

While the Hambidge Center is already a mountain home for creative genius, the new campaign will ensure that more people will know about it and benefit from it. In the week before the 2016 fire, Badoud and his staff removed

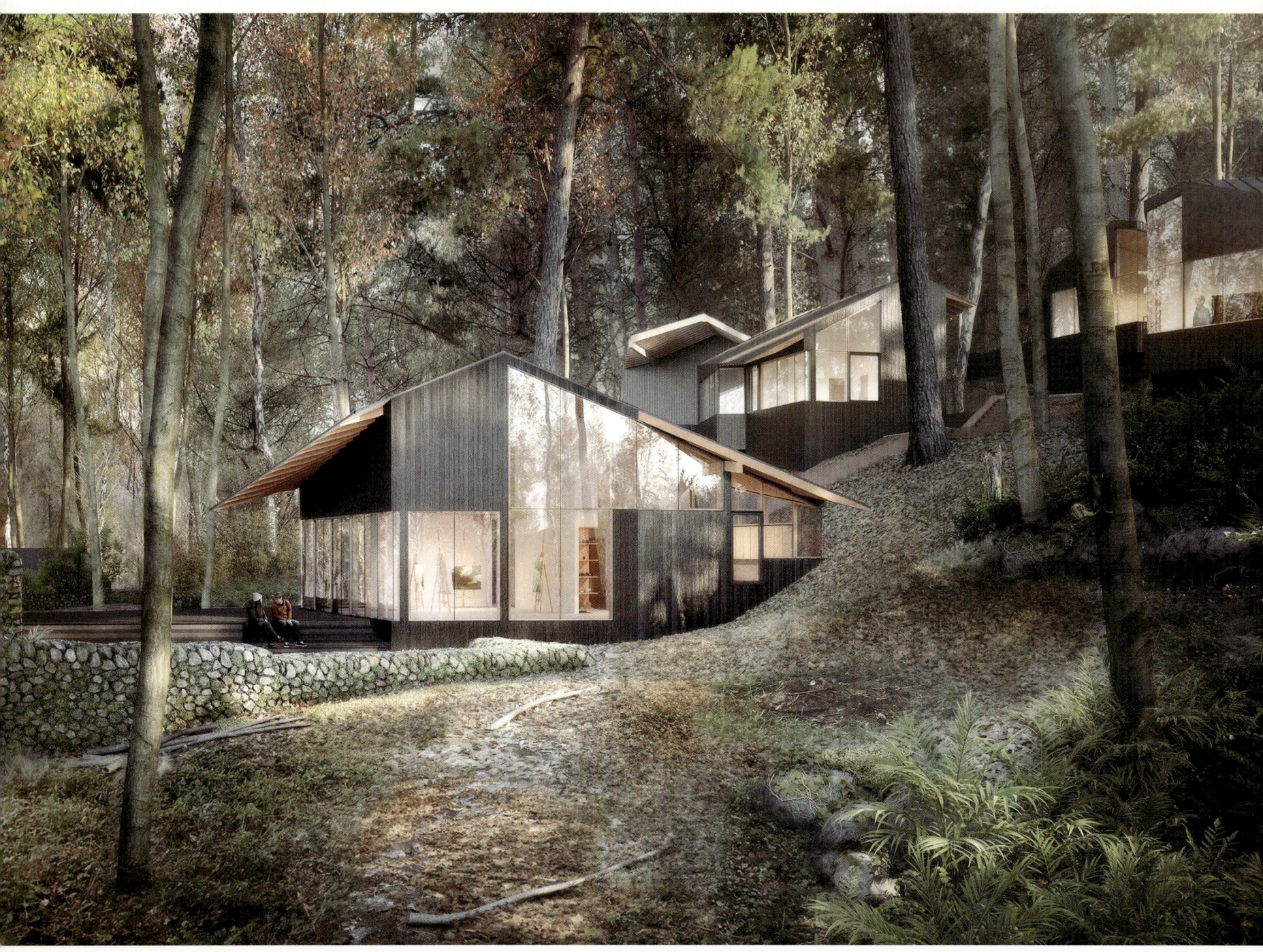

Artist rendering of the Antinori Village, part of
Hambidge 2.0. Image by ʙʟᴅɢs | DarcStudio

historic documents and artifacts from the site, including Mary Hambidge's precious weaving looms, pieces of furniture, pottery, and books. Among the hundreds of books given by "writers who have sunk their souls into them," now shelved in the home that was Mary Hambidge's, Badoud found the inspiration he needed: a dedication that offered special comfort and assurance that all would be well, regardless.[5] Not long after Badoud began his tenure as executive director in the summer of 2009, poet and Hambidge Fellow Sean Hill left his book of poems *Blood Ties & Brown Liquor*, with an inscription to Jamie and the Hambidge Center: "Thank you for the support. Here's to the memories that sustain us."

At a time when he especially needed it, Badoud was reminded of something he already knew. The most important component at Hambidge is the sustenance that people—artists specializing in dance, music, theater, visual and literary arts, or science from around the globe—take from a residency there. A sustaining sense of purpose ensures that Hambidge lives in them and in their work wherever they take it. "The beauty of that is that what's most important [about Hambidge] carries forward," Badoud said, "so that Hambidge is growing in new communities across the world," leaving a better one than we found.[6] In this time of change and turmoil, is there anything more we could ask of our arts than that?

CONCLUSION

The story of Jay Hambidge and Mary Crovatt Hambidge is fascinating, complex, and important to examine within the context of change and innovation in twentieth-century American art, design, and culture. Born during the last decades of the nineteenth century, they both lived through a world war and a pandemic while experiencing a national culture transitioning toward industrial dominance along with a growing divisiveness and diversity in American and European artistic circles. After Jay's death in 1924, Mary lived through a global depression, another world war, the Cold War, and the Vietnam War, and she saw developments in American art ranging from non-objective art to the Appalachian craft revival. Jay's and Mary's understanding and interpretation of ancient Greek art and culture was the foundation that united them and guided their endeavors.

Jay Hambidge and Mary Crovatt Hambidge collectively and separately had an impact on early twentieth-century art and design through their near-obsessive admiration for ancient Greek innovations in architecture and textiles. They sought to revive what they understood about this past by advancing it in their own work and by teaching it to others. They were artists sometimes on the periphery, sometimes in the center of developments in American art and design, and each contributed a new approach to traditional arts: Jay by maintaining a dedication to pictorial accuracy while proposing new ways to introduce the principles of Dynamic Symmetry to the decorative arts, and Mary by embracing handcrafts and promoting Dynamic Symmetry as a way to achieve a holistic lifestyle.

New facts, a more detailed timeline, and new insights from archival documents and images provide a deeper understanding of the lives and works of this eccentric couple. They began the twentieth century determined to make a mark; over the next decades they each found their calling.

What would Jay have accomplished had he not suddenly died in 1924? Would he have been able to apply his theories to the commercial enterprises he envisioned? Would he have written more books, perhaps with clearer instructions for students? He wrote in 1902: "I will have to take a great deal of care in preparing my paper so as to get the idea simply presented, because of the difficulty the ordinary mind has of comprehending a geometrical construction."[1] Yet many readers of his work had trouble comprehending his formulas and explanations, which may account for his relative obscurity later in the century.

What would Mary have done had she not received generous lifetime financial sponsorship from Eleanor Steele Reese? Would she have found other benefactors? Would she have continued to create fashionable Greek-inspired clothing of handwoven wool and silk in a time when textiles were becoming more industrialized and clothing was becoming more ready-to-wear? This type of speculation points to the amazing set of historical conditions that allowed them to accomplish what they did.

Jay Hambidge was a skilled illustrator who sought to codify a way of mathematically formalizing two-dimensional visual compositions based on his understanding of ancient Greek architectural designs and proportions. He was an author, teacher, speaker, and idealist. He held fast to his belief that painting and drawing should be representational, but he had ideas for utilizing his theories in the applied arts, which were later adopted by those working in industrial art and design. Mary was an accomplished weaver who perceived herself as a revivalist and naturalist; her identity revolved around her mastery of weaving and the dyeing of thread as well as her determination to create a functioning artistic community. She retreated from her cosmopolitan early adulthood into the life of a rural pioneer, speaking her mind through letters, poems, and lectures at every opportunity, all while creating finely constructed cloth in brilliantly dyed colors. Together they contributed to the changing face of American art in the twentieth century. This book has offered a better understanding of their accomplishments through a critical examination of their lives.

The Hambidges' legacy continues to evolve at the Hambidge Center for Creative Arts and Sciences. The chapters by Tommye Scanlin and Donna Mintz draw attention to the importance of artist residency programs, which provide dedicated workspaces, uninterrupted time to create and think, venues to exhibit and discuss work, and opportunities for creative collaboration. The Hambidge Center offers all of these things and more. Along with the carefully organized archives and object collections at the Atlanta History Center and the Hargrett Rare Book and Manuscript Library at the University of Georgia, the Hambidge Center contributes to the Hambidges' legacy by making materials available to scholars and artists and by providing a supportive place to work, thus fulfilling one of the goals that Jay Hambidge and Mary Crovatt Hambidge sought to achieve.

1867	Edward John "Jay" Hambidge born in Simcoe, Ontario, Canada, to George Hambidge and Christina Shields. He has eight siblings: Emma, Margaret (Maggie), Charles, Sarah (Sally), Cecelia (Celia), Della (Delia), Evelyn (Eva), and George, who died young.
1883	Jay Hambidge moves to the Midwest, first to Council Bluffs, Iowa, to work as a draftsman, and later to Kansas City, where he finds work as a printer's apprentice for the *Kansas City Times*.
1885	Mary Lee Crovatt born in Brunswick, Georgia, to Alfred J. Crovatt and Mary Lee Schlatter.
1888	Jay begins his career as a newspaper reporter for the *Kansas City Star*.
1889	Jay marries Cordella Selina DeLorme in Council Bluffs, Iowa. They have four children together.
1890s	Jay and Cordella move to New York City, then to Amityville, Long Island.
c. 1890s	Jay meets Peter McArthur, a neighbor in Amityville. Peter becomes editor of *Truth* magazine and hires Hambidge to illustrate. They develop a theory of design linking natural growth patterns of plants to the proportions of Classic Greek architecture, which becomes the foundation for Hambidge's theory of Dynamic Symmetry.
1893	Eleanor Steele is born in New York City.

1897	Jay is listed as attending the Chase School of Art, and he also attends the Art Students League in New York.
1900–1904	Jay exhibits at the Paris Exposition Universelle, the Pan-American Exposition, and the Louisiana Purchase Exposition.
1901–1904	Mary attends the Lee School for Girls, an academic finishing school in Cambridge, Massachusetts.
1902	In March, Jay moves the family to London to work on a project for *Century* with Peter McArthur. They plan to start a magazine, the *Originator*, focused on their design theory. Jay meets museum professionals and scholars of Greek architecture, including Francis Penrose, author of *An Investigation of the Principles of Athenian Architecture*.
1902	Jay presents his paper "The Natural Basis of Form in Greek Art" to the London Hellenic Studies Society in November.
1902	Jay shares the success of his paper in a six-page letter to Richard Gilder of *Century*.
c. 1902–1903	Jay and Peter McArthur have a creative and philosophical falling-out.
1903	*Journal of Hellenic Studies* publishes a summary of Jay's paper "The Natural Basis of Form in Greek Art."
1903	In February, the family moves back to New York, living in Richmond Hill, Queens, with Jay's studio nearby. Jay continues his career as a magazine and book illustrator for *Century*, *Collier's*, *Harper's*, *McClure's*, and *Truth*.
1903	Arthur Wesley Dow publishes *Composition: A Series of Exercises in Art Structure for the Use of Students and Teachers*.
1905–1909	Mary frequently appears in the society pages of newspapers in Atlanta, Brunswick, and Savannah, Georgia.
1907	Denman Waldo Ross publishes *A Theory of Pure Design: Harmony, Balance, Rhythm*.
1909	A *Century* article features Hambidge's illustrations *The Strait of Messina Looking North* and *Eastern Coast of Sicily*.

c. 1909	Mary begins to travel from Brunswick to New York. In New York, she pursues a career in acting, artist's modeling, and professional whistling.
c. 1910	Jay establishes an unsuccessful photography business in New York City.
1911	Mary earns a certificate from a whistling course taught by Mrs. Alice Shaw.
1911	Jay works at Carlton Illustrators agency in the Flatiron Building.
1913	Mary performs a whistling solo of "In Venice" at the Confederate Reunion Ball at the Oglethorpe Hotel in Brunswick.
1913	Jay visits the International Exhibition of Modern Art, also known as the Armory Show.
1914	Mary performs with her mockingbird, Jimmy, in New York.
1914	Jay and Gove publish "The Ancestry of Cubism" in *Century*.
1914	Jay moves his studio to New York City and begins living with two of his sisters there. Cordella and the two youngest children move in with her mother in Stockton, California.
1914	Jay meets Mary Lee Crovatt in New York.
1914	Jay develops a system of dyeing colors and making color charts for applied arts, such as rugs.
1914	Jay establishes a working relationship with New York furniture and decorative art dealer Miss Traver of C. M. Traver and Co. to provide color sketches and designs for the company's rug, tapestry, and upholstery division.
1914–1915	Mary lives at 257 West 86th Street and then at 12 Gramercy Park, New York.
1914–1924	Jay spends considerable time working on Dynamic Symmetry, a theory connecting nature and art through geometry.
c. 1917	Jay begins to study and measure the proportions of Greek vases with assistance from Gisela Richter, curator in the Department of Greek and Roman Arts at the Metropolitan Museum of Art, and Lacey D. Caskey, head of the Antiquities Department at the Museum of Fine Arts, Boston.

1917–1924	Jay lectures in New York, Boston, Chicago, and New Haven, and he creates a subscription course on Dynamic Symmetry. He develops a following of artists and illustrators, many from the Salmagundi Club in New York City.
1917	Mary's last-known whistling performance is at the home of Mrs. Charles Alexander in New York.
1918–1919	Jay receives a Samuel Sachs Research Fellowship at Harvard University to study human anatomy and Greek vases.
1919–1920	Jay's monthly publication, the *Diagonal*, runs for twelve issues, November 1919–October 1920.
1919–1921	Jay delivers papers in London at the Hellenic Studies Society.
1920	Jay's will designates Mary Lee Crovatt as executor and sole recipient of all of his property.
1920	George Bellows publishes "The Relation of Painting to Architecture," in which he defends Jay and writes about Dynamic Symmetry as an effective and efficient compositional formula.
1920	Tiffany head designer Albert Southwick utilizes the Dynamic Symmetry rectangle for storefront and object designs.
1920	Jay receives funds from Yale University and Yale University Press to travel to Athens, Greece, to measure Classic Greek temples.
1920	*Dynamic Symmetry: The Greek Vase* is published by Yale University Press.
1920	Mary attends French language classes in Paris before meeting Jay there and then traveling with him to Athens, Greece.
1920–1921	Mary is introduced to weaving at an establishment managed by Kyria Elene Avramea. She meets Eva Palmer Sikelianos, who becomes a lifelong friend.
1921	While in Greece, Mary begins a weaving notebook documenting her designs.
1921	Jay leaves Athens to embark on his most important lecture circuit; Mary stays in Athens until the fall.
1921	Maxwell Armfield publishes "Dynamic Symmetry and Its Practical Value Today."

1921	Jay writes to Mary about starting a weaving and craft enterprise to "put Dynamic Symmetry into the designs."
1921	Jay delivers the annual Scammon Lectures at the Art Institute of Chicago. His six-part series is titled "Dynamic Symmetry in Design."
1921	The League of New York Artists hosts a reception for Jay on May 10.
1921	Rhys Carpenter publishes "Dynamic Symmetry: A Criticism" in the *American Journal of Archaeology.*
1922–1929	Mary records over forty-five individual designs for dresses, coats, cloaks, and capes.
1922	Papers are recorded in Florida for the divorce of Jay and Cordella.
1922	Gisela Richter defends Hambidge's *Dynamic Symmetry: The Greek Vase*, writing that he found a "working scheme of Greek design."
1923	*Dynamic Symmetry in Composition as Used by the Artists* is published.
1923	George Parmly Day, president of Yale University Press, congratulates Jay on his recent marriage.
1924	Jay passes away at the age of fifty-seven on January 20 from a stroke while delivering a lecture.
1924	*The Parthenon and Other Greek Temples: Their Dynamic Symmetry* is published. In the preface, Caskey praises Jay's theory of Dynamic Symmetry.
1924	Denman Ross publishes "In Memoriam, Jay Hambidge" in the *Boston Transcript.*
1924	Chrysler Corporation uses the Dynamic Symmetry formula in the designs for the Chrysler Six series of automobiles.
1924–1939	Mary lives intermittently in New York City and Greenwich, Connecticut. Eva lives with Mary in Connecticut during various periods in the 1930s.
1926	Gordon Hosiery Company presents the new Gordon V Line Heel, which is described as "a stocking based on the ancient Greek principle of dynamic symmetry."

1927	Charles Mears writes a series of articles for *Women's Wear Daily*, "Application of Dynamic Symmetry to Advertising Proportions."
1927	Mary visits Rabun County and begins extended visits to Georgia. She rents a cabin, Twin Tops, in Mountain City, Georgia, and encounters Appalachian spinners and weavers. She forms a weaving collective.
c. 1928–1930	Mary meets Eleanor Steele, a wealthy arts patron and opera singer.
1930	Eleanor Steele and opera singer Hall Clovis are married.
1931	Mary designs the costumes for a production of Bach's *The Contest between Phoebus and Pan* at the Little Theater Opera Company of New York, featuring Eleanor Steele and Hall Clovis. Mary alternates living in Greenwich, Connecticut; New York City; and northeastern Georgia.
1934–1935	Mary assists Eva in weaving over one hundred costumes for her production of *The Bacchae*, performed at Bryn Mawr and Smith Colleges.
1935–1936	Mary organizes two exhibitions of woven work by the Appalachian women in New York City and at the Greenwich library.
1936	Mary leases a former hunting club retreat on Berry's Creek Road in Rabun Gap, Georgia; expands her weaving enterprise; and forms the Weavers of Rabun with monthly support from Eleanor Steele.
1937	Steele funds the start-up of a boutique in New York City selling work by Mary and the Weavers of Rabun, at first renting some temporary spaces on Madison Avenue before the official establishment of Rabun Studios at 810 Madison Avenue in 1938. Mary divides her time between Georgia, Connecticut, and New York.
1937	Mary wins a gold medal for handwoven textiles at the Paris International Exposition of Art and Technology in Modern Life.
1937–1960	Faye Thompson is the weaving studio manager.
1938	Mary visits the weaving program that Anni Albers directs at Black Mountain College.

1938	Walter Rendell Storey publishes "New Fabrics to Fit Period or Modern Rooms: Colors and Textures Reveal the Craftsman."
1939	Steele provides Mary with the funds to purchase the Betty's Creek property, which Mary refers to as the Jay Hambidge Art Foundation.
1940	Eleanor Steele and Hall Clovis divorce.
1940s	Hall Clovis and Charles Lee take a larger role in the Rabun Studios management. Mary divides her time between New York City and Rabun Gap.
1941	Eleanor Steele marries Emmet Reese, a cattle rancher, and moves to Idaho.
1941–1942	The Jay Hambidge School of Dynamic Symmetry and Weaving offers classes in weaving and crafts.
1941–1944	Eva lives with Mary at the Hambidge Center.
1944	The Jay Hambidge Art Foundation is officially incorporated.
1944	Mary has a gristmill built on the property.
1945	The Weavers of Rabun provide the drapery and upholstery fabric for President Truman's yacht, the uss *Williamsburg*.
1947	Yale University Press purchases sixty-five yards of fabric from the Weavers of Rabun to cover reprints of books by Jay Hambidge.
1947	Knoll Textiles is established.
1948–1953	Architect Philip Johnson places two orders for textiles from the Weavers of Rabun.
1949	The *New Yorker* publishes "On and Off the Avenue," in which the textiles and crafts at Rabun Studios are praised.
1950	Frances Forbes Ison publishes "The Weavers of Rabun," in which she describes Mary's talent for creating dyes.
1950s	Mary becomes increasingly disenchanted with the modern world and the encroachment of industrialization.
1950s	Mary cuts back on the amount of custom orders for the Weavers of Rabun.
1952	Brooks Wigginton plans a foundation prospectus and a board of directors for the Jay Hambidge Art Foundation.

1953	The Herman Miller textile division is established with Alexander Girard as the director.
1953–1955	Rabun Studios contributes sixteen works to the traveling exhibition *American Design for Home and Decorative Use* organized by the Museum of Modern Art.
1955	Rabun Studios relocates to 31 East 67th Street, and advertisements describe the shop as "Rabun Studios, American Arts and Crafts."
1956	Georgia O'Keeffe sends Mary some Peruvian alpaca wool with a request to have "a piece of fine material made from it for me."
1956	Weavers of Rabun textiles are featured in the *Textiles USA* exhibition at the Museum of Modern Art.
1957	The state of Georgia begins to widen and pave Betty's Creek Road, to which Mary strongly objects.
1958	Weavers of Rabun textiles are featured in an exhibition in the rotunda of the Arts and Industries Building of the Smithsonian Institution.
1958	Lees Carpet opens a plant in Rabun Gap, contributing to the depletion of Mary's workforce.
1958	Hall Clovis and Eleanor Steele Reese discontinue funding Rabun Studios. Mary relinquishes supervision. Store manager Josephine Kirpal continues to operate the shop under the Rabun Studios name. Mary takes legal action to close the operation.
1959	Andrew Ritchie publishes *Sketches of Rabun County History, 1819–1948*.
1960s–1973	Mary embraces folk and craft revivalism and seeks ways to turn the Hambidge Foundation into a working community centered on art, crafts, agriculture, and ancient Greece.
1969	Gove Hambidge writes his unpublished memoir, "Something in My Genes."
1973	Mary passes away on August 29.
1974	The Jay Hambidge Art Foundation is renamed the Hambidge Center for Creative Arts and Sciences and becomes a residential art program.

1980s   The Hambidge Center for Creative Arts and Sciences begins to offer classes on a variety of subjects and introduces other programming.

1984   The Hambidge Center reissues *Apprentice in Creation: The Way Is Beauty*, a compilation of Mary's writings assembled by her friend Aspasia Voulis.

NOTES

Abbreviations

AAA   Jay and Mary Crovatt Hambidge Papers, 1841–1973, Archives of
American Art, Smithsonian Institution, Washington, D.C.

AHC   Mary and Jay Hambidge Papers, Atlanta History Center Collections,
and Kenan Research Center at the Atlanta History Center

HCCAS   Hambidge Center for Creative Arts and Sciences, Rabun Gap, Ga.

UGA   Mary Hambidge Papers, 1885–1973; and Jay Hambidge Art Foundation
Papers, Hargrett Rare Book and Manuscript Library, University of
Georgia Libraries, Athens

Introduction. Jay Hambidge and Mary Lee Crovatt Hambidge

1   Jay Hambidge's publications include the periodical the *Diagonal*; *Dynamic
Symmetry: Fifteen Plates and Text Which Explain Some of the More Obvious
Principles of the Areas Used in Greek Design*; *Dynamic Symmetry: The
Greek Vase*; and *Dynamic Symmetry in Composition as Used by the Artists*.
Posthumous publications include *The Parthenon and Other Greek Temples:
Their Dynamic Symmetry*; *Elements of Dynamic Symmetry*, a compilation
of articles from the *Diagonal*; and *Practical Applications of Dynamic
Symmetry*, a compilation of his lectures from 1921.

2   Unpublished and undated memoirs, AHC, box 19, folder 8.

3   Leontis, *Eva Palmer Sikelianos*.

4   Jay Hambidge to Richard Gilder, December 18, 1902, Manuscripts and
Archives Division, New York Public Library; "Hambidge, Jay," New York
Public Library Digital Collections, https://digitalcollections.nypl.org/items

/097ac5c0-2f82-0135-2fff-237e4b48e912#/?uuid=098fa350-2f82-0135-b9cf
-4f1aafc979a7.

5   Green, "Promise and Peril."

6   Alvic, *Weavers of the Southern Highlands*; Kessler, "From Mission to Market."

7   Quoted in Eliot Wigginton, "Mary Hambidge," *Foxfire* 7, no. 3 (Fall 1973): 5.

8   Shevzov, "Art Expression"; Koplos and Metcalf, *Makers*.

9   Shevzov, "Art Expression," 101; letter from Georgia O'Keeffe to Mrs. Hambidge, October 16, 1956, AHC, box 45, folder 3.

10   Address to the Rotary Club, Clayton, Ga., July 22, 1954, AHC, box 19, folder 9.

11   Albers, "Work with Materials," 2.

12   Wigginton, "Mary Hambidge," *Foxfire* 7, no. 3 (Fall 1973): 8.

13   Troy, *Anni Albers*, includes an extensive discussion of this phenomenon as it relates to textiles and design.

14   Studies of Mary Hambidge include Philis Alvic, "The Weavers of Rabun," in her *Weavers of the Southern Highlands*; Magee, "Mary Hambidge"; Troy, "Great Weaver of Eternity"; Starnes, "Mary Crovatt Hambidge."

15   Walter, "Jay Hambidge and the Development," 1–8.

16   Jaffee, "Before the New Bauhaus."

17   Troy, *Modernist Textile*, includes an extensive discussion of this issue.

Chapter 1. Nineteenth-Century Foundations, Twentieth-Century Lives

The epigraph is from Mary Crovatt Hambidge, undated manuscript, Rabun Gap, Ga., AHC, box 19, folder 6.

1   Eliot Wigginton, "Mary Hambidge," *Foxfire* 7, no. 3 (Fall 1973): 2.

2   May 25, 1914, July 13, 1914, AHC, box 5, folder 1; August 1, 1914, October 15, 1914, UGA, MS3265, box 1, folder 2. See also Alvic, *Weavers of the Southern Highlands*, 97.

3   Jay Hambidge to Mary Crovatt, July 13, 1914, UGA, MS3265, box 1, folder 2.

4   Howard Giles Papers, Syracuse University, box 1; George Parmly Day to Jay Hambidge, June 23, 1923, AHC, box 24, folder 5.

5   Divorce decree, AHC, box 4, folder 2.

6   Jay's will of June 11, 1920, AHC, box 24, folder 5. In his unpublished 1967 memoir, Gove Hambidge, a son of Jay and Cordella, wrote, "At some time, I never knew when or where, he must have obtained a divorce and married Mary Cravatt [*sic*], a dancer who had been posing for him (I met her in the studio occasionally) who later was well known as a weaver." Gove Hambidge, "Something in My Genes," 91.

7   "Famous Son of Simcoe Dies Suddenly in New York," *Simcoe Reformer*, January 31, 1924, 1.

8   Mark Hambidge Brewer, "Chronology of Jay Hambidge," 2017, Hambidge Center for Creative Arts and Sciences, Rabun Gap, Ga.

9   *Who's Who in America*, vol. 3 (1903), 632.

10   Gove Hambidge, "Something in My Genes," 3–4.

11   Lucas, *Peter McArthur*, 16–20.

12   Pisano, *Students of William Merritt Chase*, 16. Walter, "Jay Hambidge and the Development," states that the short period of study with Chase may have been in 1900 or 1901. Chase taught at the Chase School of Art, which became the New York School of Art, from 1896 to 1907; he taught at the Art Students League from 1878 to 1896 and from 1907 to 1911.

13   Lucas, *Peter McArthur*, 58–60.

14   *New York Tribune*, March 15, 1902, 8. Thanks to Mark Hambidge Brewer for the manifest of the ship's passengers.

15   Jay Hambidge to Peter McArthur, July 1902, McArthur Papers, subseries 1.1, University of Western Ontario (excerpt courtesy of Mark Hambidge Brewer).

16   *Journal of Hellenic Studies* 23 (1903): xxxvii. Elizabeth Walter in her 1978 dissertation, "Jay Hambidge and the Development," 44–45, noted the paper as "Symmetry Found in Saracenic and Medieval Art."

17   Lucas, *Peter McArthur*, 60.

18   Jay Hambidge to Richard Gilder, December 18, 1902, Manuscripts and Archives Division, New York Public Library; "Hambidge, Jay," New York Public Library Digital Collections, https://digitalcollections.nypl.org/items/097ac5c0-2f82-0135-2fff-237e4b48e912#/?uuid=098fa350-2f82-0135-b9cf-4f1aafc979a7.

19   Gove Hambidge, "Something in My Genes," 88–89.

20   Walter, "Jay Hambidge and the Development," 49, states that *Century* sent him to Girgenti in 1902, yet in her chronology she notes the date as 1903–1904 (176).

21   William Sharp to Richard Gilder, June 3, 1893, in Halloran, *Life and Letters*, 1:493.

22   Sharp, "Garden of the Sun," 43.

23   March 22, 1920, AAA, box 3176, no. 1016.

24   Jay Hambidge to Robert Johnson of *Century*, April 4, 1911, Manuscripts and Archives Division, New York Public Library; "Hambidge, Jay," New York Public Library Digital Collections, https://archives.nypl.org/mss/504#c1144331.

25   Walter, "Jay Hambidge and the Development," 34.

26   Kaplan, *Art That Is Life*, 307.

27   Frank, *Denman Ross*.

28   Jaffee, "Before the New Bauhaus"; Ayres et al., *American Arts and Crafts Textiles*, 35–51.

29   Hambidge and Hambidge, "Ancestry of Cubism."

30   Gove Hambidge, "Something in My Genes," 89–92.

31   Obituary of Susan Abbott: "Sudden Death of Old Servant—For Many Years a Faithful Servant in Family of Judge Crovatt," *Brunswick Journal*, January 18, 1909.

32   Knight, *Standard History of Georgia*, 2806.

33   *Savannah Morning News*, September 7, 1902, 18.

34   AHC, box 15, folders 2–8.

35   *Biographical Souvenir*, 204–205.

36   *Jekyll Island Club Charter, Constitution, By-Laws, and Members* (New York: Cunningham, 1887), 4.

37   *Atlanta Journal*, January 6, 1905, C7.

38   *Atlanta Journal*, February 12, 1905, C3; July 23, 1905, D6; December 17, 1905, A7; June 2, 1907, B3; August 30, 1908, D1; December 27, 1908, B3; May 30, 1909, C6.

39   AHC, box 17, folder 2.

40   AHC, VIS 1.01, 02, 03.

41   *Atlanta Journal*, July 27, 1913, C9.

42   Quoted in Alvic, *Weavers of the Southern Highlands*, 96.

43   Her addresses in 1914–1915 included 257 West 86th Street and 12 Gramercy Park. August 19, 1914, April 13, 1915, AHC, box 1, folder 2.

44   *New York Tribune*, April 21, 1917, 11.

45   Letter, n.d., UGA, box 1, folder 4: 1923–1929.

46   April 1914, UGA, box 1, folder 2: 1914–1915.

47   May 1, 1914, UGA, box 1, folder 2: 1914–1915.

Chapter 2. Dynamic Symmetry

The epigraph is from Jay Hambidge, *Dynamic Symmetry in Composition*, 83.

1   Jay Hambidge, *Dynamic Symmetry in Composition*, 76–77.

2   Jay Hambidge, *Dynamic Symmetry in Composition*, 68.

3   Jaffee, "Before the New Bauhaus."

4   Jay Hambidge, *Dynamic Symmetry: The Greek Vase*, 142.

5   Jay Hambidge, *Dynamic Symmetry: The Greek Vase*, 7.

6   Quoted in Jay Hambidge, *Dynamic Symmetry: The Greek Vase*, 73.

7   Jay Hambidge, *Parthenon and Other Greek Temples*, xiii–xxii.

8   Jay's correspondence course subscribers: AHC, box 23, folder 10.

9   Armfield, "Dynamic Symmetry," 78.

10   Maxfield Parrish to Mary Hambidge, December 18, 1925, AHC, box 46, folder 2.

11 Maxfield Parrish to Mary Hambidge, September 3, 1939, AHC, box 46, folder 2.

12 Denman Ross, "In Memoriam, Jay Hambidge," *Boston Transcript*, January 25, 1924, UGA, box 27, folder 4.

13 Founded in 1896 by William Merritt Chase and named the Chase School of Art, it became the New York School of Art (1898–1909), then the New York School of Fine and Applied Art (1909–1936), and is now named the Parsons School of Design.

14 Bellows, "Relation of Painting to Architecture," 851.

15 Bellows, "Relation of Painting to Architecture," 851.

16 Carmean, "Bellows," 39; Bellows, "What Dynamic Symmetry Means," 4–7.

17 Carmean, "Bellows," 41–45; Bellows, "What Dynamic Symmetry Means," 4–7.

18 Jay Hambidge, *Dynamic Symmetry in Composition*, 36.

19 Jay Hambidge, *Dynamic Symmetry in Composition*, 36–37.

20 Edwards, *Pattern and Design*, x.

21 Edwards, *Pattern and Design*, vii.

22 Letters from Jay to Mary, August 12 and August 14, 1914, UGA, box 1, folder 2.

23 Letter from Jay to Mary, August 14, 1914.

24 Course catalogs, PC050101, New School Archives and Special Collections, New York.

25 Jay Hambidge, *Dynamic Symmetry in Composition*, 47.

26 Jay Hambidge, "Dynamic Symmetry and Life Class Work," *Diagonal* 1, no. 7 (May 1920): 138.

27 Howard Giles, "Dynamic Symmetry in the Class Room," *Diagonal* 1, no. 8 (June 1920): 155–160.

28 See *Bulletin of the Art Institute of Chicago* 15, nos. 4–5 (April–May 1921): 148–152.

29 Stahle, "New Key to Art," 107, 122.

30 Richard Guy Wilson, *Machine Age in America*, 131–135.

31 Chrysler Six advertisement, "Dynamic Symmetry in Chrysler Beauty," *House and Garden* 47 (May 1925): 62.

32 *Time*, January 14, 1929, 8.

33 Le Corbusier, "Automobiles."

34 Mears, "Application of Dynamic Symmetry," 3.

35 Frank, *Denman Ross*, 136.

36 Advertisement in *Harper's Bazaar*, n.d., AHC, MSS OS2.376.

37 Jay Hambidge, "Dynamic Symmetry of the Human Figure, Lesson IV," *Diagonal* 1, no. 4 (February 1920): 74.

38 Hay, *Paris to Providence*; Fiorentini, "Collaboration."

39 Jay Hambidge, *Dynamic Symmetry: The Greek Vase*, 11.

40 Carpenter, "Dynamic Symmetry."

41 Carpenter, "Professor Carpenter's Reply," 74–75.

42 Richter, "Dynamic Symmetry."

43 Richter, "Dynamic Symmetry," 60.

44 L. D. Caskey to Jay Hambidge, December 21, 1922, UGA, box 1, folder 3.

45 L. D. Caskey to Jay Hambidge, December 31, 1922, AHC, box 24, folder 4.

46 "Jay Hambidge," *Boston Transcript*, January 1924, typed document, AAA, box 3181, no. 781.

47 Karl K. Kitchen, "Illustrating One of the Three Easiest Ways of Acquiring Fame and Honors in New York City," unidentified newspaper clipping, n.d., AAA, box 3181, no. 963.

48 Kitchen, "Illustrating."

Chapter 3. Mary Crovatt Hambidge and the Formation of Her Handcraft Technique and Philosophy in Greece and New York, 1920–1935

The epigraph is from Jay Hambidge, letter to Mary Crovatt, March 1, 1921, AHC, box 5, folder 7.

1 Letters were addressed in care of Thomas Cook and Son, Athens, a travel company.

2 AHC, box 17, folder 6.

3 Letter from Mary Crovatt Hambidge to Mr. Zikakis, December 20, 1949, "Letter for Broadcast by the Voice of America to Greece," AAA, box 3178, no. 325.

4 Eva lived with Mary in Connecticut for periods in the 1930s and at the Hambidge Center from 1941 to 1944. Mary visited Eva at her apartments in New York in the late 1920s through the 1940s.

5 Leontis, *Eva Palmer Sikelianos*, xxiv; letter from Mary Hambidge to Kyria Elene Avramea, Odos Serifou 38, n.d., AAA, box 3178.

6 Letter from Muriel Noel to Mary Hambidge, April 21, 1921, AHC, box 5, folder 7; letters from Muriel Noel to Mary Hambidge, 1922, UGA, box 1, folder 3.

7 Letters from Jay to Mary, May 4 and May 14, 1921(AHC, box 5, folder 7), implying that Mary was staying with "Mrs. S[ikelianos]," but that Jay did not have Eva's address; letter from Jay to Mary, June 5, 1921 (box 6, folder 7), mentioning that Mary is managing "Mrs. S's" cuisine, "But be careful and not get in too deep with the cuisine."

8 Letters from Jay to Mary, August 12 and August 14, 1914, UGA, box 1, folder 2.

9 Jay Hambidge to Mary Crovatt, n.d., UGA, MS 3265, box 27, folder 2.

10 Morris, "Revival of Handicraft," 176; Kaplan, *Art That Is Life*.

11 Letter from Jay to Mary, June 25, 1921, AHC, box 6, folder 1.

12   Letter from Jay to Mary, August 9, 1921, AHC, box 6, folder 2.

13   Mary Crovatt Hambidge to Mr. Zikakis, "Letter for Broadcast."

14   Mary Hambidge to Mrs. Woodward, July 31, 1938, UGA, box 1, folder 7.

15   Letter from Jay to Mary, July 13, 1921, AHC, box 6, folder 1 ("The getting of Mrs. S's dress plans is a great darling"); letter from Berea College to Miss Croratt [*sic*], March 20, 1923, UGA, box 1, folder 4.

16   Leontis, *Eva Palmer Sikelianos*, 45.

17   Leontis, *Eva Palmer Sikelianos*, 78.

18   Sikelianos, *Upward Panic*, 78, 76.

19   Leontis, *Eva Palmer Sikelianos*, 41–63.

20   Sikelianos, *Upward Panic*, 109.

21   Cleve, "Noel Stitch." I thank Karin Schaller, former administrator at the Hambidge Center, for this information.

22   Jay Hambidge to Mary Crovatt, July 11, 1921, AHC, box 6, folder 1.

23   Undated typed page, UGA, box 27, folder 3.

24   "A Fashion Show," *Spur*, May 1, 1925, UGA, box 1, folder 4.

25   Letter from Mary Crovatt Hambidge to Eva Palmer Sikelianos, November 7, 1925, Eva Sikelianou Papers, accession no. 189, Benaki Museum/Historical Archives, Athens. Many thanks to Artemis Leontis for sending me the correspondence.

26   UGA, box 16, folder 3.

27   Notebook, 35, 41, 61, AHC, box 15, folder 6.

28   Tibol, *José Clemente Orozco*, 9, 102, 248; Leontis, *Eva Palmer Sikelianos*, xl; Jennifer Wilson, "Dynamic Symmetry."

29   Mary Hambidge to Denman Ross, undated letter [before 1929], UGA, box 1, folder 4.

30   Denman Ross to Mary Hambidge, August 31, 1932, UGA, box 1, folder 5.

31   "Cantala and Opera Buff Charm," *New York Times*, February 24, 1931, 28.

32   AHC, VIS. 1.20.

33   Young, *Killinger Collection*.

34   Mary Hambidge to Katherine Dreier, November 14, 1931, Katherine S. Dreier Papers, Société Anonyme Archive, Yale Collection of American Literature, Beinecke Rare Book and Manuscript Library, New Haven, Conn., YCAL MSS 101, box 16, folder 451.

35   Katherine Dreier to Mrs. Hambidge, November 16, 1931, Katherine S. Dreier Papers, Société Anonyme Archive, Yale Collection of American Literature, Beinecke Rare Book and Manuscript Library, New Haven, Conn., YCAL MSS 101, box 16, folder 451. See box 41, 1198, for Mary's letter to Shawn.

36   Correspondence regarding the Rowland House, 116 Field Point Road, where Mary lived from 1932 to 1939, is in AHC, box 6, folder 5. See also "Singers

Acquire Estate," *New York Times*, March 23, 1934, 28. Part of the property was donated to the Greenwich Audubon Center in 1943.

37 Leontis, *Eva Palmer Sikelianos*, 184.

38 Eva met Shawn in 1939 through Dreier. She worked with him in Florida that year on the costumes for *The Persians*, and she loaned Shawn a Delphic Festival costume for a later staging of *Prometheus Bound*. Leontis, *Eva Palmer Sikelianos*, 165–173. Mary has been credited with working on Shawn's *Prometheus Bound*, but there is no evidence of this collaboration.

39 Leontis, *Eva Palmer Sikelianos*, 184–185.

40 Letter from MPG [the woman who rented the Twin Tops cabin to Mary] to Mrs. Hambidge, October 9, 1935, AHC, box 6, folder 3.

41 Mary Crovatt Hambidge to Mr. Zikakis, "Letter for Broadcast."

42 Mary Hambidge, undated manuscript, AHC, box 19, folder 8.

43 Starnes, "Mary Crovatt Hambidge," 56.

44 Mary Hambidge, "Creative Life in the Home," address to the University of Georgia's University Women's Club, June 2, 1950, AHC, box 8, folder 2.

45 Mary Hambidge, "Creative Life in the Home."

Chapter 4. The Weavers of Rabun and Rabun Studios in Historical Context

The epigraph is from Mary Hambidge, "Creative Life in the Home," address to the University of Georgia's University Women's Club, June 2, 1950, 3, AHC, box 8, folder 2.

1 Mary Hambidge to Mrs. Woodward, July 31, 1938, UGA, box 1, folder 7.

2 Eleanor Reese Correspondence, AHC, box 53, folders 1–6: letters from Eleanor Steele Reese to Mary Hambidge (box 52, folder 3) regarding the negotiations for and sale of the Latimer property; receipt from the National Bank of Greenwich, Connecticut, for $6,005.00, February 3, 1939 (box 43, folder 6); lease for the stone house from Latimer for $50 per quarter beginning May 7, 1936 (UGA, box 1, folder 5). See Shevzov, "Art Expression," 59. The foundation was officially incorporated in 1944. After Mary's death 200 acres were sold for funds to maintain the property.

3 Letters from Eleanor Steele Reese to Mary Hambidge, July 8, 1936; April 28, 1938; April 13, 1938; June 20, 1938, AHC, box 52, folder 3.

4 Eleanor Steele Reese to Mary Hambidge, June 2, 1938, AHC, box 52, folder 3.

5 Eleanor Steele Reese to Mary Hambidge, November 21, 1938, AHC, box 52, folder 3.

6 Eleanor Steele Reese to Mary Hambidge, October 14, 1942, AHC, box 52, folder 4.

7 Tax records and foundation records, AHC, box 54, folders 9–10; board minutes, box 35, folder 16.

8   Eleanor Steele Reese to Mary Hambidge, June 4, 1941, AHC, box 52, folder 4.

9   Kaplan, *Art That Is Life*, 298–333; Kessler, "From Mission to Market,"
      127–133.

10   William Frost, letter to Anna Enberg (director of Berea's Fireside Industries),
      1911, William Goodell Frost Papers, Berea College Archives,
      box 10, folder 5. See also Broomfield, "Weaving Social Change."

11   Lucy Morgan, cited by the North Carolina Department of Natural and
      Cultural Resources, www.ncdcr.gov.

12   Alvic, *Weavers of the Southern Highlands*. See also Eaton, *Handicrafts of the
      Southern Highlands*.

13   Alvic, *Weavers of the Southern Highlands*, 1–77.

14   Ball, "Artists in North Georgia Mountains," 1–3.

15   Alvic, *Weavers of the Southern Highlands*, 96–112.

16   There were other enterprises that did not follow convention or tradition.
      For example, Zoltan and Rosa Hecht established the School for the New Age
      in 1924 in Saluda, North Carolina, to train students in creating traditional
      crafts, especially hooked rugs, with modernist designs. See Fowler, *Hooked
      Rugs*.

17   Mary Crovatt Hambidge, *Weavers of Rabun*, 1–3.

18   Ritchie, *Sketches of Rabun County History*, 417–418.

19   Mary Crovatt Hambidge, *Weavers of Rabun*, 1.

20   Mary Hambidge, "Creative Life in the Home."

21   AHC, box 2, folders 1–5.

22   Leontis, *Eva Palmer Sikelianos*, xliii.

23   Anni Albers to Mary Hambidge, February 25, 1938, Josef and Anni Albers
      Foundation, Bethany, Conn.

24   Anni Albers to Theodore Dreier, July 17, 1938 (capitalization and spelling per
      original), Josef and Anni Albers Foundation, Bethany, Conn.

25   Constantine and Larsen, *Art Fabric*; Auther, *String, Felt, Thread*.

26   Alvic, *Weavers of the Southern Highlands*, 102–103.

27   Shevzov, "Art Expression," 75–92.

28   Shevzov, "Art Expression," 67, 81–82.

29   Starnes, "Mary Crovatt Hambidge," 56.

30   Alvic, *Weavers of the Southern Highlands*, 104; Starnes, "Mary Crovatt
      Hambidge," 56.

31   Ison, "Weavers of Rabun," 162.

32   Ison, "Weavers of Rabun," 160.

33   Shevzov, "Art Expression," 97–110.

34   Shevzov, "Art Expression," 111–114.

35   Friedman, *Selling Good Design*.

36   Thompson and Lange, *Design Research*, 11–13, 174–175.

37 Storey, "New Fabrics," sm 14.

38 Shevzov, "Art Expression," 75–79, 91–92.

39 Mundy's contract was drawn in October 1937. ahc, box 46, folder 11.

40 Shevzov, "Art Expression," 75–92; Josephine Kirpal to Eleanor Steele Reese, December 29, 1945, ahc, box 47, folder 3.

41 "On and Off the Avenue," *New Yorker*, September 17, 1949, 82.

42 "On and Off the Avenue," *New Yorker*, November 26, 1949, 94–95.

43 Alvic, *Weavers of the Southern Highlands*, 105; *Williamsburg* order sheet, September 28, 1945, ahc, box 47, folder 3.

44 Alvic, *Weavers of the Southern Highlands*, 105; ahc, box 7, folder 5.

45 Shevzov, "Art Expression," 101.

46 Letter from Georgia O'Keeffe to Mrs. Hambidge, October 16, 1956, ahc, box 45, folder 3.

47 See Riley and Eigen, "Between the Museum"; Koplos and Metcalf, *Makers*; Einik et al., "Collected Essays"; Constantine and Larsen, *Art Fabric*, 7–20.

48 Advertisements in *Craft Horizons* 9, no. 3 (Autumn 1949): 19; *Craft Horizons* 17, no. 1 (February 1957): 4.

49 Inventory of Rabun materials to MoMA, July 8, 1953, Museum of Modern Art Archives, ic/ip I.b.18, ahc, box 39, folder 3.

50 Drexler and Daniels, "Textiles USA," 14–15.

51 Letter from George Christy to Mary Hambidge, September 21, 1956, aaa, box 3178, no. 976.

52 Rabun Studios advertisement, *Craft Horizons* 16, no. 6 (December 1956): 50.

53 Smithsonian Institution, news release, November 4, 1958, ahc, box 53, folder 12.

54 Letter from Grace Rogers to Mrs. Hambidge, October 17, 1958, ahc, box 53, folder 12.

55 Draft of a letter, n.d., aaa, box 3179, no. 677.

56 Petition, May 27, 1957, aaa, box 3179, no. 750.

57 Williams, "Southern Appalachians," 66.

58 Josephine Kirpal to Eleanor Reese, May 13, 1958, ahc, box 52, folder 7.

59 Alvic, *Weavers of the Southern Highlands*, 107; Josephine Kirpal to Eleanor Reese, November 8, 1958, ahc, box 52, folder 7.

60 Troy, "Textiles as the Face."

61 Eight-page prospectus, December 14, 1952, ahc, box 56, folder 2; school pamphlets, ahc, mss.os.4.91.

62 Letter from Frank Coleman to Mary Hambidge, November 25, 1970, aaa, box 3178, no. 1295.

63 Mary Crovatt Hambidge, "I am My Destiny, I am the Weaver," ahc, box 17, folder 8. See also Mary Crovatt Hambidge, *Apprentice in Creation*, 77.

Chapter 5. Memories of Hambidge Center Experiences

1   One Hundredth Anniversary of Mary Crovatt Hambidge: 1985 Calendar of Events, brochure in possession of Scanlin.

2   "Biography," American Tapestry Alliance, https://americantapestryalliance .org/exhibitions/tex_ata/jean-pierre-larochette-yael-lurie-a-study-in -national-treasures/biography/ (accessed April 27, 2020).

3   "Jean Pierre Larochette & Yael Lurie: A Study in National Treasures," American Tapestry Alliance, https://americantapestryalliance.org /exhibitions/tex_ata/jean-pierre-larochette-yael-lurie-a-study-in-national -treasures/ (accessed April 27, 2020).

4   Press release, n.d., Hambidge Center, Rabun Gap, Ga. This press release and the registration form for the workshop are in the writer's personal collection.

5   Marois's website, http://www.marcelmarois.com/index.php/en/ (accessed February 2, 2020); press release, n.d., Hambidge Center. The press release and workshop details are from the files of Janet Hart, Williamsburg, Va. Hart was one of the participants in the workshop.

6   Brennan's tapestries are the subject of an online exhibition curated by Anna Byrd Mays. "Archie Brennan," American Tapestry Alliance, https:// americantapestryalliance.org/exhibitions/tex_ata/archie-brennan / (accessed January 23, 2020).

7   Pat Williams, text message to author, January 11, 2020; *Pat Williams Makes Things*, https://www.patwilli.com/ (accessed February 2, 2020).

8   "Bio," https://www.garza-cuen.com/bio (accessed January 24, 2020).

9   Jennifer Garza-Cuen, email to author, April 27, 2020.

10 *Killers of the Dream* was a finalist for the National Book Award in nonfiction in 1950. "1950 Winners: Nonfiction," National Book Foundation, https:// www.nationalbook.org/awards-prizes/national-book-awards-1950/?cat =nonfiction (accessed January 23, 2020).

11 Bass, "Strange Life of Strange Fruit."

12 See https://www.piedmont.edu/lilliansmith-resources#other (accessed February 1, 2020).

13 Letter from Lillian Smith to parents, August 9, 1947, Piedmont College Archives, Demorest, Ga., https://www.piedmont.edu/files/docs/Letter -from-LES-to-camper-parents-08-09-1947appended.pdf (accessed January 10, 2020).

14 "Lillian E. Smith Center," Piedmont University, https://www.piedmont.edu /lillian-smith-center (accessed February 1, 2020).

15 Smith, "Dope with Lime," 3–4.

16   Some information about Mary Hambidge and Lillian Smith is included in Chirhart and Clark, *Georgia Women*: Magee, "Mary Hambidge"; and Inscoe, "Lillian Smith."

17   Mary Hambidge, *Apprentice in Creation*, 110.

Chapter 6. The Hambidge Center Today

1   See www.hambidge.org/mission-impact.
2   See www.hambidge.org.
3   See www.hambidge.org.
4   Agee and Evans, *Let Us Now Praise Famous Men*, 469.
5   Quoted in Mintz, "After Surviving Wildfire."
6   Quoted in Mintz, "After Surviving Wildfire."

Conclusion

1   Jay Hambidge to Peter McArthur, July 1902, McArthur Papers, subseries 1.1, University of Western Ontario.

BIBLIOGRAPHY

Agee, James, and Walker Evans. *Let Us Now Praise Famous Men*. Boston:
  Houghton Mifflin, 1941.

Albers, Anni. "Work with Materials." *Black Mountain College Bulletin* 5 (1938).

Allman, George Johnston. *Greek Geometry from Thales to Euclid*. Dublin: Hodges,
  Figgis, 1889.

Alvic, Philis. *Mary Hambidge, Weaver of Rabun*. 1989; rpt., Murray, Ky.: Philis
  Alvic, 1993.

——— . *Weavers of the Southern Highlands*. Lexington: University of Kentucky
  Press, 2003.

Archibald, Raymond Clare. *Notes on the Logarithmic Spiral, Golden Section and
  the Fibonacci Series*. New Haven, Conn.: Yale University Press, 1920.

Armfield, Maxwell. "Dynamic Symmetry and Its Practical Value Today."
  International Studio (November 1921): 78.

Auther, Elissa. *String, Felt, Thread: The Hierarchy and Art and Craft in American
  Art*. Minneapolis: University of Minnesota Press, 2010.

Ayres, Diane, Timothy Hansen, Tommy Arthur McPherson II, and Beth Ann
  McPherson. *American Arts and Crafts Textiles*. New York: Abrams, 2002.

Badoud, J., D. Mintz, and D. Thacker, eds. *The Hambidge Center: A Creative
  Sanctuary 80 Years in the Making*. Rabun Gap, Ga.: Hambidge Center, 2014.

Ball, Lamar. "Artists in North Georgia Mountains Work to Save Weaving as a
  Hand Craft." *Atlanta Journal Constitution*, March 9, 1941, 1–3.

Bass, Erin Z. "The Strange Life of Strange Fruit." *Deep South Magazine*, December
  12, 2012. https://deepsouthmag.com/2012/12/12/the-strange
  -life-of-strange-fruit/.

Bellows, George. "The Relation of Painting to Architecture." *American Architect*
  118, no. 2349 (December 29, 1920): 851.

———. "What Dynamic Symmetry Means to Me." *American Art Student* 3 (June 1921): 4–7.

Biographical Souvenir of the States of Georgia and Florida. Chicago, Ill.: Battey, 1889.

Blake, Edwin Mortimer. "Dynamic Symmetry: A Criticism." *Art Bulletin* 3, no. 3 (March 1921): 107–127.

Brewer, Mark Hambidge. "Chronology of Jay Hambidge, 2017." Hambidge Center for Creative Arts and Sciences, Rabun Gap, Ga.

Broomfield, Sarah. "Weaving Social Change: Berea College, Fireside Industries and Reform in Appalachia." Textile Society of America, *Proceedings*, Toronto, 2006. https://digitalcommons.unl.edu/tsaconf/297/.

Carmean, E. A., Jr. "Bellows: The Boxing Paintings." In *Bellows: The Boxing Pictures.* Edited by E. A. Carmean, John Wilmerding, Linda Ayres, and Deborah Chotner. Washington, D.C.: National Gallery of Art, 1982.

Carpenter, Rhys. "Dynamic Symmetry: A Criticism." *American Journal of Archaeology* 25, no. 1 (January–March 1921): 18–36.

———. "Professor Carpenter's Reply." *American Journal of Archaeology* 26, no. 1 (January–March 1922): 74–75.

Chirhart, Ann, and Kathleen Ann Clark. *Georgia Women: Their Lives and Times.* Vol. 2. Athens: University of Georgia Press, 2014.

Cleve, Kate van. "The Noel Stitch." *Handweaver and Craftsman* 8, no. 4 (Fall 1957).

Constantine, Mildred, and Jack Lenor Larsen. *The Art Fabric: Mainstream.* New York: Van Nostrand Reinhold, 1981.

Dow, Arthur Wesley. *Composition: A Series of Exercises in Art Structure for the Use of Students and Teachers.* Boston: J. M. Bowles, 1899.

Drexler, Arthur, and Greta Daniels. "Textiles USA." *American Fabrics*, no. 38 (Fall 1956): 14–15.

Eaton, Allen. *Handicrafts of the Southern Highlands.* New York: Russell Sage Foundation, 1937.

Edwards, Edward Bartholomew. *Pattern and Design with Dynamic Symmetry.* New York: Dover, 1967. Reprint of *Dynamarhythmic Design: A Book of Structural Pattern.* New York: Century, 1932.

Einik, Nurit, Jennifer Zwilling, Darcy Tell, Helen Drutt English, Jeannine Falino, and Abbey Nova. "Collected Essays: Development in Postwar American Craft." *Archives of American Art Journal* 50, nos. 3–4 (Fall 2011).

Fiorentini, Aurora. "The Collaboration between Thayaht and Madeleine Vionnet (1919–1925)." *Dress Study* 56 (Autumn 2009).

Fowler, Cynthia. *Hooked Rugs: Encounters in American Modern Art, Craft, and Design.* Burlington, Vt.: Ashgate, 2013.

Foxfire Fund. *Foxfire.* Vols. 1–25. Rabun Gap, Ga., 1967–1991.

——— . *Travels with Foxfire: Stories of People, Passions and Practices from Southern Appalachia*. New York: Anchor, 2018.

Frank, Marie. *Denman Ross and American Design Theory*. Lebanon, N.H.: University Press of New England, 2011.

Friedman, Marilyn. *Selling Good Design: Promoting the Modern Interior*. New York: Rizzoli, 2003.

Green, Henry. "The Promise and Peril of High Technology." In *Craft in the Machine Age: The History of Twentieth-Century American Craft, 1920–1945*. Edited by Janet Kardon, 36–39. New York: Abrams, 1995.

Halloran, William. *The Life and Letters of William Sharp and "Fiona Macleod,"* vol. 1: *1855–1894*. Cambridge England: Open Book, 2018.

Hambidge, Gove. "Something in My Genes." Unpublished memoir, 1967. In possession of the Hambidge family and Mark Hambidge Brewer.

Hambidge, Jay. *Diagonal*, vol. 1, nos. 1–12 (November 1919–October 1920).

——— . *Dynamic Symmetry in Composition as Used by the Artists*. New York: Published by the author, 1923.

——— . *Dynamic Symmetry: Fifteen Plates and Text Which Explain Some of the More Obvious Principles of the Areas Used in Greek Design*. Boston: Moosehorn, 1919.

——— . *Dynamic Symmetry: The Greek Vase*. New Haven, Conn.: Yale University Press, 1920.

——— . *Elements of Dynamic Symmetry*. New York: Brentano's, 1926.

——— . *The Parthenon and Other Greek Temples: Their Dynamic Symmetry*. New Haven, Conn.: Yale University Press, 1924.

——— . *Practical Applications of Dynamic Symmetry by Jay Hambidge*. Edited by Mary Hambidge. New Haven, Conn.: Yale University Press, 1932.

Hambidge, Jay, and Gove Hambidge. "The Ancestry of Cubism." *Century* 87 (April 1914): 869–875.

Hambidge, Mary Crovatt. *Apprentice in Creation: The Way Is Beauty*. Edited by Aspasia Voulis. 1975; rpt., Rabun Gap, Ga.: Hambidge Center, 1984.

——— . *The Weavers of Rabun*. Undated pamphlet. Tennessee State Library and Archives, 43942_01-03.

Hay, Susan. *Paris to Providence: French Couture and the Tirocchi Dressmakers Shop, 1915–1947*. Providence: Rhode Island School of Design, 2001.

Herter, Christine. *Dynamic Symmetry: A Primer*. New York: Norton, 1966.

Inscoe, John C. "Lillian Smith: Humanist." In Chirhart and Clark, *Georgia Women*, 166–189.

Ison, Frances Forbes. "The Weavers of Rabun." *Georgia Review* 4, no. 3 (Fall 1950).

Jaffee, Barbara. "Before the New Bauhaus: From Industrial Drawing to Art and Design Education in Chicago." *Design Issues* 21, no. 1 (Winter 2005): 41–62.

Jay Hambidge Art Foundation Papers. Hargrett Rare Book and Manuscript Library, University of Georgia Libraries, Athens.

Jay and Mary Crovatt Hambidge Papers, 1841–1973. Archives of American Art, Smithsonian Institution, Washington, D.C.

Kaplan, Wendy. *The Art That Is Life: The American Arts and Crafts Movement in America, 1875–1920*. New York: Abrams, 1998.

Kardon, Janet, ed. *Craft in the Machine Age: The History of Twentieth-Century American Craft, 1920–1945*. New York: Abrams, 1995.

———. *Revivals! Diverse Traditions, 1920–1945: The History of Twentieth-Century American Craft*. New York: Abrams, 1994.

Katherine S. Dreier Papers, Société Anonyme Archive. Yale Collection of American Literature, Beinecke Rare Book and Manuscript Library, New Haven, Conn.

Kessler, Jane. "From Mission to Market: Craft in the Southern Appalachians." In *Revivals! Diverse Traditions, 1920–1945*. Edited by Janet Kardon, 122–133. New York: Abrams, 1994.

Knee, Karyl M. *The Dynamic Symmetry Proportional System Is Found in Some Byzantine and Russian Icons of the Fourteenth to Sixteenth Centuries*. Redondo Beach, Calif.: Oakwood, 1988.

Knight, Lucian Lamar. *A Standard History of Georgia and Georgians*. Vol. 6. Chicago, Ill.: Lewis, 1917.

Koplos, Janet, and Bruce Metcalf. *Makers: A History of American Studio Craft*. Chapel Hill: University of North Carolina Press, 2010.

Le Corbusier. "Automobiles." In "Towards a New Architecture (Vers une Architecture)." Translated by Frederick Etchells, in *Essential Le Corbusier: L'Esprit Nouveau Articles*, 133–148. Oxford: Architectural Press, 1998.

Leontis, Artemis. *Eva Palmer Sikelianos: A Life in Ruins*. Princeton, N.J.: Princeton University Press, 2019.

Lucas, Alec. *Peter McArthur*. Boston: Twayne, 1975.

Magee, Rosemary. "Mary Hambidge: A Vision of Beauty, Symmetry, and Order." In Chirhart and Clark, *Georgia Women*, 133–148.

Mary Hambidge Papers, 1885–1973. Hargrett Rare Book and Manuscript Library, University of Georgia Libraries, Athens.

Mary and Jay Hambidge Papers. Atlanta History Center Collections, and Kenan Research Center at the Atlanta History Center, Ga.

McWinnie, Harold. "A Review of the Use of Symmetry, the Golden Section, and Dynamic Symmetry in Contemporary Art." *Journal of the International Society of the Arts, Sciences, and Technology* 19, no. 3 (1986).

Mears, Charles. "Application of Dynamic Symmetry to Advertising Proportions." *Women's Wear Daily* 34, no. 12 (January 15, 1927): 3.

Michell, John. "Dynamic Symmetry in the Work of Maxwell Armfield." In *Maxwell Armfield*. Edited by A. A. Ballard. Birmingham, England: Southampton Art Gallery, 1978.

Mintz, Donna. "After Surviving Wildfire, the Hambidge Center Fights to Get Back on Track." *ArtsATL.org*, January 31, 2017. https://www.artsatl.org /surviving-wildfire-hambidge-center-fights-track/.

Morris, William. "The Revival of Handicraft." *Fortnightly Review*, November 1888. Reprinted in *The Theory of Decorative Art: An Anthology, 1750–1940: An Anthology*. Edited by Isabelle Frank. New Haven, Conn.: Yale University Press, 2000.

Penrose, Francis. *An Investigation of the Principles of Athenian Architecture*. London: Macmillan, 1888.

Pisano, Ronald. *The Students of William Merritt Chase*. New York: Heckscher Museum, 1973.

Rhode Island School of Design, Museum of Art; Currier Gallery of Art; and Dartmouth College, Carpenter Art Galleries. *Dynamic Symmetry: A Retrospective Exhibition: Museum of Art, Rhode Island School of Design*. Providence: Rhode Island School of Design, 1961.

Richter, Gisela. "Dynamic Symmetry from the Designer's Point of View." *American Journal of Archaeology* 26, no. 1 (January–March 1922): 59–73.

Riley, Terence, and Edward Eigen. "Between the Museum and the Marketplace: Selling Good Design." In *The Museum of Modern Art at Mid-Century*. Edited by *John Elderfield*. New York: Museum of Modern Art, 1994.

Ritchie, Andrew. *Sketches of Rabun County History, 1819–1948*. 1948; rpt., Atlanta, Ga.: Foote and Davies, 1959.

Ross, Denman Waldo. *A Theory of Pure Design: Harmony, Balance, Rhythm*. Boston: Houghton Mifflin, 1907.

Sharp, William. "The Garden of the Sun: Route Notes in Sicily, Part II." *Century* 71, no. 1 (May 1906).

Shevzov, Maria. "Art Expression Built upon the Crafts: Rabun Studio and the Marketing of an Ideal." Master's thesis, University of Delaware, 2010.

Sikelianos, Eva Palmer. *Upward Panic: The Autobiography of Eva Palmer Sikelianos*. Edited by John P. Anton. Philadelphia, Pa.: Harwood, 1993.

Smith, Lillian E. "Dope with Lime." *North Georgia Review* 4, no. 1 (Spring 1939): 2–5. In Lillian E. Smith Collection, Piedmont College Library, Demorest, Ga. https://cdm17007.contentdm.oclc.org/digital/collection/Magazines01/id/809.

Southern Highland Handicraft Guild. *The Handwoven Clothing of Mary Crovatt Hambidge*. Southern Highland Handicraft Guild, Folk Art Center, May 5– August 28, 1984. Asheville, N.C.: Southern Highland Handicraft Guild, 1984.

Stahle, Norma K. "A New Key to Art: Design Problems Solved." *Arts and Decoration* 15–16 (June 1921).

Starnes, Jane Ellen. "Mary Crovatt Hambidge: Art and Nature." In *Southern Arts and Crafts, 1890–1940*. Edited by James Jordan II and Jane Ellen Starnes, 56. Charlotte, N.C.: Mint Museum of Art, 1996.

Storey, Walter Rendell. "New Fabrics to Fit Period or Modern Rooms: Colors and Textures Reveal the Craftsman." *New York Times*, October 30, 1938, SM 14.

Thompson, Jane, and Alexandra Lange. *Design Research: The Store That Brought Modern Living to American Homes*. San Francisco, Calif.: Chronicle, 2010.

Tibol, Raquel, ed. *José Clemente Orozco: Cuadernos*. Mexico City, Mexico: SEP, 1983.

Troy, Virginia Gardner. *Anni Albers and Ancient American Textiles: From Bauhaus to Black Mountain*. London: Ashgate, 2002.

——— . "The Great Weaver of Eternity: Dynamic Symmetry and Utopian Ideology in the Woven and Written Work of Mary Crovatt Hambidge." *Surface Design Journal* 23, no. 4 (Summer 1999).

——— . *The Modernist Textile: Europe and America, 1890–1940*. London: Lund Humphries, 2006.

——— . "Textiles as the Face of Modernity: Artistry and Industry in Midcentury America." *Textile History* 50, no. 1 (July 2019).

Walter, Elizabeth. "Jay Hambidge and the Development of the Theory of Dynamic Symmetry, 1902–1920." PhD diss., University of Georgia, 1978.

Williams, Jonathan. "The Southern Appalachians." *Craft Horizons* 26, no. 3 (June 1966): 66.

Wilson, Jennifer. "Dynamic Symmetry: A Mathematical Structure in New School History." Parsons School of Design, May 15, 2019, https://publicseminar.org/2019/05/dynamic-symmetry-a-mathematical-structure-in-new-school-history/.

Wilson, Kathleen Curtis. *Textile Art from Southern Appalachia: The Quiet Work of Women*. Johnson City, Tenn.: Overmountain Press, 2001.

Wilson, Richard Guy. *The Machine Age in America, 1918–1941*. New York: Abrams, 1986.

Witherspoon, Gary. *Dynamic Symmetry and Holistic Asymmetry in Navajo and Western Art and Cosmology*. New York: Lang, 1995.

Young, Tricia Henry. *The Killinger Collection: Costumes of Denishawn and Ted Shawn and His Men Dancers*. Department of Dance, Florida State University, 1999.

INDEX

Albers, Anni, 6–8, 79–80, 88, 94

Alvic, Philis, 72, 80

Appalachian weaving, 4, 66–67, 72–74

Armfield, Maxwell, 26–29

Armory Show (International Exhibition of
   Modern Art), 17

Art Deco, 39, 52

Art Institute of Chicago, 26, 36

Arts and Crafts Movement, 46, 65, 67, 79

Avramea, Kyria Elene, 3, 43–46

Beery, Mary Nikas, 95, 99

Bellows, George, 26, 30–32

Berea College, 47, 72

Biltmore Industries, 72, 79

Black Mountain College, 6, 79, 80

Blue Ridge Mountains, 4, 93, 46, 81, 118

Brennan, Archie, 102–103

British Museum, 13

Carpenter, Rhys, 40

Caskey, Lacey D., 25–26, 40

Century magazine, 1, 13–17, 26

Chrysler Corporation, 37–38

Clovis, Hall, 64–65, 80–87, 94

Columbia University, 17, 40

Crovatt, Mary. *See* Hambidge, Mary Crovatt

Cubism, 17–18

Delphic Festivals, 48–51, 65

Dinsmoor, William, 40

Dow, Arthur Wesley, 17

Dreier, Katherine, 65

Duncan, Isadora, 3, 47

Duncan, Raymond, 47–48

Dynamic Symmetry, 1–9, 13–19, 24–29,
   32–37, 46; adaptions by industry, 36–39;
   adaptions by Mary Crovatt Hambidge, 6, 42,
   47–54, 75–77; detractors, 40–42; supporters,
   26–39

Edwards, Edward B. 26, 32, 35

Forbes, Edward, 25

Foxfire, 8, 95

Gilder, Richard, 13, 15

Giles, Howard, 11, 26, 32–36

Gordon Hosiery Company, 37

Hambidge, Cordella Delorme, 12–13, 19

Hambidge, Gove, 13, 17–19

Hambidge, Jay: before 1914, 11–19; *Century*
   magazine, 1, 13–17, 26; pedagogy, lectures,
   and publications, 6, 26, 29–30, 36, 46, 143n1;
   position on handcrafts, 32–34, 46–47. *See also*
   Dynamic Symmetry

Hambidge, Mary Crovatt: before 1914, 19–23;
   discovering weaving, 3, 43, 66; weaving
   and dying techniques, 64, 76–85. *See also*
   Hambidge Center for Creative Arts and
   Sciences; Rabun Studios; Weavers of Rabun

Hambidge Center for Creative Arts and
   Sciences: Antinori Village, 103, 127–128; Jay
   Hambidge Art Foundation, 4, 69–70, 76, 94;
   Jay Hambidge School of Dynamic Symmetry
   and Weaving, 95; Residency Program, 9–10,
   94–95, 102–105, 115, 118

Harvard University, 17, 25–26, 39

Hellenic Studies Society, 14, 29, 36

Henri, Robert, 26, 30

Ison, Frances Forbes, 81

Jekyll Island Club, 20

Johnson, Philip, 6, 88

Kaufmann, Edgar, Jr., 88

Kendall, William Sergeant, 25

Kirpal, Josephine, 87–94

Kitchen, Karl K., 41–42

Le Corbusier (Charles Édouard Jeanneret), 37

Lees Carpet, 94

Leontis, Artemis, 48

Little Theater Opera Company of New York, 64–69

McArthur, Peter, 13–14

Metropolitan Museum of Art, 25–26

Mundy, Roy, 87

Museum of Fine Arts Boston, 25–26

Museum of Modern Art in New York (MoMA), 88–94

Negoro, Minnie, 88

New York School of Fine and Applied Art, 32, 34, 147n13

Noel, Muriel, 45–46, 50, 56

O'Keeffe, Georgia, 6, 22, 88

Osaki, Harry, 87

Parrish, Maxfield, 26–29

Penland School of Handicrafts, 72

Penland Weavers and Potters, 72

Penrose, Francis, 14

Rabun Gap–Nacoochee School, 72, 75, 95

Rabun Studios, 6, 68–69, 85–94

Reese, Eleanor Steele, 4, 64, 67–70, 80, 131

Richter, Gisela, 25–26, 40

Ritchie, Andrew, 75

Ross, Denman Waldo, 17, 22, 25, 29, 64

Salmagundi Club, 26

Samuel Sachs Research Fellowship, 25

Shawn, Ted, 65–66, 150n38

Sikelianos, Angelos, 47–48

Sikelianos, Eva Palmer, 3, 45–54, 64–66, 79

Sikelianos, Penelope, 47–48

Smith, Lillian E., 111–114

Smithsonian Institution, 93

Southwick, Albert, 37

studio craft movement, 6, 85–88

Tackett, LaGardo, 88

Tallulah Falls Industrial School, 72

Thayaht (Ernesto Michahelles), 39

Thompson, Faye, 80

Tiffany & Co., 37, 39

USS *Williamsburg*, 87

Weavers of Rabun, 6, 68–85, 87, 93

Wiener Werkstätte, 17

Wigginton, Eliot, 8, 94–95

Yale University Press, 12, 25, 87